METHODOLOGY IN RELIGIOUS STUDIES

McGill Studies in the History of Religions,
A Series Devoted to International Scholarship
Katherine K. Young, editor

Methodology in Religious Studies

The Interface with Women's Studies

EDITED BY
Arvind Sharma

STATE UNIVERSITY OF NEW YORK PRESS

Published by
State University of New York Press, Albany

© 2002 State University of New York

For information, address State University of New York Press,
90 State Street, Suite 700, Albany, NY 12207

Production by Cathleen Collins
Marketing by Anne Valentine

Library of Congress Cataloging in Publication Data

Methodology in religious studies : the interface with women's studies / edited by
    Arvind Sharma.
        p.   cm. — (McGill studies in the history of religions)
    Includes bibliographical references and index.
    ISBN 0-7914-5347-2 (hc. : alk. paper) — ISBN 0-7914-5348-0 (pb. : alk. paper)
    1. Religion—Study and teaching. 2. Women's studies. I. Sharma, Arvind.
    II. Series.

    BL41 .M435 2002
    200'.82—dc21
                                                                2001042647

10   9   8   7   6   5   4   3   2   1

Contents

Preface

ARVIND SHARMA

The study of religion has developed a wide range of methods to study its subject matter, ever since its establishment as an academic discipline in the 1860s. These have now become fairly well defined and may be identified, despite areas of overlap, as: the historical method; the phenomenological method; the sociological method; the psychological method; the anthropological method; the theological method; the hermeneutical method; the dialogical method; etc., in the study of religion.

Although the data base for the study of religion was considerably enlarged by increased knowledge about primal religions and religions of the East during the century stretching from the 1860s to the 1960s, the basic orientation of the data remained the same. It consisted mainly of an account of the beliefs and practices of the various religions from various parts of the world. The various methods in the study of religion enumerated earlier were applied to the study of and reflection upon such data.

Since the 1960s, a significant feature of this data has come to be widely recognized; namely, that most, if not all, of it is androcentric. This recognition led to the growth of women's studies, which has sought to correct this situation in the study of religion by recovering or reconstructing such data as pertain to women rather than men, thus attempting to redress the balance in this respect. Feminist studies pursue such an agenda even more vigorously, if at times less rigorously.

A modern student of religion sensitive to this development, as well as to the developments in the methodology of religious studies, is naturally led to ask the question: what are the implications of this development for the study of religion? Upon reflection this question points to an even broader issue. What is the nature of the relationship between the method and what constitutes the

vii

subject matter of the method? When applied in the current historical context, this general issue assumes a more precise formulation: what implications do women's studies in religion have for methodology in religious studies and vice versa? To illustrate: women's studies have led to an increased appreciation of oral history as a source of attaining fuller knowledge about a religious tradition, as most of the religious texts were typically redacted by males. Similarly, the prevalence of the worship of the Mother Goddess has raised the issue whether such worship, in historical terms, is positively associated with an improved position of women in the society in which it is prevalent, or whether it serves to merely reinforce the androcentrism of that society by fulfilling a masculine psychological need. The first illustration bears directly on the application of the historical method in the study of religion, and the second on the sociological and the psychological.

In this book eight eminent scholars of religion explore such mutual implications of subject and method in the study of religion, enriching both. We hope the reader will feel similarly enriched perusing it.

Introduction

KATHERINE K. YOUNG

The scholarly study of religion was inspired by the Age of Discovery's encounter with foreign religions and the Enlightenment's insistence that knowledge be founded on empiricism and reason. Empiricism and reason gave rise, in turn, to the development of distinctive academic disciplines beginning in the nineteenth century: history, literary criticism, sociology, psychology, anthropology, philosophy, and so on. Disciplines are defined by both their subject matter and the techniques used to gather and examine information. In its general sense, the term *method* refers to an academic discipline. Because the study of religion has drawn on many disciplines and techniques, it is really a field of studies that can be characterized as interdisciplinary. Most scholars of religion have focused on texts due to the importance of scriptures in world religions. They have generally used philological, literary, historical, phenomenological, theological, philosophical, and hermeneutic methods to understand these texts. Some, however, have used anthropological, sociological, and psychological methods. The latter are becoming increasingly important with the new interest in women and religion. The longest essay in the volume, for instance, is devoted to the interface of the psychology of religion and women's studies.

In recent years, there has been a sea change in the study of religion because of the synergism generated by women's studies, feminism, and the various disciplines that make up the field of religious studies. This can be explained partly by the fact that women's entrance into universities in large numbers, beginning in the 1960s, paralleled the second wave of feminism and the development of new departments of religion in secular universities. Women, especially those pursuing graduate studies, gradually became aware that something ever so basic was amiss in the study of religion: where were the women in this scholarship and why was universalism and human nature represented explicitly as male? To answer these questions, they criticized existing disciplines and methods, adapted them whenever possible, or invented new techniques. The result, some four decades in the making, has been to change permanently our understanding of religions along with the disciplines and methods used to study them. To analyze the methodological changes, David Kinsley examines the history of religions; Katherine K. Young, the phenomenology of religion; Rita M. Gross, the anthropology of religion; Constance A. Jones, the sociology of religion; Diane Jonte-Pace, the psychology of religion; Mary Ann Stenger, the philosophy of religion; Rosemary Radford Ruether, theology; and Elisabeth Schüssler Fiorenza, hermeneutics.

Several methodological themes can be detected in this book, although the authors do not always think about them in the same ways, an indication of the ferment over method in the study of women and religion (but also religion in general). One broad category has focused on challenging descriptions, explanations, and theories. This has included:

1. documenting women's invisibility and inequality;
2. including women and female symbols;
3. avoiding reductionism;
4. understanding differences of form or meaning;
5. reassessing theories;
6. transforming disciplines and methods.

A second, albeit related, set of issues has focused on scholarship in the service of feminist goals:

1. criticizing misogyny in scholarship;
2. using sex/gender/race as the important analytic category;
3. destabilizing traditional views of women;
4. eliminating hierarchy in the research process;
5. avoiding generalizations and essentialism;
6. seeking many perspectives;
7. challenging enlightenment thinking and scientific methods with their claims to objectivity;
8. stating authorial standpoints and social position;
9. harnessing research to social change;
10. redefining the nature of religion;
11. criticizing the lack of revolution in the disciplines;
12. transforming, reconstructing, and inventing religions.

There is consensus among the authors of this volume that the field has been dramatically challenged from its surface observations to its deep paradigms by critiques of its androcentrism. There is consensus, moreover, that this has been a good thing: good for women, of course, but also good for the methods and the very concept of knowledge. Scattered through this volume, though, are reflections and comments that suggest differences. One is between those who think that it is necessary to ask new questions, collect new data, offer new analyses, and revise or develop new theories to do justice to the findings, and others who think their primary mandate is political change. The former might be called academic reformers and the latter political revolutionaries. Thus, for some, stating one's standpoint means simply stating one's presuppositions whatever they might be, whereas for others it means testifying to one's feminist commitment. For some, adequate data, criteria, and reason still count as central to the academic method (after the gender "correction" has occurred, that is). But for others, all this talk is a thing of the past, the "old" (and erroneous) Enlightenment age, which cannot be corrected because it was so fundamentally wrong.

As this volume reveals, there are several other watersheds. Some scholars see their thinking as part of larger intellectual trends during the last century, whereas others view feminism as posing a break with all that went before. Even among those who see a break, some look to the diversity talk of postmodernism and deconstruction whereas others look to the solidarity talk of Marxism and its derivative called Critical Theory. Whereas some worry about androcentric texts reducing women to the status of "objects," others are concerned about gynocentric texts reducing men to power brokers. And whereas some think that men in the past intentionally desired to harm women by subordinating them, others think that at some point these values were so embedded in culture that it was impossible to see the subordination. Perhaps the most profound watershed of all is, however, the idea that traditional religions are so in need of reform that they need to be eliminated altogether in order that women may create a religion on their own and of their own.

1

Women's Studies in the History of Religions

DAVID KINSLEY

> On the most archaic levels of culture, *living as a human being* is in itself a *religious act*, for alimentation, sexual life, and work have a sacramental value. In other words, to be— or rather, to become—*a man* means to be "religious."
> —Mircea Eliade, *A History of Religious Ideas*

To appreciate the radical impact women's studies has had on the discipline of history of religions, it is necessary first to describe briefly how the history of religions understands its task.

The history of religions, which claims to be the objective, scientific study of religion, sets as its task nothing less than the study, in historical and cross-cultural perspective, of *all* human religious phenomena. It includes in its purview, not only sophisticated, literate, philosophical, and theological materials, but also popular expressions of human religiosity such as festivals, life cycle rituals, myths, and practices that are found only in oral traditions. The history of religions seeks to avoid an approach to human religiosity that privileges certain materials as "higher" and others as "lower." It assumes that all expressions of human religiosity are worthy of study. In the words of Mircea Eliade: "For the historian of religions, *every* manifestation of the sacred is important: every rite, every myth, every belief or divine figure reflects the experience of the sacred and hence implies the notions of *being*, of *meaning*, and of *truth*."[1]

History of religions does not seek to evaluate one religion (or religious expression) vis-à-vis another with a view to declaring one superior to the other. It is comparative in nature at times, as when particular patterns or themes are traced in cross-cultural context, but it does not seek by means of this approach to privilege certain traditions or types of spirituality as superior to others. Its

1

aim is to appreciate the religious nature of humankind by means of studying all religious phenomena objectively.

History of religions acknowledges that there are elite and popular forms of religion in many traditions, and that within many traditions there is criticism of (even disdain for) certain "popular" religious beliefs and customs on the part of elites, but history of religions is interested equally in elite and "popular" religion. It seeks to gain a complete picture of any given religious tradition, or any given religious situation, by viewing all expressions of religiosity.

Although history of religions *(Religionswissenschaft)* as practiced and founded by van der Leeuw, Wach, Kitagawa, Eliade, Long, and other scholars arose in the Western intellectual tradition, there was a self-conscious attempt in the discipline to avoid parochialism or to privilege Western religious traditions. This included avoiding making judgments on the truth claims of religious traditions being studied in order to fully appreciate the intrinsic value of all human religious expressions. In this respect, history of religions thought of itself as liberal, all-inclusive, and objective in its study of religion.

For Eliade, Kitagawa, Long, and others, one of the principal aims of the history of religions was to discover underlying types, models, themes, and structures in the overwhelming mass of religious data—to discover and articulate a religious grammar or syntax that was cross-culturally informed. In this quest, history of religions thought of itself as rigorously nonparochial, scientific, and neutral and sought to dissociate itself from any one tradition, point of view, or claim to truth. It distinguished itself from Christian theology and church history.

During the formative years of the history of religions in Europe and America, its claims to be completely objective and all-inclusive in its study of human religiosity, to be the first systematic attempt to study religion sympathetically and objectively, were heady stuff. Under the leadership of Eliade and the Chicago school, a number of scholars set about the task of creating a "new humanism" in the West, an enlightened outlook that was based on a nonparochial, unbiased, all-inclusive, and sympathetic study of human religiousness.[2] The hope was strong that the history of religions could infuse the West with a new vision of the human spirit based on a more open, catholic, and sympathetic study of non-Western religious materials.

Women's studies has had a devastating effect on many of the underlying claims of the history of religions. In general, the effect of women's studies on history of religions has not been to cast doubt on the intent of the discipline. Rather, the effect has been to show, often in shocking and dramatic ways, the extent to which history of religions has not been true to its own mandate. It has been neither all-inclusive nor objective in its study of human religousness.

History of Religions as the Study of Men's Religion

The task of including all expressions of religiosity in the purview of the history of religions, of course, is not easy. The extent to which it has failed to do so has been made embarrassingly clear by women's studies. Despite its claim to include all religious phenomena within its scope, the history of religions, like all other humanistic disciplines, in fact had a quite limited focus. What it claimed to be the religions or religious expressions of humankind were often (indeed, usually) the religions and religious expressions of males. Prior to the advent of women's studies, the history of religions was primarily the study of men's religion.

What is particularly embarrassing is that historians of religions seemed completely unaware of this state of affairs. They assumed that men's religion was synonymous with human religion. Scholarly studies of initiation were often limited to male initiation. Studies of deities were often limited to male deities, or would include a special section on "goddesses" (as if all goddesses were of one type or were a particular type of the wider, more generic category of "god" or "deity"). Studies of a culture or religious tradition would often include (usually near the end) a section on "women. " More often than not, these brief sections on women or goddesses were based on male views of women or goddesses. They were discussed primarily, if not exclusively, as adjuncts to males, according to their relationships with males: as mothers, wives, consorts, daughters, and sisters. Women were the "other"; they were objectified and spoken about from the male point of view.

The classic statement on this great lack in the history of religions was made by Rita Gross, a historian of religions and herself a student of Eliade and the Chicago school, in her article "Androcentrism and Androgyny in the Methodology of History of Religions." There she wrote:

> The unconscious androcentric presuppositions undergirding almost all work done to date in the history of religions cause serious deficiencies, especially at the primary level of data-perception and gathering, and this deficiency in turn generates serious deficiencies at the level of model-building and theorizing whenever any hint of sexuality or sexual imagery is present in the data being analyzed.[3]

From the androcentric point of view that dominated history of religions prior to women's studies, it is claimed either (a) that women are included under the generic male, and thus no special consideration need be given them, or (b) that women are other, in which case, to cite Gross again:

> [T]hey are discussed as an object exterior to mankind, needing to be explained and fitted into one's worldview, having the same ontological and epistemological status as trees, unicorns, deities or any other

object that must be discussed to make experience intelligible. They are there in the world, but they are discussed as an "other" to the human Subject attempting to understand his world (generic masculine deliberate), as the problem to be solved, not as a Co-Subject in a mutual attempt to understand human sexual differentiation and all its manifestations.[4]

Women's Religion is Different from Men's Religion

Not only did women's studies demonstrate to historians of religions that their studies were concerned almost entirely with men's religion, it demonstrated also that women's religion was often different from men's religion. Incorporating materials on women's religious practices and beliefs often resulted not so much in elaborations of previously stated generalizations about a given tradition as in subversion of such generalizations. Once historians of religions began to study women's religion with opened eyes they began to see, for example, that Hinduism for a male can be, and usually is, quite different from Hinduism for a woman. They began to appreciate that there are often quite distinct male and female subcultures within the larger culture, and that these gendered cultures are far more defining of individual character and religious expression than the shared aspects of the wider culture and religion. One scholar, speaking of Hinduism as practiced in North India, for example, has said that gender is the "most pervasive factor" in determining which religious group one belongs to, which social and religious activities one participates in, and how one understands the mythology and theology of Hindu culture.[5]

Even in the case of males and females who participate in the same religious community, or the same cultic tradition, it has become evident that religious experience can be quite different. An interesting case in point concerns the religious poetry of two sixteenth-century North Indian devotees of Krishna, one male, Sūrdās, and one female, Mīrābāī. In a comparison of their writings, it is clear that the two relate to Krishna in differing ways and use different metaphors to express their love. A dominating metaphor in Mīrā's songs is her marriage to Lord Krishna. In the songs of Sūrdās, this image is lacking, although he imagines himself to be a woman in love with Krishna. Mīrā is "at home" with the images, nuances, and particulars of the married women and uses this metaphor to describe her relationship with the Lord. Sūrdās is only comfortable with a romantic, illicit, relationship, which is the subject of most Sanskrit poetry.[6]

A similar case concerns the early religious poetry of Indian Buddhist monks and nuns. Hymns of the monks (*Theragāthā*) and nuns (*Therīgāthā*) were preserved in separate collections. Although there are numerous stylistic and formulaic similarities between the two collections, a study of the hymns shows significant differences that were probably due to gender. In the hymns of the nuns, for example, we find much more attention given to relationships. They mention their previous roles as mothers and daughters, they mention friends in the monastic order, and they discuss rivalries with other monastics. The hymns of the nuns are also much more inclined to discuss overt conflict, which probably reflects the fact that women had a more difficult time leading the monastic life due to prejudices against them at the time.[7]

The Materials Being Studied Are Created by and for Males

Women's studies also made embarrassingly apparent the great extent to which almost every culture (literate and nonliterate) is (or was) patriarchal, sexist, androcentric, and often misogynist. The problem is particularly acute in the study of texts. In most cultures (until very recently) it was primarily or exclusively males who were literate. It was the men who wrote texts, studied texts, commented on texts, and invoked texts in a variety of social situations. In some cases (for example, Hinduism) women were forbidden even to hear certain religious texts. In these texts, the primary concerns are male concerns. Women are routinely regarded as "other" and are dealt with primarily as they relate to males. Women's religion in these texts is described (if it is mentioned at all) from an outsider's point of view and is usually regarded as in some way inferior to male practice and belief. Male religious practices are regarded as prestigious and powerful, women's as lowly, crude, and relatively ineffective.

A good example of this is the recitation of the *Devī-Māhātmya*, a Hindu text in Sanskrit in praise of the goddess Durgā, at the Vindhyavāsinī temple near Mirzapur in North India. The text is recited by a variety of people there throughout the year, and on certain festival days thousands of devotees come to recite the text. Most of those who recite the text are males, and the few females who do recite the text usually do so in a vernacular language, as they do not know how to read or pronounce Sanskrit. According to the professional male reciters of the text, the recitation of the text in Hindi (or another vernacular language) does have merit, but is much less meritorious than chanting the text in the original Sanskrit. Both recitations are water, they say, but Sanskrit recitation is like Ganges water compared to the tap water of Hindi. Or Sanskrit recitation is like fresh milk, Hindi recitation like powdered milk. Sanskrit recitation of the text is like pure *ghee* (clarified butter); Hindi recitation is like Dalda (a cheap cooking oil).[8]

Prior to the advent of women's studies, the androcentric nature of many of the materials studied by historians of religions was barely noticed, and if it was, deserved little comment. The implication was that the recitation of the *Devī-Māhātmya* in Hindi, by women, was indeed less potent, religiously uplifting, and spiritually prestigious than the recitation of the text in Sanskrit by males.

Materials on Women's Religion Are Sparse or Entirely Lacking in Some Cases

Women's studies has also made clear the extent to which materials dealing with women's religion are meager or entirely lacking in some traditions. The literary records of most religious traditions are the sole source of our knowledge about them yet the texts tell us very little (sometimes nothing) about women's religious practices. It is next to impossible to reconstruct women's religious worlds on the bases of these materials. The historical record, which is so often controlled entirely by males, is sometimes silent on women. Prior to women's studies, historians of religions barely noticed this fact and would blithely generalize about the religion of the Sumerians, Hindus, Chinese, or Egyptians on the basis of descriptions of male religion. Women's religion was relegated to a few offhand remarks about what "the Hindus allow women to do, or not to do." Men's attitudes to women in ancient literary sources (typically androcentric) were the sole basis for reflections on women's religion. Women's studies has made clear the great extent to which women's voices have been silenced in the course of history, how their words have gone unspoken, and how, in many cases, they have been irretrievably lost to us. To the historian of religions this means that our descriptions of religious traditions are often incomplete and heavily biased in favor of male religion.

Materials on Women Had Been Ignored

In those religions and traditions where materials on women do exist, it was a matter of these materials having been neglected as worthy of study by historians of religion. In the late 1960s and 1970s, when an interest in women's religion began to flourish, there was a paucity of scholarly work on the subject. Those of us who taught courses on women and religion at this time had to struggle to find relevant books and articles. It was startingly clear that women's religion had not been studied, that it was an entirely new field. The title of the book edited by Nancy Auer Falk and Rita Gross, *Unspoken Worlds: Women's Religious Lives in Non-Western Cultures* (San Francisco: Harper & Row Publishers, 1980), summed up the problem. There was rich material in many traditions, but it had been ignored; it had not become the subject of history of religions.

The discovery of women's religion (it was nothing less than a discovery) unleashed an incredible effort, mostly but not entirely by women scholars, to find and reflect upon women's religion. Now, some twenty-five years later, we have an immense body of detailed data on women's religions in many traditions. A cursory look at materials being published by scholarly journals in religious studies, scholarly presses dealing with religion, the program for the

Annual Meeting of the American Academy of Religion, and the programs for other conferences dealing with religion indicates the immense amount of work now being done on women's religion. In all areas—biblical studies, Judaism, Christianity, and Islam, native, South Asian, and East Asian religions, contemporary new religious movements, and so on—there is intense, sophisticated and productive scholarship underway that is creating a huge amount of material on women's religion from all over the world and throughout much of recorded history. This has radically changed the face of religious studies in general and the history of religions in particular. We now have detailed studies of individual religious heroines,[9] women's religious cults,[10] and women's religious rites and rituals.[11]

It is not an exaggeration to say that this effort has given a depth of focus to history of religions that it entirely lacked prior to the advent of women's studies. In light of the vast amounts of materials that have been made available on women's religion in just twenty-five years, it is incredible to remember that history of religions almost entirely ignored this material prior to women's studies.

Religious Materials Are Heavily Gendered

Women's studies has taught history of religions that the data it investigates are often heavily gendered. It used to seem unproblematic to analyze, interpret, and then generalize to an entire culture about a particular myth, ritual, symbol, or theological system. The difficulties were usually described in terms of the mastery of languages, the complexity and nuance of symbolic structures, and the social or cultural setting of the materials in question. These difficulties, of course, remain. Women's studies, however, has added to the historian of religion's task the crucial aspect of cultural gendering. Historians of religion are now aware of the fact that a particular symbol, ritual, myth, or belief may be thought about in one way by males and another way by females. It is clear in many cases that it is simply not accurate to suppose that the meaning of a particular religious text, event, or symbol is the same for males and females.

A particularly vivid example of the gendered nature of the material that historians of religions study is the case of the goddess T'ien Hou (also known as Ma Tsu), who is widely worshipped along the South China coast. Among males, T'ien Hou is primarily a symbol of pacification and social order. Her cult was encouraged during the twelfth and thirteenth centuries by the state as part of a pacification program aimed at pirates and certain boat peoples dwelling along the South China coast. Stories about T'ien Hou in literary sources emphasize her defeat of socially disruptive elements such as pirates. The cult of T'ien Hou also became strongly associated with the protection of male lineages and the social hierarchy. Government officials promoted and attended her festivals. For males, she is primarily an establishment deity, a guardian of the status quo.

The way women relate to T'ien Hou is entirely different. They take no part whatsoever in the public cult of the goddess and usually do not know anything of her mythology as contained in literary sources. They relate to her individually, and the stories they know of her are primarily from local oral traditions. They bring her offerings on behalf of their families and ask favors from her. They address her as T'ien Hou Niang Niang, the suffix lending her a maternal or grandmotherly character. As a maternal confidant, T'ien Hou is especially approached for children and the protection and enrichment of the household.[12]

Another example of how religious symbols are understood quite differently by females and males concerns the nine Durgās. In Varanasi there is a group of goddesses known as the nine Durgās, each of whom has a temple. In texts, these goddesses are always listed in the same sequence: Śailaputrī, Brahmacāriṇī, Candraghaṇṭā, Kuṣmāṇḍā, Skandamātā, Kātyāyanī, Kālarātrī, Mahāgaurī, and Siddhidātrī. In his research on Durgā worship in Varanasi, Hillary Rodrigues asked both males and females how they understood these goddesses and what lent the group internal coherence. Males, for the most part, stressed the fact that all were manifestations of Durgā or the Mahādevī, that they represented her different manifestations in the world. When pressed, some males interpreted the nine goddesses as different stages in the evolution of *prakṛti* (the physical creation) or as different elements in it. Śailaputrī, for example, represents unrefined matter, Brahmacāriṇī represents the active principle in water (that which intensifies or thickens water to become semen, for example), Candraghaṇṭā is the active principle within fire, Kuṣmāṇḍā is identified with the element of air, and Skandamātā represents ether *(ākāśa)*. Kātyāyanī represents the heart or mind and is the principle of intellect *(buddhi)*. Kālarātrī is the element of time and manifests herself as ignorance *(avidyā)*. Mahāgaurī lends knowledge to the world and is identified with consciousness *(cit)*. Finally, Siddhidātrī is the aspect of ego *(ahaṁkāra)*, as well as the principle of the self *(ātman)*.

Interpretations of the nine Durgās by women differed dramatically from this rather philosophical view of the goddesses. According to certain females, the nine Durgās represent the stages in a woman's life; as one woman put it: "These nine Durgās are our life, women's life.[13] In what we might term a view of the goddesses as expressions of the female life cycle, Śailaputrī (daughter of the mountain) represents the newborn female, who is fresh and pure like the snows of the mountains. Brahmacāriṇī is a young girl who has reached puberty but has not yet menstruated. Candraghaṇṭā is the young girl who has begun to menstruate (*ghaṇṭa* means bell but can also mean a period of time in Hindi, so her name may mean "she who has periods, cycles, or phases").

Kuṣmāṇḍā is the fertile, pregnant woman who is large bellied like the pumpkin gourd (which is what her name refers to). Skandamātā (mother of Skanda) is the mother who has just given birth and sustains her young. Kātyāyanī (a name sometimes used to refer to widows) is a middle-aged widow who still looks after her children and is independent and strong. Kālarātrī (dark night) is a woman entering menopause, the dark night (or death) of her fertile powers. Mahāgaurī (great pure one) is a postmenopausal woman who has returned to the purity of a virgin *(gaurī)*; she engages in ascetic or spiritual pursuits such as pilgrimage and is no longer troubled by menstrual "pollution," which is ritually prohibiting. Finally, Siddhidātrī (she who bestows attainments or perfections) is the woman who has achieved spiritual perfection and is capable of giving perfection to others.[14]

Historians of religions, when presented with data such as this, are tempted to prefer one interpretation over another as more coherent, satisfying, and compelling (and in this particular case, I personally am strongly inclined to the interpretation given by women). The first point I wish to make with reference to the nine Durgās, however, is how males and females find different meanings in the same set of symbols and how the different meanings can enrich our understanding of religious materials. To fully appreciate the meaning and power of symbols it is often necessary to actively seek out female and male views.

Given the gendered nature of symbols and culture generally, a more forceful way of putting the matter would be to say that some symbols (or symbol sets) primarily or basically express women's experience and that when males seek to interpret them, they misinterpret them, completely failing to understand their essential meanings. Although I am not willing to say this in respect to the nine Durgās, it is a possibility that the historian of religions should keep in mind when trying to appreciate the extent to which religious data is strongly gendered.

The Hermeneutics of Suspicion

Women's studies has taught historians of religion to approach their materials with what has been termed a "hermeneutics of suspicion."[15] That is, women's studies has made clear both the biased nature of many religious materials and the biases of many historians of religion. Women's studies has taught history of religions to be suspicious of sources or scholars that condemn, belittle, or ignore women and to look harder and more critically at religious materials with a view to discovering women's religious worlds. Women's studies has made it difficult, indeed, impossible, to rest content with the conclusion that women's religious lives were either the same as men's or of no interest simply because materials written by males (whether primary or scholarly sources) do not mention women or relegate them to a secondary, "other" role. The hermeneutics of suspicion has taught the historian of religions to be cautious when reading (or writing) about "the ideal Hindu woman." Too often in the past (and in the present) historians of religions have uncritically accepted an androcentric view of women as an objective description of their values, lives, and outlooks. The view found in many Hindu writings that a woman should devote her entire life to serving her husband (the ideal of the *pativratā*), even if he is a contemptible lout, does actually describe the lives of many Hindu women. The hermeneutics of suspicion, however, asks whose view this is and whose interests are being served by idealizing women this way. It is suspicious of descriptions of women that patently serve male interests. The hermeneutics of suspicion seeks to look beyond or behind androcentric biases in both primary and scholarly sources in order to discover women's own voices, which often dissent from male stereotypes of women.

Engaged Scholarship

Women's studies has also placed a good deal of emphasis on the fact that all scholarship is subjective to some extent. It has raised doubts concerning the possibility (and the desirability) of totally disinterested, objective, detached scholarship. Many in women's studies have said that all scholarship has an agenda and that it is best to be aware of what it is. In the case of many of those in women's studies, the agenda concerns undertaking scholarship that will alleviate the oppression of women in one way or another. It is aimed at increasing the scholarly awareness of women and the androcentric nature of most past, and much present, scholarship. The aim is to undertake engaged scholarship[16]—scholarship that is aware of its agenda and pursues it with passion.

In the case of history of religions, this has meant soul searching, as it claims to be objective and scientific. In its origins it sought to disassociate itself from any theological or cultural bias or viewpoint. How successful it has been in this respect is a matter of debate. It is clear, however, that in history of religions, as in other disciplines, there are certain paradigms, preferences, and predilections that dominate its scholarship. These are rarely consciously acknowledged by those in the field and often must be pointed out by critics.[17] Women's studies has challenged history of religions to look more carefully at its underlying paradigms. It has also invited historians of religions to be more forthright in undertaking their research as part of a wider theological, social, political, moral, or economic agenda. It has invited historians of religions to make value judgments concerning what we might term good and bad religion, for example.

Goddess Religion

Women's studies has also generated a greater interest among historians of religions in goddess religion. Twenty-five years ago there was little research being conducted on goddesses. This is in striking contrast to the present, when many scholars are actively engaged in research on goddess worship and mythology. In Hinduism, for example, recent major scholarly works on goddesses include: Douglas Renfrew Brooks, *Auspicious Wisdom: The Texts and Traditions of Śrīvidyā Śākta Tantrism in South India* (Albany: State University of New York Press, 1992; C. Mackenzie Brown, *The Triumph of the Goddess: The Canonical Model and Theological Visions of the Devī-Bhāgavata Purāṇa* (Albany: State University of New York Press, 1990); Thomas Coburn, *Encountering the Goddess: A Translation of the Devī-Māhātmya and a Study of its Interpretation* (Albany: State University of New York Press: 1991); Kathleen Erndl, *Victory to the Mother: The Hindu Goddess of Northwest India in Myth, Ritual, and Symbol* (New York: Oxford University Press, 1993); Alf Hiltebeitel, *The Cult of Draupadī*, 2 vols. (Chicago: University of Chicago Press, 1988); Cynthia Ann Humes, "The Text and Temple of the Great Goddess: The *Devī-Māhātmya* and the Vindhyācal Temple of Mirzapur" (Ph.D. diss., University of Iowa, 1990); Stanley Kurtz, *All the Mothers Are One: Hindu India and the Cultural Reshaping of Psychoanalysis* (1992); Rachel Fell McDermott, "Evidence for the Transformation of the Goddess Kālī: Kamalākānta Bhaṭṭācārya and the Bengali Śākta Padāvalī Tradition" (Ph.D. diss., Harvard University, 1993); Hillary Peter Rodrigues, "The Image of the Goddess Durgā and Her Worship in Banaras" (Ph.D. diss., McMaster University, 1993); and William S. Sax, *Mountain Goddess: Gender and Politics in a Himalayan Pilgrimage* (New York: Oxford University Press, 1991). During the past twenty-five years, a large and detailed body of scholarship has been produced that gives us a rich, complex, refined picture of goddess worship in many parts of India and a clear analysis of Hindu goddess mythology.

Interest among historians of religions in goddess religion can be related to the influence of women's studies in two ways. First, because of women's studies, more women have become interested in history of religions. Women's studies has encouraged more women to pursue the academic life, which used to be completely dominated by men (the situation in history of religions was no different from any other field). Many of these women historians of religions have shown interest in goddess religion as part of a wider interest in female symbolism. Second, within women's studies itself, there has developed an intense interest in goddess religion in prehistory, which is believed to be part of a nonpatriarchal, matristic culture predating patriarchy. By focusing scholarly attention on goddess religion, women's studies has sparked an interest in goddess religion among historians of religions, both female and male.

Androgyny in the History of Religions

Rita Gross, as early as 1977, called for what she termed an *androgynous outlook* as a necessary preliminary to methodology in the history of religions.[18] The androgynous perspective involves acknowledging that any model for humanity must contain both female and male. It subverts the tendency of androcentric scholarship to "collapse the male norm and the human norm,"[19] to exclude the female altogether or to relegate the female to the status of object. Instead of studying women as adjuncts to males, or women's religion as a deviation, approximation, or curious expression of normative male religion, the androgynous approach affirms that female and male religion and spirituality are often separate and parallel. Much of male religion, as we know all too well on the basis of androcentric data and androcentric scholarship, excludes women. What is also obvious, however, is that much female religion excludes male participation. The task of the historian of religions is no longer to study women's religion as a reflection of male religion but to study women's religion in its own right, as a phenomenon that makes sense in its own terms.

Problems

Women's studies, particularly insofar as it is informed by feminist analysis and principles, poses certain difficult problems for history of religions. In much feminist analysis, human culture is perceived to be unrelievedly patriarchal, androcentric, and usually misogynist. In this analysis males are invariably the victimizers and women the victims. Women live under the shadow of male oppression and are not allowed to lead their own lives. Surely there are many examples of male oppression of women. But does it help the historian of religions in interpreting her data to operate with the view that this situation is universal and omnipresent? Is this the place to begin? It seems to me that this position is often reductionistic.

Categorizing males as oppressors and women as victims can also lead to objectifying women as a category and blinding the historian of religions to women's own voices, keeping him or her from hearing women as subjects. This has become clear in conversations between Western feminists and women in non-Western cultures concerning certain religious-cultural practices, such as clitoridectomy or Muslim women wearing the *hijab*. The temptation for Western feminists, indeed Western scholars in general, is to condemn such practices as oppressive of women and illustrative of patriarchal values. When women who practice these customs defend them, they are considered to have been brainwashed by the patriarchy. That is, they are objectified and characterized as victims. It is not easy, in my opinion, to know where the truth lies in many of these cases. It seems important to me, however, to allow the women who seek to defend these practices as significant in their own religious lives to speak to us as historians of religions.[20] The tension that sometimes exists between Western and non-Western women concerning some of these practices may suggest that Western analysis and categories sometimes tend to objectify and generalize unfairly.

A continuing problem for history of religions is the extent to which such data is unavailable for study. It is unavailable precisely because of the centrality of gender in most cultures. Part of the problem in the early history of the history of religions, when nearly all historians of religions were male, was that women's religious lives were often hidden, often deliberately hidden, from male investigators. That this problem was exacerbated by scholarly androcentrism and a general disinterest on the part of males in women's religion, goes without saying. But the problem remains, quite apart from scholarly androcentrism. Put simply: women scholars are often not welcome to study certain aspects of male religion, and male scholars are not welcome to study certain aspects of women's religion. In the end, perhaps, the only realistic conclusion is for historians of religions to accept this situation and to recognize that in many cases we can only perceive a partial picture of the whole which must be completed by colleagues of the opposite sex.

Conclusion

It is no longer possible for historians of religions to focus exclusively, or even primarily, on men's religion. Our classrooms are filled with students, both women and men, who are now quick to ask: "What about women?" Women's studies has woken up the academy to the scandal of androcentric scholarship and the adrocentrism implicit in many of the materials historians of religions study. This has greatly broadened the field of history of religions, expanding its interests into areas once ignored or neglected. Historians of religions, now well aware of the extent to which males have dominated literary sources, and also the extent to which males insist on speaking for women, are inclined to go directly to women themselves to study how they live out their religion. Historians of religions are now less inclined to generalize about all people in a tradition on the basis of literary sources alone. There is a growing interest and respect for oral tradition, in-depth interviews with women, and what was often called, somewhat disdainfully, "popular religion," which often meant religious practices and beliefs of women. Women's studies has chastened history of religions, and the discipline is much the better for it.

Notes

1. Eliade, *A History of Religious Ideas,* v. 1: *From the Stone Age to the Eleusinian Mysteries* (Chicago: University of Chicago Press, 1978), xiii.

2. To a great extent this meant, in practice, the study of Asian and "native" traditions. In the Chicago school there was a strong emphasis (to a great extent because of Eliade's own background) on South Asian and native materials, and a fairly strong bias against the biblical traditions (Judaism and Christianity) and Islam. China also tended to take second place to the religions native to India and nonliterate cultures.

3. Rita Gross, "Androcentrism and Androgyny in the Methodology of History of Religions," in *Beyond Androcentrism: New Essays on Women and Religion,* ed. Rita Gross (Missoula: Scholars Press, 1977), 7.

4. Ibid., 10.

5. Susan Wadley, *Shakti: Power in the Conceptual Structure of Karimpur Religion* (Chicago: Department of Anthropology, University of Chicago, 1975), 37.

6. See John Stratton Hawley, "Images of Gender in the Poetry of Krishna," in *Gender and Religion: On the Complexity of Symbols,* ed. Caroline Walker Bynum, Stevan Harrell, and Paula Richman (Boston: Beacon Press, 1986), 231–256.

7. See Kathryn Rennie, "The Struggle for Liberation in the Therīgāthā," MA thesis, MacMaster University, 1990, 123–124.

8. Cynthia Ann Humes, "The Text and Temple of the Great Goddess: The *Devī-Māhātmya* and the Vindhyācal Temple of Mirzapur," Ph.D. diss., University of Iowa, 1990, 517.

9. For example, Barbara Newman, *Sister of Wisdom: St. Hildegard's Theology of the Feminine* (Berkeley: University of California Press, 1987).

10. For example, the Zar cult of North Africa: Janice Boddy, *Wombs and Alien Spirits: Women, Men, and the Zar Cult in Northern Sudan* (Madison: University of Wisconsin Press, 1989).

11. Some recent works in Hinduism include: Mary McGee, "Feasting and Fasting: The Vrata Tradition and its Significance for Hindu Women," Ph.D. diss., Harvard University, 1987; Anne M. Pearson, "'Because it Gives me Peace of Mind': Functions and Meanings of *Vrats* in the Religious Lives of Hindu Women in Banaras," Ph.D. diss., McMaster University, 1992; and several articles in Julia Leslie (ed.), *Roles and Rituals for Hindu Women* (Delhi: Motilal Banarsidass, 1992).

12. James L. Watson, "Standardizing the Gods: The Promotion of T'ien Hou ('Empress of Heaven') along the South China Coast, 960–1960," in *Popular Culture in Late Imperial China,* ed. David Johnson, Andrew J. Nathan, and Evelyn S. Rawski (Berkeley: University of California Press, 1985), 292–324.

13. Hillary Peter Rodrigues, "The Image of the Goddess Durgā and Her Worship in Banāras," Ph.D. diss., McMaster University, 1993, 257.

14. Ibid., 236–260.

15. As far as I know, the first person to use this term in reference to feminist scholarship was Elisabeth Schüssler Fiorenza, *In Memory of Her: A Feminist Theological Reconstruction of Christian Origins* (New York: Crossroad, 1983), 56.

16. This term is used by Elisabeth Schüssler Fiorenza in speaking of feminist biblical scholarship (*Bread Not Stone: The Challenge of Feminist Biblical Interpretation* [Boston: Beacon Press, 1984], 46). She also uses such terms as *advocacy scholarship* and *evaluative scholarship* (ibid., 43, 66, 84–92).

17. See, for example, Gregory Schopen, "Archaeology and Protestant Presuppositions in the Study of Indian Buddhism," *History of Religions* 31, no. 1 (August, 1991): 1-23, and Edward Said, *Orientalism* (New York: Vintage Books, 1979).

18. "Androcentrism and Androgyny in the Methodology of History of Religions," in *Beyond Androcentrism: New Essays on Women and Religion,* ed. Rita Gross (Missoula: Scholars Press, 1977), 7–22.

19. Ibid., 13.

20. I am grateful to Philippa Carter for raising these issues in response to my request to reflect on the interaction between women's studies and history of religions.

2

From the Phenomenology of Religion to Feminism and Women's Studies

KATHERINE K. YOUNG

Introduction

There have been two sea-changes in the past century on the topic of religion and women. The first involved the transition from Christian perspectives with their normative (ethical and ontological) underpinnings to the *empirical* study of world religions based on insiders' views analyzed in comparative and historical frames. This sea-change was the product of the *Religionswissenschaft* school with its subdivisions: the phenomenology of the religion and the history of religions. The second involved the realization that these emic views were, in point of fact, still partial because they represented only the perspectives of elite males in the world religions. This made the scholarly claims of universals, patterns, and "essences" based on comparisons of all religions inadequate at best and misogynist at worst. This sea-change was, of course, the product of feminist critique of religions and its scholarly wing, women's studies. In this chapter, I will (1) present the major contributions of phenomenological philosophy and the phenomenology of religion; (2) compare these to feminism and women's studies; and (3) consider whether the approaches can prove mutually corrective and create a useful synergy for future studies of women and religion.

Phenomenology Explained

The phenomenology of religion as a method has its roots in the "phenomenological movement." The latter began in nineteenth-century Germany and Austria and extended through the first half of the twentieth century with the philosophical thought of Franz Brentano, Carl Stumpf, Edmund Husserl, Alexander Pfänder, Adolf Reinach, Moritz Geiger, Max Scheler, Martin Heidegger, and Nicolai Hartmann. It also spread to France, inspiring Gabriel Marcel, Jean-Paul Sartre, Maurice Merleau-Ponty, and Paul Ricoeur.[1] The term *phenomenology* is derived from the dictum that initially inspired this philosophical movement: "to the things [themselves]" *(zu den Sachen)*.

Scholars of religion sensed a kinship with the phenomenological movement, despite the latter's origins in philosophy. This was partly because of a turn toward empiricism in the study of religion and the distinction of *Religionswissenschaft* ("the scientific study of religion"), from theology and metaphysics. Among the European scholars involved were the nineteenth century figures F. Max Müller and C. P. Tiele and the twentieth century scholars W. Brede Kristensen, C. Jouco Bleeker, Rudolf Otto, Gerardus van der Leeuw, Joachim Wach, Raffaele Pettazzoni, and Mircea Eliade. By the 1950s, this phenomenological tradition was taking root in North America, especially at the University of Chicago. There, Wach, Eliade, and Ricoeur contributed to a "school" called the Phenomenology and History of Religions. Their approach involved synchronic or cross-cultural comparisons and the search for essences, or types (in other circles, this was called comparative religion), but also the historical study of religions with an emphasis on philology and texts.

As American students began to develop their linguistic skills in specific religions, and as the patterns or essences "detected" by phenomenologists came under attack as "false" representations of "real" phenomena, the phenomenology of religion began to wane. At that point, the term *history of religions* became the name of a subdiscipline in the field of religious studies. Whereas every major religion was included in early phenomenology of religion (comparative religion), the new term included in practice but not necessarily in theory every religion *except* Christianity. This division expressed the secondary status of these religions in the West and the long tradition of studying Christianity in the university (represented by faculty appointments, subdisciplines, and so on). The comparative study of world religions gradually dropped out of sight, therefore, even as general questions about the nature of religion and its status as a distinct discipline continued and books by Otto, van der Leeuw, Wach, and Eliade remained popular in the classroom.

It is striking that other disciplines in the humanities did not eliminate the comparative approach. Anthropology, for example, developed extensive data banks (the Human Resource Area files) and refined quantitative methods to describe and explain cross-cultural phenomena. Sociologists and political scientists, too, continued to use comparative methods. Gradually, in the 1990s, comparative studies in religion began to make a comeback. Now, though, the comparisons were more limited in scope.

Empiricism

Despite their many differences, phenomenological philosophers have shared a common method.[2] It begins with the particular—that is to say, the concrete. Claiming to be a legitimate form of empiricism and a descriptive science, it is based on the act of "direct" seeing and hearing. The key here is the adjective *direct,* because we usually experience phenomena through ready-made understandings created by common sense, conventional interpretations, doctrines, theories, and so forth. The latter are deeply embedded in our consciousness. They are used automatically to process experiences mediated by the senses, the unconscious, and the imagination. They seem natural, therefore, as if belonging to "the thing itself."

The idea of direct experience is captured in Wittgenstein's phrase "don't think but look," inspiring an intentional observation of any experience.[3] Phenomenologists call this precognitive concentration on experience, preceding analysis and understanding, an "intuitive" grasp of the thing itself—that is, *what* appears in experience itself and *how* it appears (that is, how it changes depending on the angle or the limitations of the physical apparatus of the eye, thus any perspectival modification—cubes that appear to be trapezoids, say, or dabs of paint that suggest objects in Impressionist paintings). The aim of a full description based directly on experience is to prevent a *premature* simplification, which is a danger of the positivist approach to empiricism.

Therefore, freeing the senses from their cultural baggage is done by becoming as self-conscious as possible about whatever has been culturally superimposed on phenomena. This is an intentional activity. It involves training, conscientious self-criticism, and methodical care. The exercise is called *epoché,* "bracketing out," for instance, the question of whether something actually exists. As a result, phenomenologists generously accept everything that comes into view as a tentative fact. By extension, *epoché* refers to the self-conscious removal of all cultural superimpositions so that the "thing itself" can be intuited.

Phenomenologists consider their own bodies the best training grounds. Husserl, unlike the scientists of his day (who were interested in anatomy, physiology, and organs), examined the nature of body-consciousness as the "life-world" *(Lebenswelt).* Sartre explored the body not only as a precognitive and automatic engagement with life, a given, but also as the source for an awareness that occasionally erupts into consciousness—especially with pain and death. For him, moreover, bodies are consciously experienced links between ourselves and others, including their awareness of our bodies. This can arouse emotions such as embarrassment or timidity and thus create another kind of bodily awareness. Merleau-Ponty described the body as the primary place for existence, for the appropriation of space, and for the emotional life related to pleasure, pain, and libido. In his *Phenomenology of Perception,*[4] he discusses the phenomenology of the body, examining its spatiality, motility, and sexuality, along with its relation to expression and speech.

Phenomenology has also been used to explore psychology. Now, by suspending the question of their reality, dreams could be taken seriously as proper topics for investigation. They are, after all, "things" that appear to the consciousness. It is no coincidence, then, that several phenomenological philosophers wrote about psychology (Brentano, Husserl, Pfänder, Geiger, Sartre, Merleau-Ponty, and Ricoeur). Moreover, because phenomenology allowed for a focus on direct experience, it created scope for scholars to appreciate claims of religious experience by individuals (what became known as the discipline of the psychology of religion). The exercise of *epoché* was especially valuable, because it precluded worry over the existence of deities, the truth claims of cosmogonic myths, or the efficaciousness of magic so that phenomenologists of religion could observe, describe, and interpret phenomenona like these—first from emic perspectives (those of insiders) and subsequently from etic ones (those of outsiders) by inductively determining a yet more complex pattern based on *all* emic perspectives.

Distinguished from, yet closely related to, this initial step of trying to experience something directly, are several analytical steps that must *precede* description. Phenomenologists make systematic comparisons to detect similarities and differences (a process Husserl called "intentional analysis").[5] In this way, they determine which features constitute a phenomenon by making it unique. They arrange similar phenomena in a series (like colors in the spectrum). Then, they determine the nodal points (such as pure colors in the spectrum). Next they systematically omit or substitute features (a process called "imaginative variation") to determine whether they are necessary or accidental ingredients. Which colors, for example, must be mixed to make the non-primary colors? Or, which features are required to form a triangle rather than a square? The phenomena so defined are arranged, in turn, from concrete, or particular, to abstract, or general (a shade of red to red as a primary color to the more general concept of color). They call these patterns, which are abstracted from particulars, "essences." These patterns allow them to establish classifications. Sometimes, new phenomena fit into existing classifications; at other times, new classifications must be created for them. Although the grounding of phenomenological empiricism is in the intimate experience of an individual body and consciousness, it is by no means contained by or restricted to these. Phenomenologists move from their own specific and concrete experiences to those of others by way of comparison. That way, they can determine whether any concrete particulars are experienced in common. They become more confident, of course, when the latter are reported—despite the epistemological gap between self and other. And when this occurs often enough, there is an empirical basis for declaring that a pattern exists. In that case, there has been a passage from the particular to the general.

For some phenomenologists, patterns consist of objective, in the sense of invariable, features. For other phenomenologists, patterns consist of common features suggestive of probabilities. They also call these patterns "essences" but view them as a "family of resemblances" rather than a set of invariable features.

The phenomenological method has been used by scholars of the *Religionswissenschaft* school because they have wanted to ground their understanding of religion in empiricism. It was especially important in connection with interreligious encounters of the eighteenth and nineteenth centuries. These clearly required a new approach, one that did not project the values, norms, theories, and classifications of Christian theology and Western metaphysics onto other religions. This had prevented scholars from describing non-Christian religions in their own terms. In fact, it fostered serious misunderstandings and contributed to the colonial mentality. The new method was obviously superior for those interested in the scholarly study of religions.[6]

Like their counterparts pursuing phenomenological philosophy, phenomenologists of religion have been interested in more general patterns. In their case, these are discovered by induction when the data of many religions are gathered and systematically compared.[7] Perhaps the most famous phenomenologist of religion was Eliade. His method involved collecting religious expressions of many natural phenomena (earth, sky, water, trees, and so forth) as well as cultural ones (myths, rituals, spiritual techniques, and so on) in various times and places. In this way, he could determine which features occur repeatedly. These constituted the types—that is, the patterns or "essences," based on a family of resemblances.

Subjectivism

Any claim to empiricism on the part of phenomenologists has had to deal with the larger issues of metaphysics, ontology, and epistemology despite *epoché* as a step in the method. Because "things" always appear in the context of human consciousness, some phenomenologists have questioned whether anything can really exist apart from it. How can that be known? By the eighteenth century, this question had already shaken the traditional foundations of metaphysics, ontology, and epistemology. As a result, their foundations shifted to the individual. Descartes provided the famous dictum: "I think, therefore I am." And Kant, in his *Critique of Pure Reason*, argued that the limits of reason made the metaphysical "no longer the *object* of knowledge but the immanent *structure* of knowledge."[8]

Some phenomenological philosophers participated in this sea–change by placing emphasis on the process of knowing, how the object appears in the consciousness depending on perspective (called the "constitution" of the object, and the "conditions of possibility" of knowledge).[9] Husserl, in particular, paid attention to the "way in which the appearances of an object were constituted in and by consciousness."[10] And that, in turn, had several effects.

One effect has been to extend the observation of how perspective changes the perception of an object to the idea that an object is constructed and deconstructed. Though the latter term was not used by phenomenologists, the idea behind it would become important as the name of a subsequent and closely related movement in the last quarter of the twentieth century—deconstruction.

A second effect has been to convince some phenomenologists (especially those interested in psychological or philosophical issues) that *consciousness* is even more important than the *things* that appear within it. They discussed consciousness first; only then did they turn to the following: (1) consciousness *of* something; (2) the grasping or seeing of that of which consciousness is conscious as a phenomenon in itself; (3) the recognition that all this is pure subjectivity; and (4) the recognition that subjectivity is "processual," belonging to a flow of consciousness, even when focused on something.

A third effect of this focus on consciousness has been to make lived human experience, the individual, and the ordinary events of daily existence the focus of philosophy (though this wasn't exactly a novum in history, because early philosophy and much of religion had always focused on daily life). Similarly, the spiritual experiences of *ordinary* individuals became important topics of investigation in the field of religious studies, thereby broadening its scope beyond ecclesiastical institutions, religious norms, and canonical texts. In a sense, the phenomenology of religions paved the way for the later deconstructive, postmodern, and feminist *challenges* to texts, norms, and institutions— which widened the scope of religious studies to include vernacular texts and marginalized groups.

Unlike some phenomenological philosophers, phenomenologists of religion have not followed the path of subjectivism. They have remained vigilant against the idea of reducing religious phenomena to the unconsciousness, imagination, or cognition. The reason, they have claimed, lies in empirical data: individuals commonly report experiences of "otherness" breaking into or arising within daily life.[11]

Idealism

The detection of general patterns has been understood as empirical induction by many phenomenologists. This has been considered a hallmark, in fact, of phenomenology. Nevertheless, some have claimed that more is at stake. Despite phenomenological philosophy's early concern with empiricism, it has developed the reputation of adhering to idealism for several reasons. One is its preoccupation with essences. Phenomenological empiricism, as noted above, has emphasized the disciplined watching of physical and mental experiences, moving by analogy from the particular to the general in order to detect common patterns or "essences." Husserl called the essence, the ideal being *(Eidos)*; the investigation of general essences, the *eidetic intuition (Wesensschau);* and the ego "which remains as an irreducible residue after having been subjected to the phenomenological reduction,"[12] the "transcendental ego." These terms have stirred considerable controversy even within the phenomenological movement. They have been suspected of introducing into the new empiricism—through the back door, as it were—either mysticism or Platonic idealism. Those who have claimed that empirical induction yields a generality that is necessary or invariable have suggested that essences represent a priori or ideal knowledge.[13]

Phenomenological philosophy has been considered idealism, moreover, because of Husserl's idea that things themselves are *constituted* by consciousness. This implies that "things" exist only in the mind (hence idealism). Not all phenomenologists have followed Husserl down this path. Merleau-Ponty, for instance, considered the method nothing more than a way of discovering the world, of catching the unique facts of existence prior to cognition and interpretation. "It denounces by implication the appeal to subjectivity and attempts to combine the subjective with the objective approach through something which might be called 'bipolar phenomenology.'"[14] Thus, for some, *epoché* is a technique by which they can make the issue of ontology temporarily irrelevant. For others, it represents an ontological decision in which "the real" becomes the mind or at least the self. Just as many phenomenologists of religion have rejected the subjectivism of some phenomenological philosophers, for instance, they have rejected idealism by refusing to explain away religious phenomena as nothing but products of the mind.

Hermeneutics

Closely related to phenomenology is the idea of hermeneutics: the "science" of interpretation. Description of human cognitive and emotional life is never devoid of meaning, because it signifies something. Whereas some meanings are obvious and belong to surface phenomena, others belong to the deep structure or less accessible layers of cultures and therefore are implicit, obscure, or even hidden. This necessitates their uncovering or an inference of meaning from the clues at hand.[15] The shift to hermeneutics began with Heidegger. In his analysis of *Dasein,* or human "being," he detected in the structure of moods a deeper meaning. This involved an interest in the nature of *being* itself and ultimately in "being-toward-death." On these depth/transcendent topics, he wrote with certainty (rather than with the tentativeness of a hypothesis to be subsequently verified). If Heidegger thought that this certainty about unseen things could be justified, suggests Spiegelberg (who does not seem to be convinced himself), it must be because he was convinced that the phenomena themselves, with their significance unveiled through the phenomenological method, had led him directly to these deeper insights about human existence. Spiegelberg (who made this comment when Heidegger was still alive) concludes that Heidegger "now seems to be in touch with 'openings' of being which reveal to him a cosmic sense about which at this stage we are still kept in suspense, especially since it seems to be no longer in our power to make 'Being' reveal it, as the initiative for such revelation has shifted to 'Being' itself."[16] Much the same could be said about Sartre's and Merleau-Ponty's "deeper insights."

Phenomenologists of religion have been comfortable with talk of being, death, and meaning. These have been the great topics of religious texts, after all, throughout the ages. Pettazzoni believed that the phenomenology of religion would elucidate the "sense" or meaning of a religion and that historical study would focus on the facts and their development. Intuiting, analyzing, understanding, and describing religious experiences led Rudolf Otto to recognize a common experience, what he termed the unique feeling of the *wholly other* or the *holy (das Heilige)*.[17] With its two prevailing characteristics—*mysterium tremendum et fascinans*—this ineffable, opaque, ultimate, and transcendent feeling erupts into everyday life. Although cultures try to express it through symbols, harness it through rituals, or recover it through spiritual exercises, it remains elusive. But because of its commonality, it is considered a general essence, and therefore a priori. Calling this the numinous or the sacred, Otto concluded that the sheer commonality of this precognitive experience suggests its a priori existence and its sui generis nature, even though it cannot be known independently of the experience of body and consciousness and its first order expressions through symbols, myths, rituals, and so forth. Subsequent phenomenologists of religion have argued that the paradox must stand: not of consciousness but through consciousness; not of the self but through the self.[18]

Eliade, too, emphasized the irreducible nature of religion. The sacred erupts into the profane in the form of kratophanies, hierophanies, or theophanies. He believed that because we can tap into the sacred by repeating myths and rituals, which have preserved as memories the primary experiences of others, we can induce the experience of the sacred. This experience is vital (judging from reports of its pervasive power), because it enables humans to orient themselves in space and time with reference to human destiny, brings order to chaos, establishes a meaningful world, overcomes the tyranny of time (especially as represented by death), provides sacred archetypal prototypes for human activities, and offers a "window" to the "real" (despite the opaqueness of the profane realm). "The sacred reveals absolute reality and at the same time makes orientation possible; hence it founds the world in the sense that it fixes the limits and establishes the order of the world."[19] Eliade defined the sacred as *absolute reality,* an "essence." His definition is based on religious data found in an enormous number of textual and anthropological reports. Despite its pervasiveness, the sacred always remains elusive, partly hidden; the observable realm is completed by these experiences of and journeys into the unobservable. As a result, scholars of religion must oppose reductionism. Eliade did not ignore the role of consciousness. He saw in the "things" of consciousness (such as precognitive experiences, symbols, myths, and rituals) possible openings to another dimension of reality. These might allow direct intuitings, as it were, of *Being.*[20] Because of its nonreductive stance (by way of both what it accepts as "facts" about human existence and its refusal to dismiss testimonies as mere fictions), the study of religion as understood by Eliade must be an autonomous discipline. He wanted it to bring about a new humanism. This would enrich Western consciousness and, possibly, enhance the human condition itself.

Today the term *hermeneutics* is associated primarily with Ricoeur. Ricoeur's interest in phenomenology began with his translation of Husserl's *Ideen.* He has both drawn ideas from the movement and been critical of it. For him phenomenology is preeminently a method that provides good description. It is not a transcendental idealism as understood by Husserl. Ricoeur has had an abiding interest in Christianity, the mystery of creation, ontology, metaphysics, and the nature of human finitude. Like Christians, he understands human beings in terms of a broken unity, the break creating ambition, hatred, and other destructive passions. He believes that modern human beings are incapable of naively believing in the doctrines of traditional religion or philosophy. On the other hand, he believes that they are by nature open to polysemic myths, symbols, and rituals. Ricoeur makes a hermeneutical "wager" on belief and restoration of the "whole soul." Through the imagination and the "surplus" meaning of literature, the sacred can be discerned. Interpreting literature, albeit with a critical awareness, leads to a new level of meaning. Ricoeur calls it the "second naiveté." With that in mind, he argues that "an *archaeology* of the decentered subject should stand in tension with a *teleology* of the fulfilled subject, childhood dreams, works of art, and religious symbols, as lived possibilities for a transformed future. In spite of its overdetermined origins, the imagination can activate these possibilities and offer the broken subject new ways of "being in the world."[21] By reading texts, which are more like performances than propositions, the "world" deepens and expands. Ricoeur examines the contexts of texts, moreover, to see how they participate in "structures of domination and ideology." Doing so is important for his project of gathering together the fragments of individual identity into a story that facilitates integration and wholeness but, at the same time, responds to the need for justice and compassion. Ricoeur refers to the power and numinous nature of the sacred. He maintains that religious beliefs have their own integrity

and believes that interpretation should take into account the self-understandings of religious communities. He argues, moreover, that the first step in
understanding religions must be to explore them on their own terms, including
linguistic ones. He places heavy emphasis on language, in fact, using religious
texts to broaden the horizons of individuals. Texts are of two basic types: the
oral traditions of primordial societies (focused on nature) and the literary ones
of complex societies (focused on history). In short, Ricoeur has shifted the
focus from "consciousness" (by the phenomenological philosophers) to texts.

Feminist and Phenomenological Methods Compared

Few feminists identify themselves as phenomenologists. Nevertheless, direct
and indirect links can be discerned when the presuppositions and methods of
feminist schools are compared with those of phenomenological ones. Phenomenologists, be they philosophers or scholars of religion, want to prevent
the unconscious superimposition of values, categories, interpretations, and
theories on things so that the nature of "things" might be revealed. Feminists
want to prevent the unconscious superimposition of *patriarchal* values, categories, interpretations, and theories—termed "false consciousness"—so that
the real facts about, and the experiences of, women might be revealed. And
just as it can be argued that masculine ways of thinking should not be projected onto women, it can be argued that "white" ones should not be projeced
onto black people, heterosexual ones onto homosexual people, and so on.
Feminists have not derived their concept of "false consciousness" from phenomenologists, of course, but from Marxists.[22] Karl Marx defined it as the
bourgeois values, beliefs, interpretations, and theories that are projected onto
other classes; eventually, they come to seem so natural, universal, and inevitable that their original sinister purpose is forgotten.[23] In other words, the
bourgeoisie constructs a culture to support its own dominance. Marx's idea of
the construction of culture has contributed to the development of hermeneutics, postmodernism, and deconstruction, all of which are de rigueur among
many feminists at the end of the twentieth century.

Take hermeneutics. Ricoeur's "hermeneutics of suspicion" has been used
by many feminists to question any suggestion of patriarchal values. All texts
written by men, in fact, should be approached with suspicion regarding latent
androcentric biases or structures of male domination. Ricoeur's emphasis on
the imagination has also proven attractive to feminists because it has legitimated
new "female" ways of seeing the world. His idea of the "surplus" of meaning
in literature and the importance of symbol and metaphor have helped to dis-
lodge the idea of the fixity of scripture and opened interpretation to polysemic
meanings (thereby creating conceptual room for feminist interpretations). His
concept of the imagination has also been useful to legitimate the act of women's

story telling as creating an authentic identity if not the actual stories as definitive of reality. Finally, Ricoeur's idea of the fragmentation of modern cultures has offered feminists ways to understand the fragmented nature of women's lives and how they can be integrated and healed through the imagination.

Just as phenomenological philosophers refer to the "construction" of things in the conscious mind, some feminists refer to the "construction" of gender, symbols, and so forth, the corollary of the idea of the bourgeoisie's creation of cultural forms to buttress its own power. For many feminists, deconstruction is the method of choice for challenging world views embedded in the consciousness, language, and culture of *men* (especially Western scientists and professionals). They have popularized the thought of Jacques Derrida (who had been a student of Ricoeur), including his critique of "logocentrism" (formerly known in philosophy as "nominalism,"[24] the idea that words refer directly to real objects in the external world and real concepts existing independently of language). This shifts attention from things or ideas "out there" (whether they be the claims of science, religion, or anything else) to language "here" (any example of which becomes a "text"). According to Derrida, language is inherently unstable: (1) its words are interdependent and "play" against each other; (2) it is filled with rhetorical devices, such as metaphors and symbols, that create "surpluses" of meaning; and (3) it is at best a "trace" of its larger significance (which becomes apparent only over time). The latter is explained as follows: "readers" bring their own experiences into the act of understanding "texts," thereby creating a plurality of meanings. But this undermines objectivity, facts, knowledge, and even logic. "Texts" are incapable of bearing facts or being used logically to make predictions, for instance, because both would depend on the truth of premises and the validity of inferences (which are supposedly impossible because of the inherently unstable nature of language).

Feminist popularizers of all this go one step further. Because there can be no truth or validity (which would imply the acknowledgment of some criterion to assess interpretations), and because there are potentially as many interpretions of a "text" as there are interpreters, one interpretation is as good as the next. In other words, all are equal. Closely related to the inherent instability of language and its relativity, they claim, is the fact that culture is constructed—and can therefore be deconstructed—by human beings. For feminist deconstructionists, this ostensible, epistemological relativism supports the belief that all interpretations must be entertained. Its corollary is that "diversity" is the only thing that matters. Its political message is that everyone, at least theoretically, must be included.

Beginning from the observation that women are marginal in the historical record and the texts that compose much of that record, feminists have been interested not so much in *what* can be known but in *why* they themselves have been virtually absent from the textual canons both as knowers and the known.

Their conclusion is that knowledge, whatever that might be, results from the power of elite men. Because knowledge has been produced by elite men, they claim, it is largely about them. Knowledge has not only been androcentric, moreover, it has been misogynistic as well. Thus, just as phenomenologists have scrutinized the conditions underlying knowledge, feminists have done the same thing in connection specifically with knowledge about women.

Unlike phenomenologists, who are interested primarily in what they presume to be the neutral idea of consciousness, feminists are interested primarily in the sex of an author and the cultural definition of gender in that society. Some feminists, in fact, have attacked the very idea of scientific neutrality. Donna Haraway called it "the view from nowhere" or the "god-trick."[25] Feminist analysis of any academic text is sure to provoke the following questions. "Whose knowledge?" "Whose authority?" "Whose evidence?" "Whose science?"[26] As a result, feminists have been suspicious, to say the least, about scientific empiricism, claiming that several factors—the questions asked, the design of research projects, the collection of evidence, and its interpretation—indicate a selection based on collective interests. Facts, in short, are not really facts at all.

Both feminists and philosophical phenomenologists have written about the phenomenology of the body, our direct experience of it, and its social reality. For phenomenologists, human beings are essentially incarnated beings. Feminists, too, have claimed that there can be no knowledge without a knower—and a knower is always "situated" in a particular body.[27] Knowledge is intimately related, they claim in addition, to its type of embodiment,[28] the differences between male and female bodies, in particular, and how these affect psychology. Mary O'Brien, in a now classic description, argues that men and women experience the reproductive cycle in very different ways. Her aim is to demonstrate that the way women experience embodiment is very different from that of men.[29] Both phenomenologists and feminists have opposed the idea that our experience of the body can be studied effectively in any mechanistic way, which they associate with positivist science. But many feminists have a much deeper antipathy to objectification of the female body by men, claiming that doing so (not only in connection with science but also, even more importantly, in connection with sexual pleasure) is a major cause of misogyny.[30]

Closely related to the phenomenology of the body is the phenomenology of the gaze. Both phenomenological philosophers and feminists focus on the "gaze." Sartre explored the human gaze,[31] a topic that grew out of the phenomenological interest in perception. The gaze is different from just seeing and being seen, observed Sartre, because it petrifies, curdles, enslaves, and expresses conflict. Feminists are interested in the *male* gaze directed toward *women*, of course, especially in pornography but also in photography, advertising, film, and television.

Some feminists go beyond phenomenological philosophy by including women's experiences.[32] Because reason and mind have been associated in Western thought with maleness and superiority, whereas body and emotion have been associated with femaleness and inferiority, some want body and emotion now to be included when experience and knowledge are discussed (and others want them not only included but viewed as superior, thereby not eliminating the hierarchy but reversing it to make women innately superior to men).

Both phenomenologists and feminists incorporate intuition, a precognitive kind of knowing, into their concepts of knowledge. For phenomenologists, this is nothing but one step, albeit a very important one, in the phenomenological method. For some feminists, though, it is a characteristic, female way of knowing comparable to the empirical way of knowing associated with men (for other feminists, it is a *superior* way of knowing).

Some phenomenological philosophers have accepted engaged knowledge. By definition, the human body is always engaged with the world. Philosophy, too, is always engaged with the world. Phenomenologists, however, have tried not to be *so* engaged that they become *engulfed* by the world and lose their capacity for critical thought. Describing Merleau-Ponty's politics, for instance, Spiegelberg observes that phenomenologists thought that they should maintain a delicate balance: "the philosopher who is both citizen and philosopher, neither a revolutionary nor a conformist, obeying and disobeying at the same time . . . [an] ambivalent position between Marxist action and Hegelian contemplation."[33] For many feminists, of course, the whole point of knowledge is engagement for the purpose of improving the status of women.

Phenomenological philosophers, as already discussed, have been among the first to draw attention to the perspectival nature of knowledge: how phenomena change with every change of perspective, because all angles cannot be seen at once. Merleau-Ponty asked the following question: "[I]s not to see always to see from somewhere? . . . I am trying to express in this way a certain manner of approaching the object, the 'gaze' in short, which is as indubitable as my own thought, as directly known by me."[34] Feminists have emphasized the fact that identity (race, sex, historical context, and so forth) creates a particular perspective. This has come to be known as "feminist standpoint theory" or "standpoint epistemology." Everyone has a standpoint and therefore a bias. Like phenomenologists, feminists expose the biases of others; they reserve their ammunition, of course, for men.

Just as phenomenologists bracket out concepts of truth and falsity (though, for some, that is just a step in the collection of data), feminists do the same thing in connection with "standpoint epistemology" (i.e., because everyone has a standpoint, there can be no universal claims to truth and falsity). Standpoint theory has been derived partly from deconstruction and postmodernism, it is true, but partly from feminist politics. After white feminists were criticized by black women for being middle-class and "hegemonic," they have intensified their focus on particularity (under the rubric of "pluralism," "diversity," or "multivocality") and emphasized the presence of minorities within the movement. In one sense, this has been a moral response: acknowledging their own power in the social structure. In another sense, though, it has been a political response: maintaining solidarity among women. Phenomenologists focus on perspectives for practical reasons (because they are aspects of "phenomena"), in short, and feminists do so for a political reason (because the "pregendered" analyses of male phenomenologists have been naive or even malicious—part of the universal plot against women).

Due to the fact that the notion of "diversity" has such theoretical and practical importance, most feminists have been reluctant to generalize about human nature. They often refuse, moreover, to generalize about the nature of women (which proves "insensitive" to particular female identities and histories). As a result, feminists usually attack any general pattern as a false "construction" that destroys the individual. Phenomenologists take a very different approach. The whole point of phenomenology is to determine "essences" or the general nature of things. Some feminists have attacked the term *essence*, taking their cue from deconstruction's stand against "logocentrism" (nominalism), and the idea that nothing can be known about anything except its linguistic form or appearance. For them logocentrism and essentialism are not only synonyms, they are the "bad guys" of epistemology (both being lies "constructed" by and for men). They are disturbed, moreover, by the claim of some phenomenologists that "essences" are a priori. Incidentally, this problem was not lost on the phenomenologists; Husserl himself noted the personalization of "being" in individuals, whereby individuals have "each-his-own-ness" *(Jemeinigkeit)*, thus constituting a monad ("the fully concrete ego with its constituted as well as its constituting components, its potentialities, its actualities, and other appurtenances of its private life").[37] So, under the influences of deconstruction, postmodernism, and the politics of identity, which focus on the particular, some feminists have ostensibly opposed the search for *any* patterns—to say nothing of general "essences."

From this discussion, it is obvious that there are many parallels between phenomenology and feminism that have come about by direct and indirect links. Sometimes a distinction is made between feminism and women's studies: the former is activism to improve the status of women (including changing the traditional religions to make them more "female-friendly"—inclusive of replacing gods with goddesses—or the creation of new, or almost new religions altogether), the latter the academic study of women and feminine imagery, especially analysis of women's marginalization or invisibility in the historical record (based on textual studies) and expanding the design of the research by documenting women's real religious lives (based on ethnographies, oral histories, and interviews). If phenomenology is compared to women's studies rather than feminism (which has been hitherto the topic of this chapter), then there are other similarities. In religious studies, the phenomenological methods of *epoché* and empathy are used to understand women in a wide variety of religions and social locations (thereby responding to the call for documenting diversity), and from the specific perspectives of women. The voices of insiders in scholarship (including those of women who both belong to a religion and are scholars of it) have become important. However, very few women's studies scholars have been open to cross-cultural comparisons.[38]

Some Concluding Thoughts

The early phenomenologists now seem hopelessly androcentric with their use of the generic "he" and their universalizing language that never asks whether the experiences of men might differ significantly from those of women, and so on. Moreover, because "essences" have been determined by male phenomenologists on the basis of male experiences alone (whether intentionally or not), women have had good reason for criticizing this kind of scholarship. But does this mean that the phenomenological method is totally inadequate and should be abandoned? What about the concept of "essence" itself? Has it no merits, as some feminists claim? Finally, what about the phenomenologists' insistence that their task be limited to description and interpretation? Is this too limited, as feminists claim, specially in the women's context in which there must be political activism to improve the status of women, if not to revolutionize societies altogether?

First, I will address the general problem of "essence." In defense of phenomenology's interest in essences, it must be granted that inherent in the very nature of language and the acquisition of knowledge is the human capacity to generalize. We could not exist if everything were an utterly discrete moment, an entirely unique entity. That would pose the many problems of solipsism or how to explain causation (also a problem for the Theravada Buddhist doctrine of "momentariness").

Spiegelberg defends the concept of essence as follows: "[W]henever particular phenomena show this kind of affinity, when, for instance, all the reds cluster together in this way," he says, "we can hardly overlook the fact that underlying it is some common pattern or essence in which they all share in varying degrees, and which they all in a sense embody. Seeing reds as red we also see redness, the general essence which is exemplified in all of them. Now it is certainly possible to see these particulars without seeing the general essence. But it is not possible to see them *as particulars* without seeing the general essence which they particularize. Thus, what happens is that on the basis of seeing particulars in their structural affinities we also become aware of the ground of their affinities, the pattern or essence."[39] In other words, we classify shades of red within the general category of red (even though precise classification can vary from one culture to another and even from one period to another). We generally know when it is important to focus on a shade such as orange or pink and when it is important to focus on the fact that they are merely shades of red. The perspective changes, depending on context; the particular and the general are not identical. Both can be useful. Yes, the change of level can cause misunderstandings and often must be clarified, but it has generally been acknowledged that the ability to generalize is not only a feature of language and thought, it is also part of being human.

By the 1990s, during the heyday of postmodernism and deconstruction with its penchant for diversity, the phenomenological method seemed dormant. Just then, Martin Marty and R. Scott Appleby edited a book called *Fundamentalisms Observed*.[40] In their introduction and conclusion, they argue for a revival of phenomenology. Not surprisingly, they include several caveats to ward off attacks on "essences," even when they are considered clusters of characteristics creating a "family of resemblances"[41] rather than a pattern determined by invariable characteristics. They move back and forth between what they call unique examples and patterns. These patterns, they argue, create a "hypothetical aggregate," a "pure fundamentalism." As if to counteract yet again the suspicions that "hypothetical" or "pure" might evoke in readers, Marty and Appleby move from the general pattern back to one particular example. They discuss this in detail, now informed by the insight of comparative analysis. This, in turn, sets the stage for some even more general comments meant to isolate and define "pure fundamentalism." Unlike older attempts at phenomenology, though, this one concludes with a section called "deconstructing pure fundamentalism." Again, as if to forestall their critics, they write that: "[t]his definition of 'pure' fundamentalism, a synthesis of extremes to which certain movements tend, hardly provides an adequate guide to, or reflection of, the complexity and variety of the global phenomena portrayed in this volume. At best it perhaps provides a point of departure for subsequent investigations that, in exploring violations and modifications of this type, will likely render this early description obsolete. Such 'violations of type' are indeed numerous in this volume, and it is worth briefly sketching some of them, not only to demonstrate the complexity of the fundamentalist phenomena but also to indicate some measure of the work that lies ahead in accounting for the almost endless variations on the central themes."[42] They go on to speak of "their tentative beginning in charting varieties of fundamentalism."[43]

This accommodation of phenomenology to postmodernism and deconstruction makes the search for "essences" not a goal but one standpoint among several (for instance, a focus on a particular). If phenomenologists maintain a dialectic between the general and the particular, acknowledge the many levels of generalization, and understand that the greater the generalization the greater the distortion of the particular, their method should continue to be productive. As I have written in another context: "To move beyond our present impasse we should use various methodologies for creating classifications and feel free to experiment with classifications at various levels of generalizations to see what insights they may reveal. It may well be that no one classification will do justice to the material. Perhaps we need Eliade's 'patterns'. . . . Perhaps it is time to learn something from the social anthropologists and their correlations of variables with a large cross-cultural sample."[44]

This takes me to the second problem. Because there is male bias lurking in many phenomenological descriptions of past scholars, does this mean that we should abandon phenomenology? I do not think so. Remember that the major phenomenologists lived in the second half of the nineteenth century and the first half of the twentieth. The major feminists who have influenced Academia have lived in the second half of the twentieth century, especially the last quarter of it. When the phenomenological movement was developing, the concepts of androcentrism and gender had not yet taken hold, though the first feminists were agitating for the vote. Thus, to impose today's analysis from the perspective of gender on the early phenomenologists without keeping this distinction in mind is to indulge in anachronism.

Moreover, despite their critiques of "essentialism," feminists are not as opposed to generalizations as they sometimes claim to be. After all, most discuss women as a group. Besides the biological classification (the fact of female bodies, gestation, and lactation), they speak of women's experiences under patriarchy (their subordination and victimization by men) as if this were a universal of the class of women (despite some evidence to the contrary). Scrutiny of feminist literature also shows a willingness to generalize about the nature of men as a class, either explicitly or implicitly, despite occasional disclaimers. A critic might claim that this is sheer expediancy: feminists talk about diversity within the sisterhood to deal with political differences but about the commonality of the sisterhood to mobilize opposition to whatever hinders women. The fact that *men* are often stereotyped, as noted above, suggests to critics that the feminist view of generalization or essentialism is, moreover, a matter of political expediency than scholarly method. Do not both phenomenologists and feminists, in short, have something to learn and unlearn about generalizations?

This takes me to one final problem for consideration. Phenomenologists of religion have insisted that their task is description and analysis. Feminists say that theirs is critical evaluation and social activism. First, it is necessary to acknowledge that the importance of activism for many feminists creates problems for feminist deconstructionists who want to accept, in good postmodern fashion, all views. The only way to reconcile these two feminist positions—

acceptance of diversity and the need for political action—is to admit that something *else* is going on just beneath the surface: the promotion of one world view. Deconstruction is used *selectively,* in short, and for the purpose of attacking political opponents. In the case of feminism, it is used to attack anything associated with "patriarchy," and (explicitly or implicitly) to promote anything associated with feminism. It is true that feminist deconstruction reveals diverse points of view among women (by rejecting any kind of essence); it is also true, however, that feminist deconstruction usually ignores or conceals the diverse points of view among men. The argument of some feminists against the concept of facts (unless, of course, they happen to support their claims) is also an example of selectivity: they argue that androcentrism, for instance, equals bias: gynocentrism, apparently, equals nothing more more than the attempt to establish "balance" and "diversity." Take yet another example. Although some feminists are quick to protest the objectification of their bodies, they hardly ever mention the many ways in which male bodies are objectified, whether as bodies in the lab, cannon fodder on the battlefield, machines in the factory, or whatever. And they seldom, if ever, ask whether objectification is appropriate in some circumstances even though it is inappropriate in others; the female readers of *Cosmopolitan* have long known, for instance, that women enjoy sex (which, by definition, involves objectification) no less than men— whether that includes "romance" or not. In short, some feminists overcome the inherent contradiction between evaluation for social change and the relativism of postmodernism by not calling attention to the conflict at the theoretical level, but rather by dealing with it at the practical level through the strategy of selection.

When evidence is found to support their political cause, they make vigorous claims about truth, often relying on statistics (even though statistics are notorious even among social scientists for their susceptibility to skewed results). When evidence does not support their political cause, however, they sometimes resort to the claim that it represents nothing but a (biased) perspective, a (hostile) standpoint. Instead of arguing for a reduction in bias of any kind, which would prevent them from advocacy (the inherent problem of "engaged scholarship"), they argue for the promotion of their own bias. In *Feminism and Religion,*[35] for example, Rita Gross claims that, as long as she has explicitly stated the biases, in effect, that guide her scholarship, she has "achieved the level of objectivity that is possible. . . . Other scholars may offer other points of view, but not greater objectivity."[36] But is objectivity merely the disclosure of bias? Is there no accountability to text or context, to empirical evidence, to formal reasoning? At least phenomenologists try to move beyond subjectivism by comparing the reports of their experiences with those of others in order to detect more general patterns (even though in hindsight they did not deal with the changes of perspective based on gender).

This feminist position is partly due to the influence of postmodernism and deconstruction. These movements have, in theory, all but equated "diversity" and relativism (although, in practice, "diversity" seldom includes opposing positions). Deconstruction opens the door to new views and provides a new authority for them (the authority for deconstruction being the inherent instability of language). The political implications go far beyond this, however, because popularizers of deconstruction use it as a convenient strategy for undermining only *some* world views (those of their adversaries) and not others (their own). This presents a contradiction. On the one hand, there can be no truth, and no ranking of interpretations. On the other hand, some criterion is obviously used to select specific world views for deconstruction.

Now back to the more general problem created by phenomenologists' insistence on description based on *epoché* of all values in order to allow the phenomenon to appear and feminist activism based on evaluation of values and an upfront admission of their own biases. What phenomologists need to do is not abandon the method but take it several steps further. First, just as we once needed a "correction" to understand the distinctive experiences of women, we now need one to understand the distinctive experiences of men. In other words, we need to eliminate the distortion of assuming that everything presented as universal by earlier phenomenologists applied to all or even most men. We need accurate and "thick" descriptions of men and their experiences, ones that are developed with empathy and *epoché* (to the point of bracketing out feminist critiques) and attention to their specific needs and vulnerabilities. If that sounds like heresy from the perspective of feminist orthodoxy, so be it. Only in this way can we ever decide which phenomena are gendered (to a greater or lesser degree) and which are truly universal (or at least very common). This could help us understand how gendered experiences influence each other, moreover, and change over time. In short, the task of adequate description is not yet complete. In fact, some feminists have tried to correct this by adopting a more inclusive approach based on the rigorous application of scientific empiricism; research would focus on women *as well as* men. Research questions would stem from the problems of women *as well as* those of men. Phenomenologists and feminists or women's studies scholars who study women and religion have much to learn from each other, not only to understand some common roots but also to refine their methods. Yes, feminists have taught us about the influence of sex, gender, and power as important variables. We can hardly return to the naiveté of the early phenomenologists (or the early social scientists, for that matter). Still, we should be alert to phenomenologists and feminists who would lead us down the road to solipsism and subjectivism in the name of "diversity" and unfair stereotypes because of androcentrism or gynocentrism.[45] And we should be alert to those who would prefer to ignore any criterion other than power, for this creates the problem of reductionism again for religion and, worse yet, secularizes the very nature of religion in unprecedented ways.

This still leaves one problem: the relation between phenomenology and women's studies (as scholarly techniques to increase knowledge) and feminism (as a political movement to increase the power of women). To bridge these two quite different orientations, we could consider them sequentially. First would come "thick phenomenological description," instigated by gender-sensitive questions about both women's and men's experiences and careful use of *epoché* of all values, including feminist ones, and empathy with the subject. Then would come critical evaluation of the information gathered, which would detect problems. Finally would come problem solving. As long as each stage were done with scholarly integrity and carefully marked, the various orientations and their respective methods could benefit the overall project.

Notes

1. Here, I am following the analysis of Herbert Spiegelberg, *The Phenomenological Movement: A Historical Introduction*, 2 vols. (The Hague: Martinus Nijhoff, 1965).

2. This is the conclusion of Spiegelberg, who has systematically analyzed the movement. See especially 2, 653–701.

3. This is not unlike the Buddhist meditative technique of *vipassana*. In this discipline, people are trained to observe the flow of consciousness, watching comings and goings as well as emotional qualities.

4. M. Merleau-Ponty, *Phenomenology of Perception*, trans. Colin Smith (London: Routledge & Kegan Paul, 1962).

5. Intentional analysis means the analysis of the property of an act which points to a referent or the property of a meaningful symbol which points to an object, therefore the act which intends and the object intended (Spiegelberg 2, 719).

6. According to Müller, for instance, *Religionswissenschaft* should be a descriptive, objective science (free from the normative context required by theological and philosophical studies of religion). Tiele argued that it should be based on the description and collection of data about religion. Kristensen, too, observed that it should be descriptive and systematic. In addition, he argued that scholars should start with the faith of believers and bracket out their own religious beliefs; they should even empathize with the believers who ascribe absolute truth to their own religions. van der Leeuw suggested that scholars begin by tentatively naming religious phenomena (preliminary classification) and then gather examples of them. Then, they should incorporate them into their own experience, consciously and sympathetically, through the exercise of imagination with self-surrendering love

(bracketing out all questions of their existence or nonexistence). Finally, they should organize the material effectively.

7. In good phenomenological fashion, Bleeker argued that the study of religion should be typological (defined by general patterns), as did van der Leeuw. His ideal types include: (1) key concepts such as power, salvation, and savior-figures; (2) humans (religious people and their communities); (3) the reciprocity between outward and inward action; (4) aspects of the world as sacred; and (5) types of religious founder.

8. Pierre Thévénaz, *What is Phenomenology? And Other Essays* (Chicago: Quadrangle Books, 1962), 150.

9. Ibid., 152.

10. Spiegelberg 1, 7.

11. van der Leeuw argued, for instance, that there is always some relation between the subject and the object "[P]henomenology . . . is not a method that has been reflectively elaborated, but is man's true vital activity consisting in losing himself neither in things nor in the ego, neither in hovering above objects like a god nor dealing with them like an animal, but in doing what is given to neither animal nor god: standing aside and understanding what appears into view" (G. van der Leeuw, *Religion in Essence and Manifestation: A Study in Phenomenology,* 2 vols. [New York: Harper & Row, 1963], 676).

12. Spiegelberg 2, 714.

13. There are obviously informal versions of this inductive process—for example, those that allow the concept of red to be acquired by a child with an adult's help, part of the acquisition of abstract language.

14. Spiegelberg 2, 535.

15. Ibid., 695.

16. Ibid., 696.

17. Rudolf Otto, *The Idea of the Holy,* trans. John W. Harvey (1923: New York: Oxford University Press, 1958).

18. For van der Leeuw (and some others), recognition of the "wholly other," the "essence" par excellence, is a power (kratophany). His recognition of its autonomy amounts to nothing other than his recognition of God. Recognition of this reality comes not merely from the claims of Christian scripture, though, but from phenomenological empiricism based on the study of other religions. Although his goal was objectivity, he realized that this could not be completely attained. The appearance of "things," he believed, is more like something seen in a mirror than something seen directly, face to face (van der Leeuw 2, 678). That, he believed, was due partly to the unconscious and partly to the elusiveness of God. Unlike Kant, who ruled out the mirror analogy in understanding the nature of things, van der Leeuw held onto it. This was possible because, in addition, he held onto theology as identifying a

final meaning. Put otherwise, the limit of meaning *is* the ultimate meaning. Paradoxically, the essence of religion remains partly concealed—even though the phenomenology of religion reveals its patterns (as if in a mirror).

Wach described the study of religion as a way of deepening our sense of the numinous, of our own religions, and of other religions. In the final analysis, this demands creative intuition. That caused some later critics (such as R. J. Zwi Werblowsky) to claim that he had ignored the boundary between phenomenology and theology (R. J. Zwi Werblowsky, "The Comparative Study of Religions—A Review Essay," *Judaism* 8.4 [1959]: 275–276).

19. Mircea Eliade, *The Sacred and the Profane: The Nature of Religion,* trans. Willard R. Trask (1957: San Diego: Harcourt, Brace Jovanovitch, 1959), 30.

20. Buddhist scholars and others have viewed Eliade's use of this term with its ontological implications as a superimposition of a Christian concept on other religions. Many schools of Buddhism, for instance, repudiate the concept of being and non-being.

21. Mark I. Wallis, "Introduction," in Paul Ricoeur, *Figuring the Sacred: Religion, Narrative, and Imagination,* trans. David Pallauer (Minneapolis: Fortress Press, 1995), 7.

22. Spiegelberg 2, 418.

23. See John Torrance, *Karl Marx's Theory of Ideas* (Cambridge: Cambridge University Press, 1995) especially 61–64 and 191–217.

24. John M. Ellis, *Against Deconstruction* (Princeton: Princeton University Press, 1989).

25. Donna Haraway, "Situated Knowledges," in Donna Haraway, ed., *Simians, Cyborgs, and Women: the Reinvention of Nature* (New York: Routledge, 1990).

26. S. Harding, *Whose Science? Whose Knowledge? Thinking from Women's Lives* (Ithaca: Cornell University Press, 1991).

27. K. Lennon and M. Whitford, eds., *Knowing the Difference: Feminist Perspectives in Epistemology* (London: Routledge, 1994); L. Alcoff and E. Potter, eds., *Feminist Epistemologies* (New York: Routledge, 1993); H. Longino, *Science as Social Knowledge* (Princeton NJ.: Princeton University Press, 1990); A. Gray and M. Pearsall, eds., *Women, Knowledge and Reality* (Boston: Unwin Hyman, 1989); H. Rose "Hand, Brain and Heart: A Feminist Epistemology for the Natural Sciences," in *Signs: Journal of Women in Culture and Society* 9, no. 11 (1983).

28. Genevieve Lloyd, *The Man of Reason: "Male " and "Female" in Western Philosophy* (London: Routledge, 1983). Also, P. H. Collins, *Black Feminist Thought: Knowledge, Consciousness, and the Politics of Empowerment* (Boston: Unwin Hyman, 1990).

29. Mary O'Brien, *The Politics of Reproduction* (London: Routledge and Kegan Paul, 1981).

30. S. Harding, *The Science Question in Feminism* (Ithaca: Cornell University Press, 1986).

31. Jean-Paul Sartre, *Being and Nothingness: An Essay in Phenomenological Ontology,* trans. Hazel E. Barnes (London: Methuen, 1957). See also Spiegelberg 2, 505–507.

32. A key figure in this transition from existential philosophy to feminism is Simone de Beauvoir, partner of Jean-Paul Sartre and author of *The Second Sex* (1968).

33. Spiegelberg 2, 527.

34. Merleau-Ponty, 67.

35. Rita M. Gross, *Feminism and Religion: An Introduction* (Boston: Beacon Press, 1996).

36. Ibid., 16.

37. Spiegelberg 2, 720.

38. I myself have experienced this ambivalence in the way feminists have reacted to my introduction for *Women in World Religions* (Albany: State University of New York Press, 1987). I looked for cross-cultural patterns and created a typology (à la Max Weber) to show how religions fare when assessed by the criterion of women's religious roles outside the home. Some readers disliked the idea of looking for common patterns, or the idea of ranking religions according to a criterion—even though I noted clearly that this was only one among many criteria that could be used.

39. Spiegelberg 2, 678.

40. Martin E. Marty and R. Scott Appleby, eds., *Fundamentalisms Observed* (Chicago: The University of Chicago Press, 1991).

41. Much of their method is standard phenomenology. They begin by identifying five characteristics of the phenomenon of fundamentalism which becomes their working definition. Moving on, they refer to various historical and phenomenological approaches. Then, they discuss the fact that the authors have bracketed out their own presuppositions, "an approach which does not mean that they successfully leave them behind, but that they become aware of them, take them into consideration, and do some compensating for them" (Marty and Appleby, x). They argue in standard phenomenological fashion that just as bracketing out presuppositions is important for adherents of one religion in trying to understand those of another, it is important for liberal or secular scholars trying to understand the alien world of fundamentalism (perceived as a phenomenon on the political right) in a balanced way. The aim of this book, they say, is to ensure that members of these fundamentalist communities can at least recognize themselves in the descriptions. They discuss

patterns that appear in the book and illustrate their findings with examples from specific chapters.

42. Marty and Appleby, 836.

43. Ibid., 839.

44. Katherine K. Young, "World Religions: A Category in the Macking?" in *Religion in History: The Word, the Idea, the Reality,* ed. Michel Despland and Gérard Vallé (Waterloo, Ont.: Wilfrid Laurier University Press, 1992), 111–130). This article discusses the problem of creating categories. Whether the category is "world religions," "human," "man," or "woman," the theoretical problems are similar.

45. See Paul Nathanson and Katherine K. Young, *Spreading Misandry: The Teaching of Contempt for Men in Popular Culture* (Montreal: McGill-Queen's University Press, 2001).

3

Feminist Issues and Methods in the Anthropology of Religion

RITA M. GROSS

The anthropology of religion is an ambiguous term linking two closely allied disciplines: anthropology and the academic study of religion. But what is the anthropology of religion? Classically thought of as the study of the religions of indigenous peoples, in some ways, it is an almost nonexistent field, lost in the interstices between religious studies and anthropology. But in other ways, as we shall see, it is becoming constitutive of genuinely cross-cultural studies in religion.

Few scholars, however, are primarily anthropologists of religion. One is either an anthropologist who sometimes studies religion and reads what other anthropologists say about religion, or one is a religious studies scholar who may do research on an indigenous religion, in which case anthropological studies of that culture become important. One's primary discipline is basic to a scholar's approach to the anthropology of religion.

Though their subject matters often overlap, only a few scholars in either anthropology or the academic study of religion read extensively in the literature of the other field.[1] In many departments of religious studies, including most Ph.D.-granting research departments, little attention is paid to the study of indigenous religions, with the result that the anthropology of religion is the first expertise of few in the academic study of religion. Most textbooks on world religions do not contain substantial chapters on indigenous religions or the so-called "little traditions" of the great classical religious civilizations, further evidence of the marginalized status of the anthropology of religion in religious studies. Many regard the anthropology of religion as more creditably within the provence of the anthropology department, which will usually include some courses on "primitive religion." But, though religion was once

41

one of the keenest subjects for anthropologists to study and debate, recent anthropological theory and field reporting are much less heavily invested in religion.

This mutual ignoring is especially the case for the feminist schools within each field. I have only rarely encountered citations of the work of feminist scholars of religion in the writings of feminist anthropologists. For example, Falk and Gross's *Unspoken Worlds: Women's Religious Lives,* a text widely used for the feminist anthropology of religion by scholars of religion is rarely cited by feminist anthropologists. In 1989 the American Anthropological Association published *Gender and Anthropology: Critical Reviews for Research and Teaching,* a "state of the art" survey at that time. But it contained no article on religion. The situation is the same for a more recent survey of feminist anthropology, Michaela di Leonardo's *Gender at the Crossroads of Knowledge: Feminist Anthropology in the Postmodern Era,* published in 1991. (An earlier, but now largely outdated resource book, *The Cross-Cultural Study of Women,* edited by Margot Dudley and Mary I. Edwards and published in 1986, did contain a chapter on religion.) The situation is the same with feminist scholars of religion. With the exception of Carol Christ's appeal to Clifford Geertz in her well-known article "Why Women Need the Goddess,"[2] few feminist scholars of religion utilize anthropology in their own work. The anthropologists who have been most influential in the academic study of religion, Clifford Geertz, Victor Turner, and Claude Levi Strauss, have not been widely utilized by feminist scholars of religion. More striking is the fact that few feminist scholars of religion are conversant with feminist anthropology and rarely cite its literature. Furthermore, because the anthropology of religion is not a large subspecialty within religious studies, there are very few feminist scholars of religion who specialize in the anthropology of religion.

Perhaps we should conclude at this point that the feminist anthropology of religion is an almost nonexistent enterprise, in part because the anthropology of religion seems to be a disappearing field. But, in fact, while anthropology of religion may be a disappearing field, both religious studies and anthropology are incorporating that subject matter in new ways. Religion is still being studied by anthropologists, but usually not as an isolated phenomenon. Instead, it is collapsed into culture in general and studied quite widely in cultural and symbolic anthropology. Even more important, the field of religious studies is changing drastically, so that material that once would have been studied primarily by anthropologists is now considered integral to religious studies.

When I was a graduate student with some specialization in the anthropology of religion, it was a very marginalized, though distinctive, subfield studying the religions of indigenous peoples—religions without texts. It was a marginalized subfield because the study of religion was overwhelmingly dominated by textual studies, even for non-Western traditions. What is now called "religion on the ground," religion as lived and experienced by ordinary people, was virtually ignored by students of the major world religions. The anthropology of religion, if by that we mean the study of those layers and types of religions that rely on oral traditions and specialize in myth and ritual, was limited to the tiny minority who studied "primitive religion," as the religions of indigenous peoples were then called. And, by definition, those who studied anthropology of religion were not expected to study India, China, Japan, or the Middle East; texts were prevalent in those areas and if one wished to study religion in one of those areas, one had to study texts.

But the stranglehold of textual studies on the field of religious studies is now being broken, especially for South Asian studies, and this major shift in the field introduces the anthropology of religion in a new way. We ask again—what is the anthropology of religion? I suggest that we take as the subject matter for the "anthropology of religion" those kinds of religious situations and phenomena best studied by the methods characteristic of anthropology—participant observer inquiries, interviews, and surveys. In other words, those dimensions of religion and those religions that one cannot understand through textual studies are the domain of the anthropology of religion. This means that the anthropology of religions is no longer limited to the study of indigenous peoples but also includes the nontextual layers of major world religions. For example, most South Asian scholars now are familiar with popular religion in modern India, not merely with religion as portrayed in classical texts. So perhaps we could say that, at least for some areas within religious studies, the anthropology of religion has not disappeared at all, but is becoming mainstream academic study of religion, even though study of the religions of indigenous peoples is still a minor theme in most departments of religion. And significant portions of this new literature mainstreaming the anthropology of religion are indeed a feminist anthropology of religion.

The feminist issues, methods, and literature of this expanded "anthropology of religion" will be my major focus in this article, though it must be understood that I approach the anthropology of religion as a religious studies scholar, not an anthropologist. By now, the general implications of feminist methodology for any discipline are somewhat well understood and I will not engage in a detailed discussion of the way in which feminist scholarly methods entail a paradigm shift in our model of humanity, as I have done in other contexts.[3]

Two tasks are as central to a feminist anthropology of religion as they are to any other field. The first is to obtain full and accurate information about women that is well integrated into our overall understanding of the religion under study. Sometimes dismissed as merely "the anthropology of women," this step is the absolutely necessary foundation for any further theoretical refinement. However, the "anthropology of women" is not the end product of genuine feminist anthropology of religion. As has often been said, feminist scholarship is more than an "add women and stir" enterprise. It is about reconceptualizing the whole field or the specific religion being studied, taking into account the newly gathered information on women. This task is immense and has led to some profound changes in long-accepted theories and interpretations. Perhaps the relationship between the anthropology of women and feminist anthropological theory could be clarified by continuing the "add women in stir" analogy a bit further. If we add women and really do stir all our information thoroughly together, rather than just adding a longer chapter on women into a new edition of an old classic, everything in our old classic will look different, just as our cookie dough looks different after the next ingredient is stirred into the batter, rather than left lying on top of first ingredients put into the bowl. Or as I have said in another context, usually the inadequacies of scholarship that ignored women cannot be corrected merely by painting in a small blank corner of the canvas; instead the whole picture has to be redrawn.[4] When this task is undertaken, the anthropology of women transforms into feminist anthropology.

It might seem that the task of gathering data about women, of doing the "anthropology or women" would have to precede the task of reconceptualizing basic theories. In some ways that is true, because more data yields more powerful theory. But in other ways, the very emergence of the "anthropology of women" presupposes intense, though often inarticulate, dissatisfaction with prevailing theories and models. These two tasks are intertwined rather than linear in the feminist anthropology of religion, even though I will deal with each in turn.

Directions in the Anthropology of Women

In the late sixties and early seventies, some scholars of religion suddenly became aware that humanity consists of two sexes, a fact their theories and descriptions of religion had heretofore ignored. The descriptive and the theoretical inadequacies deserve separate discussion.

On the one hand, descriptions of indigenous religions and popular strata of the world religions could never eclipse women as thoroughly as did studies of religion that focus on classic texts. One of the most consistent and persistent generalizations in the study of women and religion is that classical religious texts often do not accurately reflect or report women's experiences of the religion in question. Furthermore, women are often severely restricted from text-dependent religious activities and the texts in question are sometimes quite misogynistic. When texts are emphasized as the only or the most important materials for scholars of religion to study, our descriptive accounts of women and religion will be hazy, vague, inaccurate, and highly incomplete and women will often disappear altogether, which explains part of the motivation for many feminist scholars to be dissatisfied with the bias toward texts that still prevails in some segments of the academic study of religion.[5]

Women cannot disappear in the same way from descriptions of religions based on field studies, travelers' reports, etc. Since women will be about half of any population and since women and men have distinctly different gender roles in most societies, in some senses, women are highly visible. They are necessary as marriage partners, as mothers of the next generation, and in some cases as vital players in the economy. They are also often mysterious and inaccessible to the foreigner describing the culture, whether anthropologist or traveler, which in a convoluted way can make women visible by their absence, as fantasies and projections about them multiply. Therefore, no "on the ground" discussion of religion would be likely to omit completely some description of women's roles, which means that the anthropology of religion is more likely to contain some information about women's religious lives than are descriptions of a religion, such as Hinduism, solely based on classic Hindu texts.

Indeed, the literature already available to the anthropologist of religion in the late sixties and early seventies did contain significant amounts of sheer information about women and religion. But there was something distinctly unsatisfying, but very difficult to pin down, about the way in which that information was processed and presented. In retrospect it is easy to see that the unsatisfactoriness is due to the androcentric model of humanity that guided the data-collecting and data-organizing processes, but at that time, when anthropologists of religion were first beginning to be curious about women and gender, there was no conceptual alternative. One did not even have conceptual clarity to see that women, qua women, were rarely described. Instead their functions in the lives of the men of the society were much more likely to be described, which meant that one did not receive a coherent, connected account of women's religious lives and activities, but only glimpses, as they entered or left the stage of men's lives. Whether these "now you see them, now you don't" accounts of women resulted from androcentrism on the part of travelers and other observers, who literally couldn't see women as interesting human beings in their own right, or from the viewpoints native men have about women in the culture being studied, or from a combination of the two, is often unclear and would differ from one account to another. But certainly the consensus of feminist anthropology of religion is that androcentrism on the part of foreign (largely Western) observers seriously distorted our descriptions and understandings of women's lives, roles, and significance in many religious settings.

Much more serious, however, were theoretical and linguistic obstacles to seeing that humanity really contains two sexes, not one sex—men—and their objects of interest and curiosity—women. Everyone had been trained to write and think in the generic masculine so that the ubiquitous *homo religiosus* of history and anthropology of religions theory seemed straightforward to most. My first suggestion, as a graduate student in 1968 that there might some need for the construct *femina religiosa* was met with scorn, outrage, ridicule, and defensiveness. The construct *homo religiosus* has now received a great deal of criticism for its essentialism and universalism, but as a model or a type rather than an empirically existing individual, *homo religiosus* would have to be a universal, a platonic from of the type that is so out of favor today. Much more serious, especially in its own day, is the fact that *homo religiosus* is clearly a universal of the male gender in most of Eliade's writings. Most of the time, Eliade writes about women as symbols to *homo religiosus*, rather than as real people. When he does, infrequently, write about women as real people, it is because their behavior represents a special case that doesn't fit his general descriptions or theories.[6] The point is not to participate in the currently fashionable debunking of one of the giants of religious studies in the twentieth century, but to point out how massive were the conceptual blinders that made gathering data about women so sporadic and that made reconceptualizing some of the most basic assumptions of the field so vitally necessary.

My early questions about *femina religiosa* led to my 1975 dissertation *Exclusion and Participation: The Role of Women in Aboriqinal Australian Religion,* probably the earliest longer document in feminist anthropology of religion, and this work led to a series of methodological articles that have been somewhat influential[7] and to *Unspoken Worlds: Women's Religious Lives,*[8] a highly influential book that remains surprisingly relevant fifteen years after its initial publication. These works directly in anthropology of religion are paralleled by important early publications in feminist anthropology, such as Michelle Rosaldo and Louise Lamphere's *Women, Culture, and Society* (1974) and Rayna Rapp Reiter's *Toward an Anthropology of Women* (1975), which were extremely important for anthropologists, but have not been widely used by religious studies scholars. Together these books and the issues raised in them delineate the concerns important to anthropology of religion with reference to the anthropology of women.[9] Emphases differ considerably between those who are primarily religionists working in the anthropology of religion and the anthropologists.

For those of us primarily oriented to religion, the first barrier to be overcome was the widespread early prejudice that women had almost nothing to do with religion and, therefore, one could generate few data and surely nothing interesting or important by attempting to investigate a non-subject. This widespread conviction undoubtedly is part of the distorted picture of religion produced by the heavy bias toward the study of religion as the study of classic texts. This bias also results in a decided emphasis on the world religions, which tend to be rather male dominated.

Conceptually, it was necessary to challenge the presupposition that only the dominant members of a religious community are interesting or important for adequate knowledge and understanding of that community. One does not understand a religion by studying only its elite or powerful strata. Furthermore, no religious community consists only of its dominant or preferred males but also includes women who have religious lives of some sort. In world religions, such as Hinduism or Islam, women are indeed technically subservient to and under the control of men. But that does not end the question of their religious lives. In the past ten years, a wealth of studies has demonstrated that women in India have extensive, rich, and significant religious lives despite the fact that their religious practices usually are not closely linked with classic texts or undertaken with men present.[10] Similarly, for Middle Eastern studies, new research has shown significant women's religious activities[11] and also discussed the interesting problem of how women cope with often pronounced male dominance.[12] In addition, the widespread claim that aboriginal Australian women simply did not have any meaningful religious life turned out to be completely incorrect, since women have extensive religious ceremonies that parallel the much more frequently studied men's ceremonies.[13] It seems that the frequent perception of women's lack of involvement with religion on the part of many religious studies scholars has more to do with what texts say about women and with certain Western cultural expectations than with religion as lived reality.

Conceding that it might be important and interesting to gather the data about women's religious lives is only the first issue for feminist scholarship in the anthropology of religion. If it is important to gather this data, who has access to the data? At first it seemed obvious that reason for such spotty, male-oriented data about women and religion was the male near-monopoly on the field. Surely if more women did field work, we would know more about women. Behind that expectation lie three assumptions that are troublesome. The first is that women would be interested in doing research on women. The second is that only women are able to do research on women. The third is that women bring a unique perspective to their studies, different from that of male scholars in the field. How one deals with these three assumptions is intimately involved with questions about the nature and validity of feminism as a scholarly enterprise.

The issue of women wanting to do research on women is tricky. It has turned out, since the advent and relative success of feminist scholarship, that many women do want to do scholarship on women, often because of a keen personal involvement with gender issues in their own culture. But, given that the field is quite androcentric, it can still be a dangerous career move to specialize in women studies in religion, especially if one brings feminist values to one's studies. Twenty years ago, most women scholars were advised to steer

clear of studying women to avoid having their work ghettoized and trivialized. My own initial response to Mircea Eliade's suggestion that I turn my
first feminist paper on aboriginal Australian religions into my dissertation is
telling: "Oh! No! I want to do my dissertation on something important."
Even feminist anthropologists, working in a field that has always been far
more friendly to women than religious studies, claim that their work is sometimes not taken seriously. One reports a recent encounter in which a male colleague invited her to lunch, wishing to inform her that feminist anthropology
was simply "'trivial me-tooism'"[14]

If that barrier is negotiated, a woman field researcher does have access to
materials that, in most cases, simply would not be available to her male colleague. This is one of the strongest elements in the argument that male scholars, by themselves, cannot give us the whole picture of a culture, one reason
why anthropology of religion in the mid-sixties was so sketchy regarding
women. Some might complain of bias, exclusion, and unfairness, especially if
the study of women were to bring prestige and job opportunities. But women's
special access to women's religious lives simply mirrors the sex segregation
characteristic of many religions investigated by an anthropologist of religion.

Clearly, the early scholarship of aboriginal Australian religions suffered
greatly because even male anthropologists who were interested in women,
simply could not find out anything about women's religious lives, leading to
the erroneous, but widely held conclusion, that women were considered profane in aboriginal culture and had no religious lives.[15] The stark contrast
between what male field researchers claimed and the findings of Diane Bell in
one of the very few sustained field research projects specifically focused on
women done by a woman is astounding. She writes:

> Some Arnhem Land specialists regard my claims to women's high
> status in the Central Desert with open amazement. . . . When I
> returned from the field and began enumerating the institutions and
> rituals which women controlled and maintained, our discussions con-
> tinued. "But," he countered, "they don't have sacred sites." "Yes,
> they do," I assured him. "Well, he said in triumph, "they don't have
> incised boards." "Sorry," I replied. "In that case," he observed, "they
> got the anthropologist they deserve."[16]

The lack of attention to women's sustained religious lives in India and
the Middle East and the widespread assumption that Hindu and Muslim
women are uninvolved in religion surely resulted from the same causes. As
anyone familiar these societies knows, sex segregation is relatively high.
Most of the vast new literature on women and religion cited earlier was
researched by women and probably could only have been discovered by
women.

Finally, it is impossible to imagine that one of the most important recent works in feminist anthropology of religion, Karen Brown's *Mama Lola: A Vodou Priestess in Brooklyn* (1991), could have been researched by a man. The level of intimate friendship and self-revelation between Karen Brown and Mama Lola, so integral to the book's unique insights into Vodou, would be nearly impossible in a cross-gender, cross-cultural research project.

It is one thing to claim that women scholars will have unique access to women's religious practices simply because they are women. It is quite another to claim that they bring special perspectives to their research because of their own womanhood. This claim takes two forms, the first of which suggests that women bring special perspectives to their studies because of their experiences as women rather than men in their own culture. The second claim turns on an assumption that women understand other women because of the universal nature of female experience. I will suggest that the first form of this claim has cogency while the second is highly questionable.

I first encountered the first version of this claim very early in a memorable event. When Mircea Eliade encouraged me to continue my research on aboriginal Australian women, his reason was that I was seeing things in the data that he as a man had not seen. He was correct, but I believe that I was seeing different things than he because of my cultural experiences as a female in a Western academic and religious environment, not because of essential male and female natures that preordained each of us to see what we did. There is no question that feminist scholarship is in part due to women's intense dissatisfaction with the gender role stereotypes to which we had been socialized and the difficulties we faced as religious studies scholars in a discipline that did not particularly want us there. In my own case, that was precisely the initial motivation.

There is also no question that many scholars share the experience that being female in our academic culture affects our scholarship.[17] Our cultural experience of femaleness often encourages us to do research and to write in ways that are not characteristic of academia. Many of us are quite uncomfortable with the neutrality, distance, and disinterest in our subject matter thought to be important in some segments of academia. We often write in the first person and insist on explaining and justifying our standpoints, rather than writing as if our experiences were irrelevant to our interests and conclusions as scholars. That such an approach does not detract from scholarship but enhances it is a case I have often made.[18]

Keen interest in and empathy for, even personal involvement with, those about whom we write also often characterize feminist anthropology of religion. Karen Brown is especially outspoken and cogent about the importance of her friendship with Mama Lola, the emotional closeness between them, and her growing inability to regard Mama Lola simply as the object of her scholarship. In addition, Karen Brown openly narrates her own growing involvement in Vodou religion, as she passed beyond simply observing its rituals to being initiated herself. The success of her book demonstrates that these heretical methodological stances, which may have something to do with the experience of being female in this culture, can no longer be dismissed. However, though all these scholarly tendencies are more likely to occur in the scholarship of women than of men at the present time, that they cannot be attributed to a "female nature" is amply demonstrated by the fact that other women scholars are embarrassed by such tactics.

The second claim regarding what women bring to the scholarly enterprise—their unique insight as females into "the female experience"—is now largely discredited by postmodern anti-essentialism. Early feminist scholarship is often accused of having posited a "female experience" that was as universalistic and monolithic as the generic masculine or Eliade's *homo religiosus* and was utterly insensitive to local variations of women's experiences, especially as they are influenced by factors other than gender, such as race and class. In such scholarship, male and female essential natures are then invoked to explain cross-cultural universals, which were assumed to exist. Such scholarship is now ridiculed by postmodernism's wariness regarding any generalizations.

While I think the postmodern criticism of early feminist scholarship is overstated, I would agree that the idea of a monolithic "women's experience" makes no sense. I cannot imagine that anyone seriously involved in cross-cultural comparative religious scholarship would be prone to the position called "essentialism"—the view that there are male and female natures and traits that all men or all women share across cultural boundaries. Insofar as I am familiar with the literature, essentialism or the search for cross-cultural universals has not been a serious pursuit in the feminist anthropology of religion.

Feminist anthropology, however, did seriously entertain several hypotheses about cross-cultural universals, which were not sought in male and female essential natures; rather they assumed universal male dominance which they sought to explain by differing social processes argued to be universal. Three theses were especially important in feminist anthropology. Two of the explanations were first published in the influential volume *Women, Culture, and Society*, already discussed. Michelle Rosaldo's lead-off essay suggested that women's status varied with the degree of separation between the public and the private domains, with every society valuing the male-dominated public realm more highly. Sherry Ortner's essay "Is Male to Female as Culture is to Nature?" answered her question positively and explained universal male dominance by a universal valuing of culture (a male specialization) over nature, which is universally associated with femaleness. The third major player in feminist anthropology was Marxist anthropology, which revisited Engels's theory that the development of private property led to the development of the patriarchal family, which led to male dominance.[19]

None of these theses were ever taken up in any serious way by feminists in the anthropology of religion. By and large, feminist anthropology of religion has tended to eschew grand theory in favor of empathetic detailed studies of specific situations. When *Unspoken Worlds* was published in 1980 at the height of grand theorizing about cross-cultural universals, we warned of the difficulty of making generalizations about women and religion, even within one religion, let alone across religion in general. But we did not suggest the other extreme—of no widely observable patterns either. Two themes seem quite dominant cross-culturally. One is that religion can either call women away from their ordinary domestic concerns, or it can validate and support women in their everyday lives. The other is that religions vary greatly in the level of support either kind of woman finds in her religious environment. That is to say, both extraordinary and ordinary women can experience anything from a high level of support to outright hostility in their religious lives.[20] This modest proposal for understanding women and religion in worldwide perspective has not been tested rigorously, but might well hold up and be helpful.

Another approach to the feminist anthropology of religion was utilized by Susan Starr Sered in her recent book *Priestess, Mother, Sacred Sister: Religions Dominated by Women* (1994). Exploring only one pattern—that of religious complexes in which women usually take leadership roles and often are the majority of participants—she systematically compares twelve cross-cultural examples of such religions. (It is important to point out that, despite her title, her subject matter is not *religions* dominated by women, but religious practices, often found within larger, male-dominated religious settings, that are women's special domain.) Looking for common features of such female-dominated religious practices, she concludes that such religious practices tend to occur in matrifocal societies, that is, in societies in which a woman and her children are a dominant social unit. She also finds that such religions tend to focus especially on women's concerns as mothers, and that such women's religions tend to be this-worldly, without a significant distinction between sacred and profane spheres.[21]

If religious studies scholars who study the anthropology of religion have a failing, it is not the tendency to posit grand universals about women's experience. It is, rather, the tendency to collapse women into cultural stereotypes about women or into goddesses. Both tendencies have plagued the literature about women and religion from the beginning. Because of the Western tendency to view religion as a doctrinal system, it is very easy to write about "the Buddhist view of women" and assume that one has written about Buddhist women. The difficulty of recovering information about women in many historical periods and the pressure in the field of religious studies to do historical scholarship if one is to be taken seriously intensify this tendency.[22] For different reasons, many in religious studies, especially those less anthropologically trained, also tend to conflate and confuse women and goddesses, assuming more direct mirroring between them than is often warranted. Happy exceptions to this generalization include Kathleen Erndl's *Victory to the Mother* (1993), which carefully explores the relationship between a goddess and her devotees, female as well as male, in north India, and Cynthia Ellor's *Living in the Lap of the Goddess* (1992), a careful anthropological account of the contemporary feminist spirituality movement which discusses at length the relationship between the goddess of that movement and her devotees.

Feminist Anthropology Redraws the Picture: Some Case Studies

Gathering the data about women would be less urgent if all that were at stake was more knowledge about women. This comment is not meant to trivialize the importance of knowing about women, but to emphasize that knowledge about women is not an optional extra best left to marginalized feminists. Rather, as several case studies cogently demonstrate, knowledge about women is an essential element in understanding any culture, or any religious phenomenon, or any major theory in the anthropology of religion, or even major new developments in a whole subfield of religious studies. In this section of this chapter, I will summarize some feminist contributions to each of these four major areas of study with one case study.

Beginning with a case study concerning a specific religious culture, I will discuss aboriginal Australian religions, about which an especially strong case could be made that the information gathered by men about men gives us a rather incomplete understanding of the religion. Two facts about aboriginal religion make this clear. First, men and women practice their rituals quite separately; second, secret knowledge gained through initiation is critical to an accurate portrayal of religion—whether women's or men's. Therefore, male researchers simply could not learn about women's rituals. The story of Geza Roheim attempting quite unsuccessfully to elicit sacred songs from the older women is often cited.[23]

But this inability to gather data did not deter early theoreticians; utilizing extensive descriptions of men's ceremonies (which are very important to the men and to the whole culture) and the fact that women were often excluded from these ceremonies, they drew two conclusions. First, women do not have any religious life but only a few ceremonies "that seem to be pale imitations of masculine ceremonies and . . . [to] play little part in tribal life."[24] Second, the sexual dichotomy so obvious in ritual is interpreted as evidence of sexual hierarchy in which men represent the sacred and ritual cleanness while women represent the profane and ritual uncleanness.[25] Given the widespread understanding that various ceremonies performed throughout the life cycle gradually transform a "profane" immature ignorant person into a "sacred" respected knowledgeable elder, and that women's ceremonies were so incompletely known, many drew the conclusion "that women make little sacred progress through life,"[26] and it is easy to see that most uncritical scholars of a prefeminist era would assume that aboriginal religion is intensely male dominated.

One could go about redrawing this picture in two ways. One is to attack the logic of the premise that the sexual dichotomy indicates sexual hierarchy and to look for evidence that women have parallel religious practices, as well as evidence that separate ceremonies have nothing to do with men being sacred and women being profane. Since I have pursued this approach in other contexts,[27] here I will pursue the second alternative, involving reports of participant-observer studies that successfully do find out about women's rituals and women's attitudes about their religious experiences. The works of Diane Bell are an excellent resource in this regard.[28]

Diane Bell's work is useful for anthropology of religion because of her sustained observations of Aboriginal women's rituals. She was the first anthropologist of an appropriate age and status (an older woman with children but without a husband) to be primarily interested in women's lives. She also engaged in behaviors, such as not trying to study men's rituals, that made her trustworthy[29] to the older women who alone could teach her, or even permit her to witness the ceremonies she records. Because of the importance of secrecy and initiation, these qualifications cannot be overemphasized.

Bell consistently emphasizes throughout her work that women simply do not see themselves as submissive or dependent to men in ritual. Instead, women are quite independent, have their own links with the Dreamtime which they frequently act out in rituals, their own sacred designs, dances, sites, and incised boards. They devote significant time and energy to these performances. She also stresses that the women do not see their ceremonies as "playing little part in tribal life." She writes:

> I came to understand that in ritual women emphasize their role as nurturers of people, land, and relationships. Through their *yawulyu* (land-based ceremonies) they nurture land; through their health and curing rituals they resolve conflict and restore social harmony, and through *yilpinji* (love rituals) they manage emotions. Thus in women's rituals their major responsibilities in the ares of love, land and health fuse in the nurturance motif with its twin themes of the "growing up" of people and the maintenance of harmonious relationships between people and country.[30]

Bell also learned how to take part as a woman in the boys' initiation ceremonies that loom so large in the standard ethnographies. Far from finding women to be helpless pawns, ritual adjuncts, "whose heads cowered, in fear of death, run to and fro the male initiation ground,"[31] she reports that women make many important decisions during the process of initiation. Complementarity and interdependence, much more than male dominance, characterizes boys' initiations, in her experience. But male researchers are not in a position to make those discoveries.

> The male observer would see the women appear and disappear, but could not track them into their ceremonial camps. Here, working from women's domain out, we see initiation as a time when women make certain statements about their importance in the presence of men, and do so in a way consonant with their construct of women in *yawulyu*.[32]

According to her report about these male initiation ceremonies, women's knowledge about and involvement in the ceremonies, as well as sexual segregation, are both pronounced. Bell reports that each afternoon of the ceremony, men and women gathered together on the same ritual ground to prepare themselves and the ritual objects for the upcoming ceremonies. But nevertheless, women and men each maintain secrecy about their ritual knowledge in each other's presence. For example, one of the men asked a woman, highly respected for her ritual knowledge, how to make certain designs. "She responded, 'Don't ask me, I'm a woman.' Half an hour before she had been teaching the women just those details."[33]

These testimonies are a clear example of how much changes when accurate information about women's religious lives, which in this case only a woman could learn, is added to our picture of the religion. It is also easy to see how male field workers, especially if their research is guided by an androcentric mindset, would deduce female inferiority and ignorance from the information available to them. In this case, adding women results in a diametrically opposite picture of the whole religion from that available when only men are studied. Instead of overwhelming male dominance, we see complementarity and interdependence; instead of women so deprived that they don't even have religious practices, we see women who have rich religious lives of their own and key positions in some of the important ceremonies from which they are supposedly excluded.

Nancy Jay's highly acclaimed book *Throughout Your Generations Forever: Sacrifice Religion and Paternity* (1992) is an example of feminist research that changes scholarly understandings of an important religious phemonenon—sacrifice, in this case. She agrees that "feminist scholarship is correctly committed to recovering women's silenced voices, but it must also look critically at all the varied methods for silencing them."[34] To do so, she engages in theoretical analyses of existing literature rather than field work. And rather than trying to illumine religion by including information about women, she sheds new light on the widespread phenomenon of sacrifice by asking why women are so frequently absent from sacrifice, not only in many ancient societies, but also in those versions of Christianity that understand the Eucharist to be a real sacrifice.

Her work begins by highlighting the well-known but widely ignored facts that women almost never participate in sacrificial ritual, that many traditions oppose childbirth or childbearing women and sacrifice, and that sacrifice repeatedly involves father son themes. Most theoreticians, she claims, have seen these facts as so obvious that they do not need comment or explanation; therefore, their theories of sacrifice proceed without reference to these facts. By contrast, Nancy Jay brings a feminist's interest in women to the question of why these facts hang together and why sacrificial practices so routinely exclude women.

In a nutshell, her thesis is that sacrifice "remedies having-been-born-of-woman, establishing bonds of intergenerational continuity between males that transcend their absolute dependence on childbearing women."[35] This explanation of sacrifice depends on her generalization that "sacrificial religions are very much features of their own social contexts, and they thrive in societies with certain kinds of family structure." She goes on to point out that "sacrifice is at home in societies where families are integrated into extended kin groups of various kinds: lineages, clans, sibs, and so on."[36] Such societies flourish in agrarian and pastoral settings, she notes, but are quite uncommon in foraging or industrial settings. But what makes extended families important to agrarian or pastoral contexts? Such societies, she claims, have some technological development, and rights in durable property are highly valued in them. In such societies durable property needs to be transferred from generation to generation, whereas foraging societies collect little durable property, and monetary media of exchange replace durable property in industrial societies, leading to the decline of extended family groups.[37] The usual solution to the problem of transfer of durable property is the creation of unilineal descent groups, either through the father or the mother, more commonly the father.

The patrilineal descent group, in particular, faces several problems which can be solved by sacrificial practices that exclude women. First is that biological paternity is uncertain but membership in the unilineal descent group must be clear and certain.

> What is needed . . . is an act as definite and available to the senses as is birth. When membership in patrilineal descent groups is identified by rights of participation in blood sacrifice, evidence of "paternity" is created which is as certain as evidence of maternity, but far more flexible.[38]

But why should women be excluded from the sacrificing group? This brings up the second problem of a patrilineal descent group. The group is utterly dependent on alien women to produce the next generation. "But if descent from these women were given full social recognition, the patrilineage would have no boundaries, no identity, and no recognizable continuity." The existence of a distinct lineage, within which rights in durable property may be transferred from generation to generation, depends on the exclusion of some and the inclusion of others. By sacrificing together men create such a group that transcends their birth from women, who, by definition, are not part of the group and do not sacrifice with the group.[39]

Finally, sacrifice can remedy another problem attendant on being born of woman. Mortality is commonly thought to be part of what one inherits from the mother. Because one is born, physically from a woman, one is destined to die. But rituals of sacrifice integrate men "into an 'eternal' social order that to a degree transcends mortality."[40] Even in situations in which women are included in the "eternal social order," such as certain Christian groups, the sacrifice is "birth done better, under a deliberate purposeful control, and on a more exalted level than ordinary mothers do it."[41]

> Sacrifice can expiate, get rid of, the consequences of having been born of woman . . . and at the same time integrate the pure and eternal patrilineage. Sacrificially constituted descent, incorporating women's mortal children into an "eternal" (enduring through generations) kin group, in which membership is recognized by participation in sacrificial ritual, not merely birth, enables a patrilineal group to transcend mortality in the same process in which it transcends birth. In this sense, sacrifice is doubly a remedy for having been born of woman.[42]

Whether or not one regards as helpful such theorizing, which provides reasons for religious behaviors that would never be offered or agreed upon by those who participate in the behaviors, it has a venerable history in the anthropology of religion. This case study demonstrates that if one is interested in such theorizing, then gender must be a factor that is taken into account. Specifically, exploring the absence of women, rather than taking it as normal and not worth mentioning, "lights up what has not been hidden but only ignored, has not been invisible but only irrelevant." In this case, "aspects of sacrifice that have been regularly left in darkness" are illuminated.[43]

The two case studies surveyed thus far suggest that our picture of a single religious situation or phenomenon can change radically when one adds women to that picture. But one of the most important discussions in feminist anthropology has more far reaching implications, as a major theory comes under suspicion. Serious interest in women has led to drastic changes in theories of

early human society, as the "just-so" story of "man the hunter" has been demol-
ished, to be replaced by a more plausible portrait of the interdependence of
men and women as foragers. According to this picture, not only is gathering at
least as important to human survival as hunting; both women and men engage
in both to some extent. Though this discussion in feminist anthropology has
not been taken up by anthropologists of religion, it has spun off important and
hotly contested discussions in feminist theories of religion, especially concerning early supposedly "matrifocal" religions. Since I have extensively reviewed
this debate in another context, I will only summarize it here.[44]

Anthropological theory in the 1950s and '60s was quite androcentric.
Portraits of the earliest humans focused on men and their hunting activities as
the sole force driving human evolution and assuring human survival; women
were assumed to be dependent childbearers who docilely waited by the fire
for the returning hunters. The development of tools, language, religion, and
art were all supposed to have been stimulated by men who hunted. In hindsight, the way in which this picture of prehistoric humanity reflected the idealized patriarchal family of the 1950s is quite laughable, but at the time androcentrism was taken for granted. With the women's movement and resulting
feminist scholarship in the 1960s and '70s, such portraits seemed entirely less
plausible. In particular, it became clear that gathering, rather than hunting, is
often the economic mainstay, with hunting providing occasional delicacies,
and that women contribute significantly to group survival as the result of their
gathering activities. They also hunt when possible, though usually long distance
hunting of large game is a male specialty. But even that domain is threatened
by more attention to communal hunts in which women and children participate
in driving large animals into traps or pits. In addition, women make tools—bas-
kets, carrying slings, digging sticks, etc.,—and they decorate them artistically,
just as men do. In short, bringing women into the picture of human origins and
development renders implausible the portrait of man the hunter.[45]

This insight, however, raises another question, which has been intensely
interesting to some feminist religious theoreticians. If man the hunter has not
always dominated women, if foraging societies are characterized by interdependence and complementarity, what explains the origins of sexual inequality? With this question, the focus shifts from earlier feminist anthropological
attempts to explain universal male dominance as due to eternal patterns in
male-female relations to consideration of the shifts in technology or environment that first trigger male dominance. Anthropologists have answered this
question in one way; ancient Near Eastern scholars in another, though the
transitions from horticulture to agriculture and from tribal to state societies
figure large in both.

In my view, the most successful and sophisticated account of the origins of
male dominance is Peggy Reeves Sanday's *Female Power and Male Dominance,*

because her account is not unileanear, isolating only one causal factor, nor are her explanations Eurocentric. Relying on data from 156 societies listed in the Human Relations Area Files, she locates cultural patterns that tend to correlate with male dominance or with female power. Chief among her findings is that it is possible to talk of female power and male-female equality when women have economic and political decision-making powers, which they do in about 32 percent of societies studied. Only 28 percent of the societies in her large sample are clearly male dominated. The remaining 40 percent are neither clearly egalitarian nor male dominated, but fall between those opposites.[46] She studies many factors that play into the level of male dominance in a society. If the environment is beneficent, then women and men tend to work together, men spend time with young children, and people develop what she calls an "inner orientation," including a symbol system that features female creative beings. Such societies are not usually male dominant. By contrast, if the environment is harsher and providing basic necessities produces stress, or if livelihood centers around large animals or migration, people develop an "outer orientation," in which the creative powers are male. Male dominance is likely in these societies, in part because men and women do not work together and men spend little time with children. But these lines of explanation are not neat and unilinear. Though, in some cases, one can "establish a causal relationship between depleting resources, cultural disruption, migration, and the oppression of women," male domination of women, when it occurs, "is a complex question, for which no one answer suffices."[47]

Feminists in the study of religion have been intensely interested in the question of the oriqins of male dominance, studying it especially keenly in the ancient Near Eastern theater. However, many of these studies are based more in mythology and theology than in anthropology and their results would be questioned seriously by many with serious anthropological training. An especially popular thesis attributing the emergence of male dominance to the decline of goddesses and the emergence of dominant male deities has prospered recently.[48] In my own detailed analysis of this argument, published elsewhere,[49] I have suggested that this thesis reverses cause and effect, in that the decline of the goddesses reflects social changes that have already occurred rather than causing them. Following Gerda Lerner[50] and others, I suggest that the chain of cause and effect leading to male dominance is initiated with some of the technological and environmental factors discussed by Peggy Reeves Sanday and others.

However, internal disagreements among those who discuss the origins of male dominance are not the major concern in this context. The major concern is that, once again, we see that taking women seriously changes our entire picture of what we are studying. Feminists, interested in women as cultural actors, asked how the human species could ever have survived if the earliest women had been utterly dependent on man the hunter for everything from all the food they ate to their own increasing brain size. Redrawing the picture of early humans as a portrait of interdependent foragers suggests that other assumptions common to the anthropology of religion need to be rethought. Primary among them is the need to explain male dominance, when it occurs, rather than to assume its universality, as had been common in earlier accounts of ancient religions and the anthropology of religion. Alternative explanations of the origins of male dominance in religion have led to one of the liveliest debates in contemporary religious studies.

Finally, in my view, important new directions in South Asian studies are, in part, due to the rise of feminist anthropology of religion in South Asian studies. The new emphasis in the study of religion in South Asia on lived religion, on religion "on the ground," rather than merely as presented in texts, has transformed the way Indian religions are taught and understood. As already noted, this trend represents the most profound methodological advance in South Asian studies in many decades. And one the of most important elements in this new approach to South Asian studies involves study of women's religious lives, which cannot be researched through textual study but must be approached using the methods of the anthropology of religions. As noted already, increased knowledge of women's religious lives in South Asia has added almost as much to our portrait of South Asia as to our portrait of aboriginal Australia. But since women's lives could be studied successfully only if textual studies were supplemented and augmented by anthropological research, those who wanted to study South Asian women's religious lives had to use anthropological methods and materials. Thus, while one could not say that the feminist anthropology of religion alone caused South Asian studies to go beyond its previous text bias, certainly adding information about women to the data about religion in South Asia has aided and abetted a major methodological corrective in the field. In this case, we see on a very large scale, that adding information about women encourages major transformations within a whole subfield of religious studies, rather than remaining merely a footnote in the margins of the field.

Emerging Issues in the Contemporary Feminist Anthropology of Religion

The anthropology of women, the exercise of gathering information about women, is now somewhat well established; certainly much more knowldege about women and religion is much better integrated into both anthropology and religious studies than was the case thirty years ago. Feminist anthropology, the exercise of rethinking major questions and areas of study in the light of this increased knowledge about women is also somewhat well established, despite holdouts against feminist scholarship, both in anthropology and in religious

studies. As we look forward rather than backward in the feminist anthropology of religion, what issues come to the fore currently? What concerns are
likely to dominate the literature of the next decade or more?

I suggest that two major concerns emerge in the current discussions.
Both of them represent some maturity in feminist scholarship, some ability to
begin to contextualize the anthropology of women and feminist anthropology
within a cluster of other issues. The first concern is to integrate gender into a
matrix of other identities that are important to both women and men, rather
than to focus on gender alone. Many now regard a total focus on gender, to
the exclusion of other determinants of identity, as somewhat artificial. The second cluster of concerns involves reconsidering power, dominance, and women.
Rather than the stark contrast of powerful men and powerless women often
conjured up by terms such as "male dominance," newer scholarship suggests
that formal male dominance often hides real power on the part of women and
that discussions of men, women, and power need to be much more nuanced.
This discussion of feminism and the anthropology of religion will conclude
with some brief comments on each of these concerns.

Two watchwords sum up the first concern—the concern to study gender
as one factor among others important to understanding any specific woman
or her culture. These words are "embeddedness" and "difference."

Rather than seeing gender as completely determinative, contemporary
scholars are much more likely to see gender as one among several factors that
figure into a person's identity and strategies. The gender dichotomy is extremely
obvious in every culture, but it is not the only factor determining a person's
identity and interests. Thus, gender is embedded into a number of other equally
determinative variables. Age and social or economic status are especially important factors and it is claimed that women's actions and attitudes are not merely
a result of their gender, but also of these other determinants. For example,
Diane Bell, whose work has been referred to frequently in this chapter, suggests that her own success in learning about Australian aboriginal women's
rituals resulted not only from her gender but from her age, since only older
women have the knowledge she sought and that knowledge is not shared with
young women. To study aboriginal women's religious lives only with respect to
gender constraints while ignoring age would thus be futile and foolhardy, leading nowhere.

The concern for gender's enmeshment with other major components of
identity easily leads to the concern for "difference," for concern with the ways
in which different women in different situations construct their worlds.
Rather than the sweeping universals and generalities about gender that were
so predominant in the beginnings of feminist theory in general, contemporary
scholars are much more attuned to the particular, to this unique situation dis-
playing its own blend of gender, age, status, etc. This tendency results from

the postmodern claim that the category "woman" has no meaning because any essential "womanhood" common to all women is rendered implausible by endless variations among women. Whether or not one agrees with this rather counterintuitive philosophical claim, there is no question that the mood of the times calls for exploration of the particular embedded into its unique cultural matrix, not only in anthropology and the anthropology of religion, but in disciplines as different from anthropology as is theology.

Finally, the second major topic of discussion in current conversations involves a more subtle consideration of issues of men, women, and power. Scholars have become less satisfied with crude generalizations about powerful men and powerless women in the face of the fact that almost nowhere are women subservient helpless pawns with no strategies to further their own interests and needs. Some refinement of the notion of male dominance seems warranted.

One suggestion introduces the category of "mythical male dominance," and differentiates dominance from power. This distinction involves the recognition that while men may hold formal dominance, in that everyone agrees that they should be in control, in fact women have considerable power, both formally and informally, to influence decisions, and everyone, both women and men, knows this to be the case.[51] This kind of "mythical" male dominance would be unnoticed in textual studies of a religion, since the texts would reflect the formal authority conferred on men rather than the accommodations of everyday life. And it would also be unnoticed in casual observations of a society, which would put on a public face of formal male dominance. It might also be unnoticed by androcentric male field workers, who would be more likely to notice male posturing than the accommodations of shared power. Furthermore, even some feminists would be likely to downplay or scorn this distinction between male dominance and female power, since it does not involve women's rights, but only customary practice, which could be violated and does not involve the kind of power many Western women seek and want. Nevertheless, as a descriptive tool, it will yield far more subtle and accurate results than too much belief in the reality of unrelieved male dominance.

Others suggest that female-male complementarity may well be much greater than has previously been recognized, especially for some religions. It is claimed that what has been misread as dominance is actually complementary difference. Men and women have very different roles even religiously, it is argued, but these differences were not viewed indigenously as giving men dominance over women. It is now quite common for insiders, especially women from cultures that have been marginalized by colonialism, to claim that they are not oppressed within their own culture,[52] that they have been seriously mislabeled by outsiders who did not understand what they were seeing, even that Western judgments about indigenous women's oppression reflects Western imperialism and chauvinism. In other cases, a sympathetic female outsider who has lived with indigenous women paints a very attractive picture of women who by all other accounts are marginalized and oppressed.[53]

The subjectivity and relativism inherent in such judgments are obvious. Probably consensus or certainty regarding them is impossible, but they enrich the discussion of men, women, and power. Claims about complementarity are justifiably regarded with suspicion by many feminists because male authorities have always claimed that gender hierarchies are natural complementarities and because alleged complementarity often benefits men much more than it benefits women. On the other hand, certainly Western observers, with their tendency to understand every difference as a hierarchy, may well be quite subject to the misjudgment that if men and women do different things, then men dominate women. In the last thirty years, the anthropology of women has demonstrated that most situations are considerably more complex.

But another complication is introduced by the fact that those who have been marginalized and colonized often eagerly defend *all* features of their culture without exception, even if certain customs seem to be cruel and unjust to a wide spectrum of commentators and observers. Often the most controversial such customs involve women, as is indicated by the current controversies over Muslim veiling of women and sub-Saharan African female genital operations. I am reluctant to take at face value every insiders' claim that what looks to outsiders like male dominance and female oppression in fact is not. I am too familiar in my own culture with women's willingness to justify and defend male dominance and the oppression of women to accept without skepticism all such claims made by women simply because they come from another culture.

These contemporary discussions reflect how much groundwork has been done in the anthropology of women in religion and in feminist anthropology of religion. If the information regarding women were still uncollected, and if scholars still thought one could understand religion or culture without integrating information about women into their theories, we would not be discussing gender as one category among others important to women as they negotiate their religious lives. Nor would we be emphasizing differences between different women's religious lives and guarding against the danger of too many generalizations. Nor could we have any clues as to whether alleged male dominance is real or "mythic" and we could not even begin to entertain the possibility that differences between men's and women's roles and activities may be genuinely complementary in some cases.

Notes

1. For a recent attempt to bring the fields into conversation, with the conversation being initiated from the side of the academic study of religion, see

Robert L. Moore and Frank E. Reynolds, eds., *Anthropology and the Study of Religion* (Chicago: Center for the Scientific Study of Religion, 1984).

2. Carol P. Christ, "Why Women Need the Goddess: Phenomonological, Psychological, and Political Reflections," in *Womanspirit Rising: A Feminist Reader in Religion,* ed. Carol Christ and Judith Plaskow (San Francisco: Harper and Row, 1979).

3. Rita M. Gross, "Here I Stand: Feminism as Academic Method and as Social Vision," in *Buddhism After Patriarchy: A Feminist History. Analysis, and Reconstruction of Buddhism* (Albany: State University of New York Press, 1993), 291–304.

4. Rita M. Gross, *Feminism and Religion—An Introduction* (Boston: Beacon Press, 1996) forthcoming.

5. For an excellent critique of the way in which models and theories of Indian religions based solely on elite texts have distorted Western understandings of Indian religions and eclipsed women, see Nancy Auer Falk, forthcoming.

6. For example, see the table of contents of his *Patterns in Comparative Religion* (Cleveland and New York: World Publishing Co., 1963), in which "woman" finds her place after the sun, the moon, the waters, sacred stones, and the earth but before vegetation, sacred places, and sacred time as a primary symbol in his famous phenomenology of religion. In *Rites and Symbols of Initiation: The Mysteries of Birth and Rebirth* (New York: Harper and Row, 1958), women's initiations are dealt with in seven pages. These examples could easily be multiplied.

7. Ursala King, ed., *Religion and Gender* (Cambridge, Mass.: Blackwell, 1995), pp. 21–22.

8. Nancy Auer Falk and Rita M. Gross, eds., *Unspoken Worlds: Women's Religious Lives,* first published by Harper and Row in 1980 and reissued in an expanded version by Wadsworth in 1989.

9. For an informative survey of the most influential writers and issues in feminist anthropology, very few of whom wrote about religion, Micaela di Leonardo, "Introduction," *Gender at the Crossroads of Knowledge: Feminist Anthropology in the Postmodern Era,* 1–36.

10. For a bibliography see Nancy Auer Falk, *Women and Religion in India: An Annotated Bibliography of Sources in English, 1975–92* (Kalamazoo: Western Michigan University, 1994). Specific sources include: Kathleen M. Erndl, *Victory to the Mother: The Hindu Goddess of Northwest India in Myth, Ritual, and Symbol* (New York: Oxford University Press, 1993); Anne Feldhaus, *Water and Womanhood* (New York: Oxford, 1995); Lindsey Harlan and Paul B. Courtright, eds., *From the Margins of Hindu Marriage: Essays on Gender, Religion, and Culture* (New York: Oxford, 1995); Lindsay Harlan, *Religion and Rajput Women: The Ethic of Protection in Contemporary Narratives* (Berkeley: University of California Press, 1992); Doranne Jacobson

and Susan Wadley, *Women in India: Two Perspectives* (New Delhi: Manohar, 1986); Julia Leslie, *Roles and Rituals for Hindu Women* (New Delhi: Motilal Barnarsidass, 1992); Frederique Apffel Marglin, *Wives of the God-Kind: The Rituals of the Devadasis of Puri* (New Delhi: Oxford University Press, 1985); Sarah S. Mitter, *Dharma's Dauqhters* (New Brusnwick, N.J.:, Rutgers University Press, 1991); Gloria Goddwin Raheja and Ann Grodzins Gold, *Listen to the Heron's Words: Reinagining Gender and Kinship in North India* (Berkeley: University of California Press, 1994); William Sax, *Mountain Goddess: Gender and Politics in a Himalayan Pilgrimage* (New York: Oxford University Press, 1991); and Susan S. Wadley, ed., *The Powers of Tamil Women* (Syracuse: Syracuse University, 1980).

11. For example, see Donna Lee Bowen and Evelyn A. Early, *Everyday Life in the Muslim Middle East* (Bloomington: Indiana University Press, 1993); Elizabeth Warnock Fernea, *Women and the Family in the Middle East: New Voices of Change* (Austin: University of Texas Press, 1985); Fernea and Basima Qattan Bezirgan, eds., *Middle Eastern Muslim Women Speak* (Austin: University of Texas Press, 1977); Erika Friedl, *Women of Deh Koh* (Washington: Smithsonian Institution Press, 1989); Fatima Mernissi, *Beyond the Veil: Male-Female Dynamics in Modern Muslim Society* (Bloomington: Indiana University Press, 1987); Bouthaina Shaaban, *Both Right and Left Handed: Arab Women Talk About Their Lives* (Bloomington: University of Indiana Press, 1991); and Unni Wikan, *Behind the Veil in Arabia: Women in Oman* (Chicago: University of Chicago Press, 1982).

12. See especially Fatima Mernissi, "Women, Saints and Sanctuaries in Morocco," and Erika Friedl, "Women and Islam in a Tribal Village in Iran," in *Unspoken Worlds,* 112–133.

13. See my "Tribal Religions: Aboriginal Australia," in *Women in World Religions,* ed. Arvind Sharma (Albany: State University of New York Press, 1987), 37–58; and Diane Bell, *Daughters of the Dreaming* (Minneapolis: U. of Minnesota Press, 1993), first published in 1983, based on study done in 1976–1982.

14. Micaela di Leonardo, "Women, Culture, and Society Revisited," in *The Knowledge Explosion: Generations of Feminist Scholarship,* ed. Cheris Kraemer and Dale Spender (New York: Teachers College Press, 1992), 118–124.

15. Rita M. Gross, "Menstruation and Childbirth as Ritual and Religious Experience among Native Australians," in *Unspoken Worlds,* 257–259.

16. Bell, 250.

17. For a useful personal account, see Kim Knott, "Women Researching, Women Researched: Gender as an Issue in the Empirical Study of Religion," in *Gender and Religion,* 199–218.

18. See especially, "Religious Experience and the Study of Religion: The History of Religions," in *Buddhism After Patriarchy,* 305–317 and chapter 1

"Defining Feminism, Religion, and Religious Studies," in *Feminism and Religion—An Introduction* (Boston: Beacon Press, forthcoming).

19. See di Leonardo, 6–17 for a helpful discussion of these essays as well as other feminist anthropological theories of the day.

20. Falk and Gross, xvi–xviii.

21. Susan Starr Sered, *Priestess, Mother, Sacred Sister: Religions Dominated by Women* (New York: Oxford University Press, 1994), 3–10.

22. I encountered this problem quite extensively when researching the historical section of *Buddhism After Patriarchy*.

23. Bell, 232.

24. A. P. Abbie, *The Original Australian* (New York: American Elsevier, 1969), 125.

25. For a quotation of the most influential statement of this thesis see Gross, "Menstruation and Childbirth," in *Unspoken Worlds*, 258.

26. Bell, *Daughters of the Dreaming*, 229, quoting Lloyd Warner.

27. Rita Gross, "Menstruation and Childbirth . . ." in *Unspoken Worlds*, 257–266 and Rita Gross, "Tribal Religions: Aboriginal Australia," in *Women in World Religions*, 37–58.

28. See especially *Daughters of the Dreaming*, and Bell, "Aboriginal Women's Religion," in *Today's Woman in World Religions*, ed. Arvind Sharma (Albany: State University of New York Press, 1994), 39–76.

29. Bell, "Aboriginal Women's Religion," 47–48.

30. Bell, *Daughters*, 21.

31. Bell, "Aboriginal Women's Religion," 68.

32. Ibid., 67.

33. Bell, "Aboriginal Women's Religion," 62.

34. Nancy Jay, *Throughout Your Generations Forever: Sacrifice, Religion, and Paternity,* (Chicago, University of Chicago Press, 1992), 150.

35. Ibid., 147.

36. Ibid., xxiv.

37. Ibid., 34–35.

38. Ibid., 36.

39. Ibid., 40.

40. Ibid., 39.

41. Ibid., xxiv.

42. Ibid., 40.

43. Ibid., 147.

44. For more detail, see "The Pre-patriarchal Hypothesis: An Assessment," in *Religion and Gender: Essays from the XVII Congress of the History of Religions*, ed. Sylvia Marcos (London: Blackwell, forthcoming). See also my "Has It Always Been That Way? Re-reading the Past," in *Feminism and Religion—An Introduction*.

45. For more detailed discussions, see Frances Dahlberg, ed., *Woman the Gatherer* (New Haven: Yale University Press, 1981); Adrienne L. Zihlman, "Woman the Gatherer; The Role of Women in Early Hominid Development," in *Gender and Anthropology*, 21–40; and Margaret Ehrenberg, *Women in Prehistory* (Norman and London: University of Oklahoma Press, 1989).

46. Sanday, 165.

47. Ibid., 8.

48. For a typical semipopular account, see Elinor Gadon, *The Once and Future Goddess* (San Francisco: Harper and Row, 1989).

49. Gross, *Feminism and Religious Studies* (forthcoming).

50. Gerda Lerner, *The Creation of Patriarchy* (Oxford: Oxford University Press, 1986).

51. Sanday, 165.

52. See for example the work of Inez Talamantez and Paula Gunn Allen.

53. The best known case is the work of Elizabeth Fernea in *Guests of the Sheik* and *Streets of Marakesh*. Some have claimed that her work is highly romanticized, in the way that only a guest who can go home again could romanticize a difficult situation.

4

Feminist Research in the Sociology of Religion

CONSTANCE A. JONES

Beginning several decades ago with the rise of the modern feminist movement, feminist scholars began to develop new historical analyses, to pose new questions about the assumptions and values of established scientific inquiry, and to call for a more complete understanding of women's position in society and place in nature. As part of the larger feminist enterprise, feminist scholarship in the sociology of religion has grappled with these issues, has undergone considerable self-scrutiny, and, in the process, has offered a critique and expansion of established social science models for research and theorizing.

This chapter surveys significant contributions to feminist thought and practice in the sociology of religion. The first section outlines feminist perspectives, the lenses through which scholarship is conducted, analyzed, and critiqued. The second section describes major elements of feminist research, including examination of women's experience in both institutionalized and noninstitutionalized religions, theoretical contributions, expanded methods, research as a factor in social action, and feminist dialogue with classical sociology. Finally, this essay summarizes women's participation in the research establishment of the sociology of religion.

Feminist Perspectives

Although feminist research in the sociology of religion has not reached a consensus on "feminist theory" or "feminist method," the evolution of feminist scholarship has included progressively more sophisticated challenges to established social scientific models of inquiry and has expanded the lenses through which science views religious phenomena.[1] Unlike the situations within the larger frameworks of sociology and anthropology in general, feminist work in the sociology of religion does not constitute a revolutionary movement designed to supplant existing research models, nor has it offered a large-scale indictment of empirical methods and survey research as factors that serve to marginalize women. Instead, feminist contributions are more properly defined as expanding and revising existing models.[2] Although we cannot define a univocal "school" devoted to feminist methods, we can speak of feminist contributions to theory and method as "feminist perspectives," scholars who employ these perspectives as "feminist scholars," and the collected research of these scholars as "feminist scholarship."

A well-known model outlines three stages in the development of feminist perspectives in a discipline: Stage 1 documents and critiques the invisibility and inequality of women. Stage 2 includes research on women that uses concepts and paradigms developed in scholarship based on men, the "add women and stir" model, named by Charlotte Bunch.[3] Stage 3 produces studies that employ gender as a basic analytic category and, thus, lead to paradigm shifts in the discipline. These three stages appear clearly in feminist research in the sociology of religion. In the first stage, early feminist analyses of both religious behavior and sociological method focused on the inequality of women and the absence of women as both researchers and objects of research. During the second stage, existing theories, such as Marxism, liberalism, and psychoanalysis were revised to "add women and stir" or "bring women back in," by adding gender as a variable without changing the conceptual frame of inquiry.[4] Later, in the third stage, as a result of methodological and epistemological debates among feminist researchers, this task of "bringing women back in" evolved into a revisionary critique that questions the basic assumptions of traditional science, women's place in both science and religion, and the very definitions of religious experience.

A primary element in this critique is recognition of the complexity and diversity of human experience. Following the lead of more general feminist analyses, feminist research in religion gives attention to groups and experiences previously overlooked. Investigation of marginalized groups and subjective experience demonstrates the limits of past theory that purported to understand human religious experience through the study of dominant groups, primarily white men, and shows how release from assumptions of their experience as "normative" provides fresh perspectives and new data for expanded inquiry.

As feminist researchers have uncovered the androcentric bias that has "equated the masculine with the universal,"[5] they have established gender as a valid category of study, recognized women as legitimate subjects of research, and investigated the power dynamics that underlie social relations as well as scientific inquiry. Feminist deconstruction of this "false universalism" demonstrates that, in addition to women, other marginalized groups, defined by race, class, ethnicity, and sexuality, have also been excluded as subjects and pro-ducers of knowledge. Universalistic assumptions inherent in all stages of the research process have functioned to exclude women of color, lesbians, and ethnic minorities as subjects of research; power relations have functioned to exclude these groups from the research establishment.

With the recognition of gender, race, and class as interlocking factors in all social research, feminist scholarship in religion draws upon the seminal contributions in theory and epistemology of black feminist scholars Angela Davis, Barbara Smith, Bonnie Dill, Deborah King, Patricia Collins, and Rose Brewer.[6] Each of these scholars points to the special responsibility of feminist research to be inclusive and holistic in modeling a pluralistic and multipara-digmatic view of the world. Black sociologists of religion Cheryl Gilkes and Delores Williams[7] build upon these ideals of multiperspectivity as sources of strength, rather than sources of division, in their studies of race, gender, and religious experience.

Part of the growing attention to social complexity is the feminist recogni-tion of the social construction of all experience and knowledge. As feminist scholars inquire into the social location of behavior, they consider ever more seriously the social positions of both researcher and subject and take into account factors of diversity and difference. Explanation of the constructedness of experience and knowledge includes a number of considerations; feminist researchers, in the main, have been concerned with a systematic inclusion of gender, race, class, and power relations as particularly important. An appreci-ation of the gendering of all social relations and an understanding of power as pivotal in the production of scientific knowledge lead to a feminist reframing of traditional research questions. Two processes occur simultaneously. First, a "contextualizing" of scientific analysis demonstrates the social construction of knowledge in the research project. Second, feminist reframing of research questions challenges traditional assumptions about gender roles and "women's place."[8]

Another major criticism of traditional sociology of religion by feminist scholarship is the discipline's focus on institutional analysis to the neglect of microsociological inquiry. Feminists argue that concentration on macro- and middle-range theories, a legacy of classical sociology that is also an element in false universalism, presents a view of religion that obscures the experiences of marginalized groups and distorts the complexity of religious experience.[9]

Our understanding of religious experience is also distorted, according to Anthony Blasi,[10] as a result of a hegemony in the scientific study of religion that devalues and negates the spirit of transcendent mystery associated with the religious mentality. This position is part of the larger, long-standing critique of reductionism in the study of religion that argues for an expanded under-standing of religious experience and behavior, specifically an understanding of religion from phenomenological perspectives. Feminist scholars draw upon this argument in an effort to undo centuries of neglect of the religious and spiritual experiences of women. They use hermeneutic and phenomenological inquiry to redress the limitations of a reductionist stance and the omission of women's experience. Feminist researchers assert that an expanded use of qualitative methods provides an opening to greater appreciation of the subjective states of themselves both as researchers and the subjects of research. Further, their reflexive examination into method demonstrates that the interaction between the researcher and the subject of research is also meaningful and influences the quality of data acquired as well as analyses of these data. In short, these methods uncover aspects of experience that would remain inaccessible through objective data collection alone.

To summarize, feminist perspectives on research involve a sequence of processes, namely, the processes of moving from a perceived need for appreciation of women's experience, to an expansion of research design, to an inclusion of alternative methods, to a reflexive examination of the research project, and finally to a more interpretive analysis. Further, as part of feminist praxis, the research process itself and research findings are dedicated to positive social action.

Fortunately, six recently published essays on the sociology of religion, taken as a whole, survey almost all of the feminist enterprise within the subdiscipline. Readers are advised to consult these essays in their entirety for their insights, feminist perspectives, and extensive bibliographies. Short reviews of these essays follow as a survey of the "state of the art" in the sociology of religion.

The first contribution is Mary Jo Neitz's introduction to a special issue of *The American Sociologist* (1989), "Feminist Scholarship in Sociology."[11] As editor of the volume, she sets out a chronological outline of feminist developments in sociology and places each succeeding article within the larger framework of transformative research. As she reflects upon the history of feminist scholarship, she describes the agenda set out in the 1970s for creation and evolution of a feminist revisionism, the debates involved in defining feminist theory, and the creation of organizations and publications to explore these issues. Neitz shows how feminist discourse moved from an early acceptance of and dialogue with Marxist theory to a feminist critique of materialism that involved progressively more refined definitions and conceptualizations of social variables. Very quickly, by the mid-seventies, the pivotal conceptualization of a sex-gender system by Joan Kelly-Gadol and Gayle Rubin[12] opened feminist discourse to exploration of the social structures and cultural processes that "engender" human thought and behavior. Sociological understanding of relations between men and women and women's place in society was articulated in feminist terms. The controversies over definitions of feminist method, feminist theory, and feminist practice that ensued are laid out deftly by Neitz.

This article and the other contributions to the special issue provide an excellent overview of the history and current debates surrounding feminist scholarship.

A second contribution, from the special issue mentioned above, is Rose Brewer's "Black Women and Feminist Sociology: The Emerging Perspective." Brewer argues that a major critique of social science emanates from the writings of a black feminist intelligentsia. The theoretical basis for this critique is an expanding appreciation of the intersection of race, class, and gender in all social phenomena and the unconscious incorporation of dominant, that is, colonizing, perspectives in the discipline of sociology. As Brewer examines the belief in assimilation and the colonization of black women's intellectual lives, she calls for a new sociological paradigm that will be informed by black women's experiences and historical positioning. Elements of this argument are included below under "Research on Women's History and Experience."

The third contribution, Ruth Wallace's "Feminism: Expanding the Horizons of the Sociology of Religion," examines the "containment of feminism" in the sociology of religion. The notion of "containment," originally put forward by Judith Stacey and Barrie Thorne,[13] argues that feminist sociologists have achieved some success in correcting sexist biases in the discipline, but have not been successful in reconstructing basic sociological paradigms. Wallace examines the containment model by demonstrating how feminist contributions have critiqued and reevaluated existing theories, particularly those of Talcott Parsons and Max Weber. She further notes how "missing" theoretical issues, brought to the fore and analyzed by feminist scholars, can be significant in the sociological understanding of religion. These issues will be discussed below under "Theoretical Contributions."

The fourth contribution to feminist discourse on the scientific study of religion is "Gender and Power in New Religious Movements" by Janet Jacobs.[14] Drawing on general feminist theory, particularly feminist deconstruction of androcentric assumptions, Jacobs explores the scientific principles that inform feminist analysis, with a view toward developing a revisionist paradigm for research. She examines in depth the concept of "false universalism" and the assumptions of neutrality and objectivity that undergird traditional scientific inquiry. She then applies these feminist contributions to contemporary studies of new religious movements. Jacobs's analysis is particularly powerful in demonstrating the unnoted biases of past research and in reworking previous scholarship in light of feminist insight. Much of her argument is included below under the rubric "Theoretical Contributions."

The fifth essay, Mary Jo Neitz's "Inequality and Difference: Feminist Research in the Sociology of Religion"[15] offers a wide-ranging review of the literature in the sociology of religion. She summarizes a vast amount of research, covering women in the ministry, Catholic feminists, women laity, converts to Orthodox Judaism, and women in historically black churches. Her section on "women-centered religious groups and practices," in which she examines spiritualism and goddess religion, combines feminist theory and research findings into an appreciation of the subjective experiences of women in religious contexts. Some of her contributions are included below under "Research on Women's History and Experience."

Another essay by Neitz[16] examines feminist theory and religious experience in greater depth. Here Neitz explores the social psychology of women's religious experience by creating a phenomenology of autonomy and submission in religious contexts. Her discussion is informed by more general feminist contributions in developmental psychology, so that she offers the reader useful tools with which to view women's religious experience in a variety of venues. Drawing on an extensive knowledge of goddess religion, Neitz demonstrates how feminist religion is expanding traditional definitions of religion, transcendence, and the value of the body. These changes are discussed below under "Theoretical Contributions."

These six essays indicate the tenor and influence of feminist thought in the social scientific research on religion. Each contribution incorporates feminist theory and method into a revisionist discourse that broadens the scope of traditional sociological models and explores ways in which feminist perspectives contribute to interdisciplinary cooperation.

Elements of Feminist Research

As elaborations of the perspectives described above, five elements characterize feminist scholarship in the sociology of religion: research on women's history and experience; theoretical contributions; expanded methods; research as an element of social action; and dialogue with classical sociology. The feminist themes that interpenetrate these elements move sociological inquiry into a more holistic mode, relieving traditional scientific dualisms, of theory and method, scholarship and activism, and research and application.

Research on Women's History and Experience

The critical change due to feminist influence is the inclusion of women and women's experience as objects of research and theory. In the last twenty years, research topics in religion reflect a growing interest in gender roles and patriarchy in the larger society. Increasingly more studies report on women's participation in and perceptions of religion. The following review of published research demonstrates this interest in both institutionalized and noninstitutionalized contexts.

As with other major institutions of society, the institution of religion creates, perpetuates, and reflects gendered relations. Religious organizations, however, have the added force of being agents of legitimation, with the ability to define behavior and belief as normative or non-normative. The feminist project is to document these gendered relations and their religious justifications and to understand how gender interacts with other social variables, particularly race, class, and ethnicity, in relations of power and dominance.

Institutionalized Religion. Within mainline Protestant denominations in the United States women have served historically as ministers. Studies of these women examine their ministerial careers, their effectiveness in positions of influence, and persisting inequities that limit their participation.[17] Although ordained as clergywomen by their respective denominations, women, even in liberal denominations, experience curtailed access to modes of influence and to complete acceptance by all congregants. Their influence and acceptance grows greater as women occupy more leadership roles and have increasing contact with those they serve.[18] Recent studies of ministerial style find that no clear distinction between masculine and feminine styles of ministry exist independently of other qualifying variables, most notably, race, ethnicity, and subculture.[19] As Protestant clergywomen grow in numbers and affect congregations with their consensual leadership styles, sociologists ponder how religious institutions may change because of women's participation in positions of power.[20]

Within Pentecostal and holiness denominations, women have been historically integral to the leadership of congregations, serving as founders and ministers of various faiths.[21] But their actual power within denominations has suffered from the conflict between charisma, which women often display, and bureaucracy, which men most often lead.[22] Even when women are in leadership positions, appeals to traditional gender roles keep women submissive and self-effacing.[23]

But we must be cautious in generalizing to all women, even within the same religious contexts. Significant differences in power and subjective experience occur among women. For example, although Pentecostal clergywomen minister differently than men, their experiences in moving toward a "religion of wholeness" show considerable variation, depending upon their life histories.[24] Women's styles of preaching and their sermon topics also vary consistently, depending upon the women's status, as pastor of a congregation or itinerant evangelist.[25] We must also be cautious in ascribing all feminist activism to women. Clergywomen report a growing number of male clergy who are involved in promoting feminist goals.[26]

Among lay women, the interaction of religious belief and gender role ideology is demonstrated by the effect of evangelical and fundamentalist ideologies on women's attitudes[27] and search for certainty in an uncertain world.[28] Feminist and fundamentalist values are mixed in some women who are redefining gender roles and family patterns.[29] The much-publicized contribution of conservative Christian ideology to public debates on family and sexuality continues to be documented in a number of studies.[30]

Other research demonstrates how race, ethnicity, and gender interact to affect women's leadership. Throughout American history, black churches have provided African American women with leadership positions, authority, and career pathways outside the official pastorate, yet not in totally uniform ways. Denominations influenced by European Christian ideologies differ from denominations influenced by dual-sex political systems of West African societies in ascription of gender roles, division of labor by gender, and power relationships.[31]

Within the Roman Catholic Church, while women's participation has increased considerably since the Second Vatican Council,[32] attitudes toward women and the positions open to women are still influenced by implicit assumptions about gender role. Priestless parishes headed by women lay ministers are witnessing a decline in hierarchical leadership and an increase in the autonomy of women pastors.[33] Still, the Church's division of labor, which defines "women's work" and "men's work," embodies traditional gender role ideologies and mirrors women's work in the larger society.[34] Gender role ideology also affects women's attitudes toward church teachings on sex and morality.[35] Among both Catholic men and women, gender role ideology more strongly affects attitudes toward abortion than does gender itself.[36] Among Catholic charismatics, gender roles are associated with the transition of God images from authoritarian patriarch to loving father[37] and with a perceived demand among women to support traditional roles of dominance for men.[38]

As with Catholicism in the United States, a pervasive, conservative gender role ideology within the Church of England explains opposition to the ordination of women as priests that cannot be accounted for solely by scriptural and theological beliefs.[39] Beyond attitudes, women clergy in the Church of England face sexism in denominational structure and organizational maintenance.[40]

Research into women's return to Orthodox Judaism demonstrates that significant differences among life circumstances are correlated with reasons for conversion. Debra Kaufman[41] finds that some female converts seek refuge from the larger society, which they perceive as dominated by decadent Western values. Orthodoxy is an opportunity to celebrate women's spirituality in defiance of the values of the larger society. Lynn Davidman, in several studies,[42] examines women's motives for conversion to Jewish orthodoxy, and finds that some women convert with the goal of maintaining independent lives of work and autonomy, while other women search for one all-encompassing community that limits their autonomy.

Lynn Davidman has joined with Shelly Tenenbaum to edit an excellent volume, *Feminist Perspectives on Jewish Studies*,[43] evaluating the impact of feminist scholarship on several of the academic disciplines encompassed by Jewish studies. These collected essays reflect new areas of thematic inquiry that have emerged from feminist analyses. Of particular import is the editors' essay that traces the history of American Jewish studies and critically reviews sociological studies of American Jews. Davidman and Tenenbaum have begun an interdisciplinary, gender-sensitive research focus to which they invite other feminist scholars to contribute.

While a thorough review of studies devoted to women's place in institutionalized religions is not possible here, this discussion has highlighted some of the variables of interest to researchers in the field. One anthology, edited by William Swatos[44] and drawn from articles previously published in *Sociology of Religion,* demonstrates a variety of perspectives used to study women in institutionalized religions. Generally, findings indicate increased participation by women, often in ways unpredictable from past research and in styles inconsistent with conventional theory. Within institutionalized religion, women are participating in tradition-affirming movements that accept women's subordinate role in religious organizations,[45] reform movements that call for significant change with respect to women's roles, while affirming the tradition itself,[46] and feminist spirituality movements that offer women healing and empowerment.[47] The substantial variation within women's religious sensibilities and the creation of new spheres of influence for women testify to the need for more understanding of how women make meaning and create practice as they engage with institutionalized forms of religion.

New Religious Movements. Since the 1960s and the rise of many new religious movements, feminist analysis has been prominent in the study of noninstitutionalized religion.[48] Scholarship in new religious movements has included analysis of all aspects of membership: conversion, socialization, adaptation, and disaffiliation. Women's perceptions of these processes are particularly interesting because many new religions hold gender role ideologies that are decidedly sexist.

As the literature on new religious movements shows, women join new religions with both extremely conservative and radical gender role ideologies. Feminist scholars ask how and why contemporary women find meaning in these diverse contexts and how their socialization into the larger patriarchal culture affects their affiliation. Variables of interest in feminist research include the institutionalization of power and dominance in new religions, the legitimation of male authority through theological symbols of male power, and women's perceptions of power relations.

The association of the divine with a masculine symbol of power has implications for the gendering of religious experience.[49] Especially in situations of extreme control over members' lives, paternalistic theological images can be combined with male dominance to produce authoritarian control. Such a situation occurred in Jonestown, Guyana among members of the Peoples Temple, when Jim Jones superimposed authoritarian control onto gender relations by cultivating a paternal image of himself that was both divine and fatherly.[50] In other, female-headed movements, the inconsistency between sexist tradition and charisma embodied in a woman leader results in socially constructed gender relations that often contain contradictions.[51]

In her analysis of the relationship between followers and charismatic leaders from an object relations perspective, Janet Jacobs[52] argues that the charismatic authority attributed to the leader is a fusion of three images: the symbol of the divine, an idealized parental image, and an idealized self. The mystical goal of merging with the divine then involves unconscious operations in which internalized images of the charismatic leader, one's ego ideal, and one's understanding of gendered relations become blurred. Jacobs's research shows that the experience of mystical union is far more common among men than among women. Instead, women more often report a sense of subordination and submission to the leader that is often accompanied by feelings of exploitation and abuse. Jacobs ties this gender difference to the larger cultural context of gendered relations in which men are socialized to seek transcendence, while women are expected to be submissive.

The recent rash of "guru scandals" involving sexual relations between Eastern teachers and Western devotees includes other significant factors in the study of gender roles in new religious movements, particularly the role of culture in specifying normative gender relations and the role of religious belief in defining the nature of a spiritual adept. In the cross-cultural milieu formed by an Eastern teacher and Western disciples, assumptions about spiritual authority, morality, and ethical behavior are superimposed on a leader-follower relationship that is characterized by a great disparity of power and considerable potential for abuse. Some feminist analyses find that power dimensions within groups and socialization to submission function as structural and psychological mechanisms that limit women's autonomy.[53] Other analyses show how authoritarian communities validate and spiritualize women's experiences that are not valued in the larger society, such as female leadership, rejection of traditional female roles, and experimental sexual relationships.[54]

Analyses of religious movements over time have demonstrated extreme variability in gendered relations. In new religious movements that have been relatively open to women's leadership and participation, such as spiritualist groups, feminine styles of influence, including diffuse authority and shared power, have been in effect for generations.[55] Other analyses delineate how the transplantation of a religious movement from a patriarchal, agricultural milieu to a nonfamilial, urban locale, as is the case with Haitian Vodou, mirrors the respective social contexts within the movement itself, including significant alteration of gender relations.[56]

In comparison to authoritarian movements, the feminist spirituality movement offers an alternative model of personal agency and structural hierarchy derived from a revisioning of gender roles. Its short history has produced a variety of new theological images, innovative organizational styles, and redefinitions of engendering the sacred. Adherents from both Eastern and Western traditions have joined in this movement to share in creating nonsexist perspectives on religion and spirituality and to draw upon long-repressed images of women as divine, as healers, as embodiments of the sacred, and as relational selves in dialogue and communion.

Feminist spirituality is particularly interesting to feminist researchers because of the authority it accords women to define themselves and their experience. In its quest to find personal and communal power as alternatives to hierarchical forms of leadership, feminist spirituality provides a startling contrast to patriarchal religions in gender role ascriptions, power relations, and religious imagery.[57] Within the Goddess movement, the Goddess is identified as the symbol for the legitimacy of female power as beneficent and independent.[58]

Within contemporary witchcraft, women are creating rituals, affirming female divinity, and constructing community.[59] Ritual creation is particularly important because it serves several functions, including group cohesion and the healing of social, psychological, and cultural marginalization.[60] Wicca has also been examined as a cultural movement with significant differences in meaning between its two branches—Dianic (women only) and Neopagan (women and men).[61] Among Dianic Wiccans the attempt to overcome social marginalization and the search for empowerment has led to social activism in the larger society.[62]

The literature on new religious movements describes associations of gendered relations and religious styles in many more contexts than can be reported here. In each context, feminist researchers examine organization forms and cognitive styles with new vision and insight, increasing, through their efforts, our appreciation of the complexity of religious experience.

Theoretical Contributions

"Feminist theory" has been a matter of debate. While some writers have questioned the labeling of a theory as feminist and have debated the criteria of feminist theory, others have denied even its existence. But, since 1988 when Janet Chafetz published her explanation of feminist theory, her perspective has been implicit in most feminist writings. She argues that a theory is feminist if it can be used to define, challenge, or revise a status quo that devalues or discriminates against women. In particular,

First, gender comprises a central focus or subject matter of the theory. Feminist theory seeks ultimately to understand the gendered nature of virtually all social relations, institutions, and processes. Second, gender relations are viewed as a problem. By this I mean that feminist theory seeks to understand how gender is related to social inequities, strains, and contradictions. Finally, gender relations are not viewed as either natural or immutable. Rather, the gender-related status quo is viewed as the product of sociocultural and historical forces which have been created, and are constantly re-created by humans, and therefore can potentially be changed by human agency.[63]

Feminist theorists interested in religious phenomena would, therefore, seek to document the gendered nature of religion as an institution, how all processes of religion are permeated by gender, and how religious definitions and legitimations are gendered.

In the past women have been the passive subjects of institutional processes and social change and, as such, have not been the definers of their reality. They have not appropriated their own history. Feminist theories are constructed to examine both historical and current themes of women's religious experience and consciousness, thereby outlining a dynamic, evolving whole that provides a context for understanding the actions of, as well as the treatment of, women.[64] In this project of discovery and interpretation, feminist theorists move women from the category of "other," which gains definition and agency in contrast with men, to the category of "self," which participates in its own becoming through control of definitions and the knowledge-producing process.

Feminist recognition of the need to locate socially both researcher and research subject involves the use of standpoint theory, originally described by Sandra Harding.[65] One uses standpoint theory when one reflexively analyzes one's own inquiry or another's experience by taking into account the dimensions of gender, race, and power. The use of standpoint theory demonstrates how these social variables inform all aspects of the research project, including the selection of research topics and the cognitive framework within which a research problem is interpreted. Using a feminist standpoint, researchers inquire into the subjective experience of groups often overlooked in traditional analysis, and, in the process, uncover a multiplicity of subjective truths.

Janet Jacobs's[66] analysis of scholarship on the Children of God illustrates how standpoint theory can be used to uncover implicit androcentric assumptions in past research. She points out that research published in the 1960s on this religious movement's use of sex by women members to recruit male members is examined only in regard to its usefulness to the organization, and that, throughout the research report, the detailed sexual exploitation of women is either trivialized or discounted as a serious area of inquiry. The implicit assumption contained in the standpoint of the male researcher is that control over female sexuality and the sexual objectification of women are normative. As Jacobs explains, a feminist analysis of this practice would assume a different standpoint, probably asking women members how they perceived and responded to the demands of exploitation and objectification.

This use of standpoint theory is an excellent example of how implicit biases and assumptions can be made explicit. Jacobs's analysis of research on the Children of God helped to shift the focus of research into new religious movements to female members and their experiences of the abuse of power. In her study of the International Society of Krishna Consciousness, Jacobs[67] used a feminist approach to interview women who were subjected to demands for soliciting funds and recruiting. She found that women had very strong reactions to their sexualized role in the movement. Her inquiry into the subjective reality of women validated the experience of the relatively less powerful and added a much-needed perspective to analyses of new religions.

Another theoretical contribution offered by feminist analysis is an expansion of traditional definitions of religion to include as sacred, experiences previously defined as secular. Feminist sensibilities about the sacred often focus on everyday activities, women's bodies, and human relationships as sources of religious inspiration and moral concern.[68] As the life cycle is imbued with spiritual significance, menarche, birthing, and menopause are defined as religious, both in their immanent manifestations and as instruments to transcendence.[69]

Feminist concern with power and dominance is also reflected in expanded conceptualizations of religion. Past research considers the empowerment functions of religion as latent and, in the case of political empowerment, as byproducts of religion, not its manifest goal.[70] The role of religious organizations in the empowerment of women is a different matter. Women use religion to create powerful local and national organizations to express their particular anxieties and demands.[71] Within institutionalized religions, empowerment is central to the meaning of religion for women who lack other sources of power.[72] Within new religions, sociologists now consider "empowerment" as a core element of religious experience, in spiritualist groups,[73] in healing groups,[74] in neo-Paganism,[75] and in new religions in general.[76] In addition, feminist research into power relations is redefining the attitudes of submission and surrender, conventionally accepted as "universal" religious ideals, as gendered and, therefore, not universal.[77]

Ruth Wallace[78] identifies four "missing theoretical issues" which feminist theories have begun to include. First is "tokenism," defined by Rosabeth Moss Kanter in her study of women in corporations.[79] Wallace reminds us that tokenism is a useful concept in examination of women in religious organizations. The second missing theoretical issue is "role expansion," Janet Chafetz's[80] term for social change that occurs when previously prohibited roles are opened to a social group. Wallace points to the growing number of women who experience role expansion in institutionalized as well as noninstitutionalized religion. The third theoretical issue is that of emotionality, a human universal only recently examined in depth by sociologists. Drawing on Arlie Hochschild's pathbreaking work in the sociology of emotions,[81] Wallace points to the particular suitability of a scientific examination of emotions in relation to religious experience. Fourth, Wallace mentions friendship as a missing theoretical issue discovered by feminist theorists. She cites Jessie Bernard's work on female-female relationships and the incalculable effect they have on the lives of women and the structure of the female world.[82] Friendships undoubtedly play significant roles in many religious experiences, such as conversion, devotion, and defection. Feminist attention to friendship could, according to Wallace, add considerable depth of understanding to our perspectives on religion.

As part of the larger interdisciplinary movement of women's studies that is challenging the dominant narrative of the Western world, feminist analysts are engaging in serious inquiry into the theoretical assumptions that legitimate the prevailing world view. Briefly, the dominant narrative assumes that a stable, coherent self is embodied in an individual who uses reason as the primary faculty of knowledge to discover a "truth" that lies outside the self and that can be discerned through "objective" research. Challenges to this narrative occur in natural science, the humanities, the fine arts, and the social sciences, and are extensive enough to constitute a crisis of legitimation.[83]

Several of these challenges are supported by feminist research, with broad implications for the sociology of religion. Feminist contributions to developmental psychology describe a self that, contrary to a stable, autonomous self, is connected to others in relationship, both during its formation and during later life.[84] Mary Jo Neitz offers a thoughtful discussion on how this model of self in relation to others has ramifications for the sociology of religion.[85] The model can be applied fruitfully to research on religious conversion, in that women, more often than men, are recruited through social networks.[86] Similarly, research on deconversion demonstrates that women's religious commitment involves more emotional than intellectual investment and is experienced in relationship.[87]

The assumption that reason is the primary human medium for knowledge is being challenged by a new appreciation of the body as a vital instrument of knowing and as a location of the sacred.[88] As Meredith McGuire points out, our acceptance of the Enlightenment legacy has served to embed us in an epistemological tradition in which things of the spirit are radically split from material things and in which mind is considered separate from body. A renewed appreciation of embodiedness in religious research would require that we explore the body's importance in self-experience, the body's role in the creation of social meanings, and the body's significance as the subject and object of power relations.

The assumptions of a knowable "truth" and the existence of a "reality" independent of subjective experience are other assumptions of the dominant narrative being challenged by feminist research. Feminist acceptance of standpoint theory and the social construction of reality, both discussed above, place feminist perspectives clearly within the ranks of challengers to the Western metanarrative.

Finally, feminist theorizing in the sociology of religion is ideally holistic and interdisciplinary. Thus, we ask, with Ruth Wallace, if there are feminist theorists who have "tried their hands at new syntheses."[89] She offers three for consideration: Janet Chafetz, Rae Lesser Blumberg, and Dorothy Smith. Janet Chafetz[90] combines Marx, exchange theory, cognitive dissonance, and reference group theory in her model of gender equality. Blumberg[91] draws on macro- and micro-sociological approaches in her feminist theory of development. Smith[92] includes the materialism of Marx and Engels and Garfinkel's ethnomethodology in her theoretical work. Wallace foresees a new theoretical synthesis emerging from these contributions which can enrich interdisciplinary dialogue.

Expanded Methods

As Shulamit Reinharz writes in her survey of feminist research methods, feminist thinking about methods involves "questions of *identity* (what are feminist research methods?) and of *difference* (what is the difference between feminist research methods and other research methods; how do feminist research methods differ from one another?)."[93] As we examine these questions, we find, with Reinharz, that, instead of a unitary research paradigm, feminist research practices constitute a plurality, including multiple themes and methods.

Reinharz's volume surveys feminist practices in research and the theoretical questions associated with choosing a method. She includes quantitative and qualitative designs, concentrating on the feminist expansion of qualitative methods as well as the creation of "original feminist methods." As each method is discussed, the reader acquires a progressively more inclusive understanding of feminist perspectives and how these perspectives, rather than particular methods, are the defining characteristics of feminist research. That is, quite traditional methods can be used in the service of a feminist perspective and feminist scholarship will be the result.

While some feminist researchers support the use of traditional quantitative methods, the larger portion of researchers emphasize the value of qualitative methods, such as ethnography, interviewing, cross-cultural analysis, oral history, case studies, and content analysis.[94] Feminist scholars mistrust the exclusive use of positivist, quantitative research methods, and call instead for a new perspective on problem conception and new methods for research. One reason for this call is the "containment of feminism" detailed by Judith Stacey and Barrie Thorne, in which quantitative studies tend to use gender as a variable, rather than as an analytic category.[95] The incorporation of gender as an analytic category in theories and research designs demands a critical reevaluation of statistical approaches and an inclusion of methods that tap the construal of meaning.

Two recent addresses to the Religious Research Association illustrate this renewed emphasis on the reflective and interpretive methods of research—the *verstehen* tradition of understanding. Wade Clark Roof's 1992 Presidential Address "Religion and Narrative" examines his discovery of story telling as a research method that affirms "who we are and what gives identity, purpose, and meaning to our existence."[96] In his view, story telling liberates us from the world of facticity and opens us to symbolic worlds of meaning. The creation of narrative brings order and significance to life events, forcing questions of interpretation. As part of the growing concern with interpretation and context, shaped in part by poststructuralist thinking and literary criticism, analysis framed from the stories of individuals reveals nuance and shades of subtlety that can contradict prevailing cultural analyses inferred from the study of institutions alone. Quoting Bellah, Madsen, Sullivan, Swidler, and Tipton[97] and Robert Wuthnow,[98] Roof demonstrates how research through narrative embodies real characters whose personal styles and beliefs cannot be understood through social correlates and broad cultural analysis. In Roof's words, "We do ourselves and religious study generally a disservice when we assume stereotypical unities that do not exist, and at the same time overlook phenomenological unities that do." Attention to narrative brings a richness and coherence to multilayered meaning systems by interweaving subjective motifs. At a larger social level, this greater appreciation of individuals' changing commitments integrates the study of religion with the study of culture and offers a more genuine comprehension of social change and religious pluralism.

The second address, "Telling Congregational Stories," by Nancy Ammerman reminds us that this is a time in the sociology of religion when "we need to hear many voices."[99] Her call to "listen from the margins" means that theories can be built from the bottom up, "by listening to the stories of those whose ideas never make it into libraries and whose practices simply get them through everyday life." Ammerman argues that the theory of secularization has become the core myth defining the sociological study of religion. She holds that the popularity and perseverance of the myth of secularization derive from analysis of institutions and the larger cultural sphere, not from examination of the religious behavior of the masses. As Ammerman listened from the margins to individuals from a wide range of Protestant congregations, she discovered that the theory of secularization could not account for the stories of individuals who derive practical shape and meaning in their lives through religious beliefs and associations. As with Roof's analysis, Ammerman's study demonstrates that, beneath the public, accepted cultural myth, lies a complex reality in which religious and activist stances, previously defined as contradictory by secularization theory, coexist quite harmoniously and efficiently within individuals.

As Roof and Ammerman note, qualitative methods often open questions of epistemology by pointing to the subject being studied as a source of knowledge. Since the pioneering work by Belenky et al. feminist researchers have been increasingly aware of alternative epistemologies in research subjects and of the value of designing methods to access these ways of knowing. The use of unstructured or semistructured qualitative methods are increasing in feminist research because they allow exploration of subjects' views of reality and allow the researcher to generate theory rather than to test hypotheses. By accessing subjects' ideas, thoughts, and experiences in their own words rather than in the words of the researcher, these qualitative methods serve as an antidote to centuries of ignoring women's ideas or having men speak for women.[100]

In each of the qualitative methods mentioned above, feminist researchers stress the value of establishing trust between the researcher and the subject. Since the researcher is dominant over the subject in the research process, hierarchical relations can bias subjects' responses. By establishing trust, the effect of hierarchy is recognized and ideally minimized so that the subject's experience can be accurately depicted.

As part of a growing sophistication in understanding epistemology, feminists use standpoint theory to question the possibility of a neutral and objective inquiry. Instead, they call for a reflexivity that examines the perspective of the researcher and names this perspective in the research report. In contrast to traditional goals of researcher indifference and total separation from research subjects, feminist goals include a "conscious partiality" that acknowledges the researcher's standpoint and values the relationship between researcher and subject.[101] This argument values the empathic understanding that accrues from some degree of identification with research subjects, a conscious participation in their experience of religion, and a mutuality between researcher and subject.

Several exemplary research projects embody these methods of feminist research. Elaine Lawless uses life stories, impressionistic observations, traditional narratives, and sermon themes to conduct phenomenological inquiry into the experience and mission of Pentecostal women preachers.[102] After reflection on her initial research, Lawless in a later work discusses the changes in her perspective and her consequent change in method. Her later work on women in the pastorate in mainline denominations, involves field work through what she calls "reciprocal ethnography," a method which produces work of "shared authorship, not of the actual words on the page and their representation to a potential reader, but in the development and consensus of our evolving discourse."[103] Lawless offers a thoughtful discussion of this new method, which she considers inherently feminist, humanistic, and reflexive in its emphasis on dialogue as a process in understanding and knowledge retrieval. She identifies the method as feminist because it "insists on a denial of hierarchical constructs that place the scholar at some apex of knowledge and understanding and her 'subjects' in some inferior, less knowledgeable position." Thus, no voice is privileged over another and dialogue is used as the key to understanding and illumination. Lawless goes on to acknowledge a political mission in her work—the goal of making the reader cognizant of blatant discrimination against women in religious institutions. In this method, Lawless is meeting the intention of her interviewees—women seeking to be whole, who advocate holistic ministries, theologies, and spiritualities—with a holistic method that includes "hearing (her subjects) into being."[104]

Other important research projects that offer insight into feminist methods as well as excellent analyses include works by Janet Jacobs, Lynn Davidman, Mary Jo Neitz, and Cheryl Gilkes.[105]

As part of the feminist value placed upon subjective experience, authors are increasingly relating their past experience and perceived standpoint as integral to research reports. If, they reason, the researcher's perspective is influenced by social location, why not inform the reader of this location and, in the process, gain self-understanding from the reflexivity that comes from pondering one's perspective. An early book in this genre relates the faith journeys of women scholars of religion as they reconstruct their lives in an attempt to bring meaning to their experiences.[106] In the ten years since publication of Meadow and Rayburn's volume, feminist researchers have integrated progressively more autobiographical accounts into their work. These accounts develop a relationship, however partial, between the reader and the researcher. This practice has a salutary effect on the authority of the discipline as well as the confidence of the reader.

Research as an Element of Social Action

An overarching goal of feminist research is reciprocal benefit of researcher and subject. As part of an activist stance, the tenet of reciprocal benefit specifies that feminist methods be used in advocacy for relatively less powerful subjects by providing them with access to the research process and its findings. In the religious context, research serves the interests of subjects by documenting the dominance, exploitation, and oppression of women within religious organizations. The "spectator" stance of traditional science is replaced by a participatory stance that involves the researcher in actions, movements, and struggles alongside subjects.[107] As ethical and political goals are combined with scientific considerations, activist research becomes a tool for uncovering the roots of injustice and the mechanisms by which injustice is perpetuated through theological justification, structural configurations, and omission of women's voices.[108] In feminist research, the scale of investigation often shifts from the macrosociological level of institutional analysis to the microsociological level of phenomenological inquiry in order to illustrate how oppressive structures are experienced subjectively. In its engagement with the struggles for recognition and emancipation of oppressed groups, feminist research creates a praxis and a new dialectic between knowing and doing.

Feminist research also participates in the development of "conscientization." First applied to the process of problem formulation by Paulo Freire, the method of conscientization specifies that the study of an oppressive reality is conducted by the objects of the oppression rather than disengaged, "objective" observers.[109] Oppressed peoples and classes, formerly defined as objects of research, become subjects who research and analyze their own positions with the assistance of professional social scientists and their research tools.

As feminist scholars accept the action oriented approach and method, we need to articulate more clearly how our research functions to strengthen the women's movement. In addition, we need to show how our particular research addresses women's issues in religion and how our different experiences, approaches, and commitments interrelate and reinforce each other. As we study the complex interplay of forces in individual human lives, what Karen McCarthy Brown calls the "passion and power issues,"[110] we must recognize our influence in and obligation to the initiation of social change.

Dialogue with Classical Sociology

Religion and its relationships to the other institutional structures of society was a major concern for sociological theorists in the early years of the discipline. Emile Durkheim (1858–1917), Karl Marx (1818–1883), George Simmel (1858–1918), and Max Weber (1864–1920) all focused on the relationship between religion and society and sought to explain religion as a social phenomenon, related to all other social phenomena.[111] The legacy of these "masters" has been a focus on religion as an institution that can be studied objectively through empirical methods, objective observation, and critical analysis. Feminists find this legacy limiting in both its institutional focus and its reliance on empirical method. Consequently, feminist scholars face the questions of whether and how to include the masters' contributions in their thinking. Both rejection and acceptance are found among feminist scholars.

Feminist dialogue with the male "masters" is only beginning. Victoria Erickson, a feminist steeped in understanding and appreciation of the contributions of classical sociologists, has explored their treatment of gender in classical theory as well as their personal associations with women in society.[112] Erickson's work values dialogue with the classical tradition, for the explanatory power it draws from traditional analysis and for the insight gained into our contemporary usage of classical concepts. For example, in her re-reading of Durkheim and Weber, she points to the way in which sacred-profane dualism in classical theory is associated with masculine-feminine dualism and thus serves as the basis for sexism in the sociology of religion.

Engagement with classical theory, traditional methods, and the legacy of the "masters" delineates the limitations of historical standpoints and the effects of androcentric assumptions upon the development of the discipline. Yet, dialogue with the classical tradition also brings power and inclusiveness to contemporary thinking, by extending the temporal and conceptual frames of analysis.[113] Feminist researchers have much to critique in the work of the "masters," and, at the same time, many valuable insights to integrate into our current models.

Women's Participation in the Sociology of Religion

Even a cursory examination of the architecture of the social sciences reveals that women have been excluded from its research and its establishment, as research subjects, as published researchers, and as contributors to theoretical perspectives. Academic journals that report social scientific investigations in religion are still dominated by male authors and the "objective science" perspective. Feminist perspectives on religion, while extant in a growing number of research reports and monographs, are rarely included in the designs of major denominational studies that are the most substantially funded of all research projects.

A review of major texts in the sociology of religion published in the last five years yields a pattern typical of the last twenty years—a chapter on women and religion and little mention of feminist theories apart from contributions to feminist spirituality. These texts mention women's exclusion from positions of power in religious institutions, new definitions of women's spirituality, and women's contributions to feminist theology, yet few note the dearth of feminist analysis in the social science establishment. As Rosemary Radford Ruether points out in this volume, this androcentric bias in all academic disciplines reflects the basic social situation in the production and control of knowledge in which men have had an almost total monopoly.

A review of major journals in the sociology of religion (*Journal for the Scientific Study of Religion, Sociological Analysis, and Review of Religious Research*) published in the last five years yields a general lack of women as senior authors, gender as a significant variable in research design, and feminist theory as central to analysis.

Although more women are participating as theorists and researchers in the subdiscipline, they serve primarily at a junior level. Because the recent influx of women in the field is largely of young women, publications in major journals report only a few more articles by women. Additionally, women often publish outside of these journals, finding that monographs and edited volumes provide greater access for their perspectives and methods.

Leadership in professional organizations reflects a much greater participation by women than a review of major journals would suggest. All of the professional organizations that discuss the sociology of religion—Association for the Sociology of Religion, Society for the Scientific Study of Religion, and Religious Research Association and a recently created section of the American Sociological Association—have historically elected women to their major offices, councils, and editorial staffs. In her discussion of women in the American Catholic Sociological Society (renamed the Association for the Sociology of Religion in 1970), Ruth Wallace argues that this organization surpasses the American Sociological Association in rates of women's leadership.[114] Using election to the position of president as the measure of leadership, Wallace shows that, as of 1988, ACSS/ASR has had seven women presidents out of fifty-one (14 percent), whereas ASA has had only four women presidents out of seventy-nine (5 percent). Of the first five women presidents of the ACSS/ASR, four were members of religious communities, whereas only fifteen of the forty-five men presidents were priests or brothers. This comparison demonstrates the value of religious communities in soliciting women for and training women in the sociology of religion. As religious communities needed staffing for their women's colleges, members enrolled in graduate programs of sociology, increasing the numbers of sociologists and expanding the numbers of women professors and researchers, particularly in the sociology of religion.

Throughout the history of each organization devoted to the sociology of religion, women have played significant roles in all levels of leadership and have been integral to all activities. In addition, women's caucuses are influential, young women scholars discuss their work in a variety of forums, and the themes of annual meetings address women's issues.

Conclusion

The perspectives and methods of feminist research are progressively used to expand and enrich sociological understanding of religion. As part of the larger transformative discipline of women's studies, feminist researchers in the sociology of religion delineate the oppressive effects of universalistic assumptions that are similar in biology, politics, ecology, and social science, determining the nature of inquiry as well as the participants in research projects. Feminist analysis offers new tools with which to examine past and present

biases in scientific inquiry and to open scientific analysis to reflexive examination. In the process, women's narratives and feminist analyses enable dialogues
that are shared with the larger community and which become instruments for
positive social action.

Notes

I am most grateful to Nancy Ammerman, Lynn Davidman, Victoria Erickson,
    Janet Jacobs, Adair Lummis; Mary Jo Neitz, Roland Robertson, Tom
    Robbins, Bill Swatos, and Ruth Wallace for their suggestions and
    opinions on this essay.

    1. Thomas Robbins and Roland Robertson, "Studying Religion Today:
Controversiality and 'Objectivity' in the Sociology of Religion," *Religion* 21
(1991): 319–337.

    2. Sandra Harding and Merrill B. Hintikka, eds., *Discovering Reality:
Feminist Perspectives on Epistemology, Metaphysics, Methodology, and Philosophy of Science* (Boston: D. Reidel, 1983); Sandra Harding, ed., "Introduction: Is There a Feminist Method?" in *Feminism and Methodology*, ed. Sandra
Harding (Blomington: University of Indiana Press, 1987).

    3. Charlotte Bunch, *Passionate Politics: Essays 1968–1986—Feminist
Theory and Action* (New York: St. Martin's, 1987).

    4. Mary Jo Neitz, "Feminist Theory and Religious Experience," in
Handbook of Religious Experience: Theory and Practice, ed. Ralph W. Hood
Jr. (Birmingham, Ala.: Religious Education Press, 1994).

    5. Judith A. Cook and Mary Margaret Fonow, "Knowledge and
Women's Interests: Issues of Epistemology and Methodology in Feminist
Sociological Research," in *Feminist Research Methods: Exemplary Readings in
the Social Sciences,* ed. Joyce M. Nielsen (Boulder: Westview Press7 1990).

    6. Angela Y. Davis, *Women, Race, and Class* (New York: Random
House, 1981); Barbara Smith, "Toward a Black Feminist Criticism," in *But
Some of Us Are Brave: Black Women's Studies* (Old Westbury, N.Y.: Feminist
Press, 1982); Bonnie T. Dill, "Class, Race, and Gender: Prospects for an All
Inclusive Sisterhood," *Feminist Studies* 9 (1983): 131–150; Deborah K. King,
"Multiple Jeopardy, Multiple Consciousness: The Context of Black Feminist
Ideology," *Signs* 1 (1988): 809–824; Patricia H. Collins, "The Social Construc-
tion of Black Feminist Thought," *Signs* 14, no.4 (1989): 745–773 and *Black
Feminist Thought* (New York: Routledge, 1991); Rose M. Brewer, "Black
Women and Feminist Sociology: The Emerging Perspective," *The American
Sociologist* 20, no. 1 (Spring 1989): 57–70.

    7. Cheryl T. Gilkes, "Roundtable Discussion: On Feminist Method-
ology," *Journal of Feminist Studies in Religion* 1, no.2 (Fall 1985): 73–88 and
"'Together in Harness': Women's Traditions in the Sanctified Church," *Signs*

10 (Summer 1985): 678–699; Delores Williams, "Women's Oppression and Lifeline Politics in Black Women's Religious Narratives," *Journal of Feminist Studies in Religion* 1, no 2: 59–72.

8. Judith Lorber and Susan A. Farrell, eds., *The Social Construction of Gender* (Newbury Park, Cal.: Sage, 1991).

9. Nancy Ammerman, "Telling Congregational Stories," *Review of Religious Research* 35, no.4 (June 1994): 289–301; Ruth A. Wallace, *Feminism and Sociological Theory* (Newbury Park, Cal.: Sage, 1989) and "Feminism: Expanding the Horizons of the Sociology of Religion," in *Religion and the Social Order*, vol. 1, ed. David G. Bromley (Greenwich, Conn.: JAI Press, 1991).

10. Anthony J. Blasi, *A Phenomenological Transformation of the Social Scientific Study of Religion* (New York: Peter Lang, 1985).

11 "Sociology and Feminist Scholarship," *The American Sociologist* 20, no. l (Spring 1989): 3–13.

12. Joan Kelly-Gadol, "The Social Relations of the Sexes: Methodological Implications for Women's History," *Signs* 1 (1976): 809–824; Gayle Rubin, "The Traffic in Women," in *Toward an Anthropology of Women*, ed. Rayna R. Reiter (New York: Monthly Review Press, 1975).

13. Judith Stacey and Barrie Thorne, "The Missing Feminist Revolution in Sociology," *Social Problems* 32 (1985): 301–316.

14. Janet L. Jacobs, "Gender and Power in New Religious Movements: A Feminist Discourse on the Scientific Study of Religion," *Religion* 21 (1991): 345–356.

15. Mary Jo Neitz, "Inequality and Difference: Feminist Research in the Sociology of Religion," in *A Future for Religion? New Paradigms for Social Analysis*, ed. William H. Swatos Jr. (Newbury Park, Cal.: Sage, 1993).

16. "Feminist Theory and Religious Experience."

17. Jackson Carroll, Barbara Hargrove, and Adair Lummus, *Women of the Cloth* (San Francisco: Harper and Row, 1983) .

18. Edward C. Lehman Jr., *Women Clergy: Breaking through Gender Barriers* (New Brunswick, N.J.: Transaction, 1985).

19. Edward C. Lehman Jr., *Gender and Work: The Case of the Clergy* (Albany: State University of New York Press, 1993) and "Gender and Ministry Style: Things not What They Seem," *Sociology of Religion* 51, no. l (Spring 1993): 1–11.

20. Martha Long Ice, *Clergywomen and Their Worldviews: Calling for a New Age* (New York: Praeger, 1987).

21. Charles A. Barfoot and Gerald T. Sheppard, "Prophetic vs. Priestly Religion: The Changing Role of Women Clergy in Classical Pentecostal Churches," *Review of Religious Research* 22, no. l (1980): 2–17.

22. Margaret Poloma, *Assemblies of God at the Crossroads* (Knoxville: University of Tennessee Press, 1989).

23. Elaine J. Lawless, *Handmaidens of the Lord: Pentecostal Women Preachers and Traditional Religion* (Philadelphia: University of Pennsylvania Press, 1988); S. Kwilecki, "Contemporary Pentecostal Clergywomen," *Journal of Feminist Studies in Religion* 3 (1987): 57–75.

24. Elaine J. Lawless, *Holy Women, Wholly Women: Sharing Ministries through Life Stories and Reciprocal Ethnography* (Philadelphia: University of Pennsylvania Press, 1993).

25. Lawless, *Handmaidens of the Lord.*

26. Lawless, *Holy Women, Wholly Women.*

27. Zillah R. Eisenstein, "The Sexual Politics of the New Right: Understanding the 'Crisis of Liberalism' for the 1980's," *Signs* 7, no.3 (1982): 567–588; C. V. Pohli, "Church Closets and Back Doors," *Feminist Studies* 9 (1983): 529–558; Margaret L. Bendroth, *Fundamentalism and Gender: 1875 to the Present* (New Haven: Yale University Press, 1994).

28. Angela A. Aidala, "Social Change, Gender Roles, and New Religious Movements," *Sociological Analysis* 46 (1985): 287–314; Mary W. Harder, James T. Richardson, and Robert B. Simmons, "Life Style, Courtship, Marriage, and Family in a Changing Jesus Movement Organization," *International Review of Modern Sociology* 6 (1976): 155–177.

29. Judith Stacey, *Brave New Families* (New York: Basic Books, 1990).

30. Nancy Ammerman, *Bible Believers* (New Brunswick: Rutgers University Press, 1987); Kristen Luker, *Abortion and the Politics of Motherhood* (Berkeley: University of California Press, 1984); Patrick H. McNamara, "The New Christian Right's View of the Family and Its Social Science Critics," *Journal of Marriage and the Family* 47 (1985): 449–458; Mary Jo Neitz, "Family, State, and God: Ideologies of the Right-to-Life Movement," *Sociological Analysis* 42 (Fall 1981): 265–276; Susan D. Rose, "Women Warriors: The Negotiation of Gender in a Charismatic Community," *Sociological Analysis* 48, no.3 (1987): 245–258; Stacey, *Brave New Families.*

31. Cheryl T. Gilkes, "Together in Harness" and "The Roles of Church and Community Mothers," *Journal of Feminist Studies in Religion* 2 (1986): 41–60, Jualyne E. Dodson and Cheryl T. Gilkes, "Something Within: Social Change and Collective Endurance in the Sacred World of Black Christian Women," in *Women and Religion in America,* vol. 3. ed. Rosemary Ruether and Rosemary S. Keller (San Francisco: Harper and Row, 1986).

32. Ruth A. Wallace, "Catholic Women and the Creation of a New Reality," *Gender and Society* 2 (1988): 24–38, *They Call Her Pastor* (Albany: State University of New York Press 1992), and "The Social Construction of a New Leadership Role: Catholic Women Pastors," *Sociology of Religion* 54, no. 1 (Spring 1993): 31–42; D. Trebbi, "Women-Church," in *In Gods We Trust:*

New Patterns of Religious Pluralism in America, 2nd ed., ed Thomas Robbins and Dick Anthony (New Brunswick, N.J.: Transaction, 1990).

33. Wallace, *They Call Her Pastor.*

34. Patricia Wittberg, "The Dual Labor Market in the Catholic Church: Expanding a Speculative Inquiry," *Review of Religious Research* 30, no.3 (March 1989): 287–294.

35. J. Patrick Browne and Timothy J. Lukes, "Women Called Catholics," *Journal for the Scientific Study of Religion* 27, no.2 (June 1988): 284–290.

36. Ted G. Jelen, "Changes in the Attitudinal Correlations of Opposition to Abortion, 1977–1985," *Journal for the Scientific Study of Religion* 27, no.2 (June 1988): 211–228.

37. Maly Jo Neitz, *Charisma and Community: A Study of Religious Commitment within the Catholic Charismatic Renewal* (New Brunswick, N.J.: Transaction, 1987).

38. Rose, *Women Warriors.*

39. Nancy Nason-Clark, "Ordaining Women as Priests: Religious vs. Sexist Explanations for Clerical Attitudes," *Sociological Analysis* 48, no.3 (1987): 259–273 and "Are Women Changing the Image of the Ministry?" *Review of Religious Research* 28 (1987): 330–340.

40. Edward C. Lehman Jr., *Women Clergy in England: Modern Consciousness, and Church Viability* (Lewiston, N.Y.: Edwin Mellen Press, 1987).

41. Debra R. Kaufman, "Women Who Return to Orthodox Judaism," *Journal of Marriage and the Family* 47 (1985): 543–555 and *Rachel's Daughters: Newly Orthodox Jewish Women* (New Brunswick: Rutgers University Press, 1991).

42. Lynn Davidmann, "Accommodation and Resistance to Modernity: A Comparison of Two Contemporary Orthodox Jewish Groups," *Sociological Analysis* 51, no.1 (Spring 1990) 35–51; "Women's Search for Family and Roots: A Jewish Religious Solution to a Modern Dilemma," in *In Gods We Trust: New Patterns of Religious Pluralism in America,* 2nd ed., ed. Thomas Robbins and Dick Anthony (New Brunswick, N.J.: Transaction, 1990); and *Tradition in a Rootless World: Women Turn to Orthodox Judaism* (Berkeley: University of California Press, 1991).

43. Lynn Davidman and Shelly Tenebaum, eds., *Feminist Perspectives on Jewish Studies* (New Haven: Yale University Press, 1994).

44. William H. Swatos Jr., ed., *Gender and Religion* (New Brunswick, N.J.: Transaction, 1994).

45. Lynn Davidman and Arthur L. Greil, "Gender and the Experience of Conversion: The Case of 'Returnees' to Modern Orthodox Judaism," *Sociology of Religion* 54, no.1 (Spring 1993): 83–100.

46. Wallace, *They Call Her Pastor.*

47. Janet L. Jacobs, "The Effects of Ritual Healing on Female Victims of Abuse: A Study of Empowerment and Transformation," *Sociological Analysis* 50 (1989): 265–279.

48. Lynn Davidman and Janet Jacobs, "Feminist Perspectives on New Religious Movements," in *A Handbook of Sects and Cults in America*, ed. David G. Bromley and Jeffrey K. Hadden (Greenwich, Conn.: JAI Press, 1992).

49. Janet L. Jacobs, *Divine Disenchantment* (Bloomington: Indiana University Press, 1991) and "Gender and Power in New Religious Movements", Rosemary R. Ruether, *Woman-Church* (New York: Harper and Row, 1985); Mary Daly, "Why Speak about God?" in *Womanspirit Rising: A Feminist Reader in Religion*, ed. Carol Christ and Judith Laskow (New York: Harper and Row, 1979).

50. Constance A. Jones, "Exemplary Dualism and Authoritarianism at Jonestown," in *New Religious Movements, Mass Suicide, and Peoples Temple: Scholarly Perspectives on a Tragedy*, ed. Rebecca Moore and Fielding McGehee (Lewiston, N.Y.: Edwin Mellen Press, 1989).

51. Catherine Wessinger, "The Legitimation of Feminine Religious Authority: The Siddha Yoga Case." Paper presented at the Society for Scientific Study of Religion, Virginia Beach. Va., 1990 and (ed.) *Women's Leadership in Marginal Religions: Explorations Outside the Mainstream* (Urbana: University of Illinois Press, 1993); Constance A. Jones, "Church Universal and Triumphant: A Demographic Profile," in *Church Universal and Triumphant in Scholarly Perspective*, ed. James R. Lewis and J. Gordon Melton (Stanford: Center for Academic Publication, 1994).

52. Jacobs, "The Effects of Ritual Healing."

53. Ibid., Constance A. Jones, "Revolutionary Sex at Jonestown " Paper presented at the Society for Scientific Study of Religion, Virginia Beach, Va., 1990 and "A Cross-Cultural Issue Concerning Women and Religion: The Case of Eastern Religious Teachers and American Devotees." Paper presented at the Southeastern Psychological Association annual meeting, New Orleans, 1991.

54. Susan J. Palmer and Arvind Sharma, eds., *The Rajneesh Papers: Studies in a New Religious Movement* (Delhi: Motilal Banarsidass Publishers).

55. Carol Lois Haywood, "The Authority and Empowerment of Women among Spiritualist Groups," *Journal for the Scientific Study of Religion* 21 (1983): 26–36; Hans A. Baer, "The Limited Empowerment of Women in Black Spiritual Churches: An Alternative Vehicle to Religious Leadership," *Sociology of Religion* 54, no.1 (Spring 1993): 65–82.

56. Karen M. Brown, *Mama Lola: A Vodou Priestess in Brooklyn* (Berkeley: University of California Press, 1991).

57. Emily Culpepper, "The Spiritual Movement of Radical Feminist Consciousness," in *Understanding the New Religions*, ed. George Baker and

Jacob Needleman (New York: Society Press, 1978); Jacobs, "The Effects of Ritual Healing"; Mary Jo Neitz, "In Goddess We Trust," in *In Gods We Trust: New Patterns of Religious Pluralism in America*, 2nd ed., ed Thomas Robbins and Dick Anthony (New Brunswick, N.J.: Transaction, 1990) and "Quasi-Religions and Cultural Movements: Contemporary Witchcraft as a Churchless Religion," in *Religion and the Social Order*, vol. 4 (Greenwich, Conn.: JAI Press).

58. Carol Christ, "Why Women Need the Goddess: Phenomenological, Psychological, and Spiritual Reflections," in *The Politics of Women's Spirituality*, ed. Charlene Spretnak (Garden City, N.Y.: Anchor, 1982).

59. Neitz, "In Goddess We Trust."

60. Jacobs, "The Effects of Ritual Healing" and "Women-Centered Healing Rites: A Study of Alienation and Reintegration," in *In Gods We Trust: New Patterns of Religious Pluralism in America*, 2nd ed., ed. Thomas Robbins and Dick Anthony (New Brunswick, N.J.: Transaction, 1990).

61. Neitz, "Quasi-Religions and Cultural Movements."

62. Nancy Finley, "Political Activism and Feminist Spirituality," *Sociological Analysis* 52 no.3 (1991): 349–362.

63. Janet S. Chafetz, *Feminist Sociology: An Overview of Contemporary Theories* (Itasca, Ill.: F. E. Peacock, 1988).

64. Yvonne Y. Haddad and Ellison B. Findly, *Women, Religion, and Social Change* (Albany: State University of New York Press, 1985).

65. Harding, "Introduction: Is There a Feminist Method?"

66. Jacobs, "Gender and Power."

67. Jacobs, "The Effects of Ritual Healing."

68. Sheila Collins, "Theology in Politics of Appalachian Women," in *Womanspirit Rising: A Feminist Reader in Religion*, ed. Carol Christ and Judith Plaskow (San Francisco: Harper and Row, 1979); Rosemary R. Ruether, *Sexism and God-Talk: Toward a Feminist Theology* (Boston: Beacon Press, 1983) .

69. Neitz, "Feminist Theory."

70. Steven Warner, "Toward a New Paradigm for the Sociology of Religion in American Society," *American Journal of Sociology* 98 (1993): 1044–1093.

71. Ibid.

72. Meredith McGuire, *Pentecostal Catholics: Power, Charisma, and Order in a Religious Movement* (Philadelphia: Temple University Press, 1982) and "Discovering Religious Power," *Sociological Analysis* 44 (1983): 1–10; Gilkes, "'Together in Harness'" and "The Roles of Church and Community Mothers"; Williams, "Women's Oppression"; Ruether, *Woman-Church*; Neitz, *Charisma and Community* and "In Goddess We Trust"; Lawless, *Handmaidens of the Lord*; Davidman, *Tradition in a Rootless World*; Judith Stacey and Susan

E. Gerard, "'We Are not Doormats': The Influence of Feminism on Contemporary Evangelicals in the United States," in *Uncertain Terms*, ed. Faye Ginsburg (Boston: Beacon Press, 1991).

73. Haywood, "The Authority and Empowerment of Women."

74. McGuire, "Discovering Religious Power."

75. Starhawk, *Dreaming the Dark* (Boston: Beacon Press, 1982).

76. James A. Beckford, "The Restoration of Power to the Sociology of Religion," *Sociological Analysis* 44 (1983): 11–32; Thomas Robbins, "The Transformative Impact of the Study of New Religions on the Sociology of Religion," *Journal for the Scientific Study of Religion* 27, no.1 (1988): 12–31.

77. Neitz, "Feminist Theory."

78. Wallace,"Feminism."

79. Rosabeth M. Kanter, *Men and Women of the Corporation* (New York: Basic Books, 1977).

80. Janet S. Chafetz, "Gender Equality: Toward a Theory of Change," in *Feminism and Sociological Theory*, ed. Ruth A. Wallace (Newbury Park, Cal.: Sage, 1989).

81. Arlie Hochschild, *The Managed Heart: Commercialization of Human Feeling* (Berkeley: University of California Press, 1983).

82. Jessie S. Bernard, *The Female World* (New York: Free Press, 1981).

83. Jane Flax, *Thinking Fragments: Psychoanalysis, Feminism, and Postmodernism in the Contemporary West* (Berkeley: University of California Press, 1990), Susan S. Hekman, *Hermeneutics and the Sociology of Knowledge* (Notre Dame: University of Notre Dame Press, 1986).

84. Nancy J. Chodorow, *Reproduction of Mothering* (Los Angeles: University of California Press, 1978); Carol Gilligan, *In a Different Voice* (Cambridge, Mass.: Harvard University Press, 1982); Mary F. Belenky et al., *Women's Ways of Knowing: The Development of Self, Voice, and Mind* (New York: Basic Books, 1986).

85. Neitz, "Inequality and Difference."

86. E. Burke Rochford, *Hare Krishna in America* (New Brunswick: Rutgers University Press, 1985).

87. Janet L. Jacobs, "The Economy of Love in Religious Commitment," *Journal for the Scientific Study of Religion* 23 (1984): 155–171.

88. Meredith McGuire, "Religion and the Body," *Journal for the Scientific Study of Religion* 29 (1990): 283–296; Susan S. Sered, "Rachel's Tomb and the Milk Grotto of the Virgin Mary," *Journal of Feminist Studies in Religion* 2 (1986): 6–22 and "Religious Rituals and Secular Rituals: Interpenetrating Models of Childbirth an a Modern, Israeli Context," *Sociology of Religion* 54, no.1 (Spring 1993): 101–114.

89. Wallace,"Feminism."

90. Chafetz, "Gender Equality."

91. Rae L. Blumberg, "From the African Food Crisis to the Israeli Kibbutz: Toward a Feminist Theory of Development," in *Feminism and Sociological Theory*, ed. Ruth A. Wallace (Newbury Park, Cal.: Sage, 1989).

92. Dorothy E. Smith, "A Sociology for Women," in *The Prism of Sex: Essays in the Sociology of Knowledge*, ed. Julia A. Sherman and Evelyn Torten Beck (Madison: University of Wisconsin Press, 1979) and "Sociological Theory: Methods of Writing Patriarchy," in *Feminism and Sociological Theory*, ed. Ruth A. Wallace (Newbury Park, Cal.: Sage, 1989).

93. Shulamit Reinharz, *Feminist Methods in Social Research* (New York: Oxford University Press, 1992), 3–5.

94. Ibid.

95. Stacey and Thorne, "The Missing Feminist Revolution."

96. Wade Clark Roof, "Religion and Narrative," *Review of Religious Research* 34, no.4 (June 1993): 297–310.

97. Robert N. Bellah et al., *Habits of the Heart* (Berkeley: University of California Press, 1985).

98. Robert Wuthnow, *Acts of Compassion: Caring for Others and Helping Ourselves* (Princeton: Princeton University Press, 1991).

99. Ammerman, "Telling Congregational Stories."

100. Reinharz, *Feminist Methods*

101. Maria Mies, "Towards a Methodology for Feminist Research," in *Theories of Women's Studies*, ed. G. Bowles and R. Klein (Boston: Routledge and Kegan Paul, 1993), 38; Donna Haraway, "Situated Knowledges: The Science Question on Feminism and the Privilege of Partial Perspective," *Feminist Studies* 14 (1988): 575–599.

102. Lawless, *Handmaidens of the Lord*.

103. Lawless, *Holy Women, Wholly Women*, 4.

104. Ibid., 5.

105. Jacobs, "Women-Centered Healing Rites"; Davidman, *Tradition in a Rootless World*; Neitz, "Inequality and Difference"; Gilkes, "Roundtable Discussion."

106. Mary Jo Meadow and Carole A Rayburn, eds., *A Time to Weep, a Time to Sing: Faith Journeys of Women Scholars of Religion* (Minneapolis: Winston Press, 1985).

107. Maria Mies and Vandana Shiva, *Ecofeminism* (Halifax, N.S.: Fernwood, 1993).

108. Elisabeth Schüssler Fiorenza, "Roundtable Discussion: On Feminist Methodology," *Journal of Feminist Studies in Religion* 1, no.2 (Fall 1985): 73–88.

109. Paulo Freire, *Pedagogy of the Oppressed*, trans. M. Ramos (New York: Continuum, 1981).

110. Karen M. Brown, "Roundtable Discussion: On Feminist Methodology," *Journal of Feminist Studies in Religion* 1, no.2 (Fall 1985): 73–88.

111. Durkheim, in a variety of works addressing religion, was interested in the integrative and normative functions of religion, which he saw as essential to social cohesion. In his studies of suicide and the elementary forms of religion, Durkheim wrote that religion is one of the main mechanisms that bind individuals to the larger social whole and that social integration will suffer as religion loses sway under conditions of modernization.

Similarly, Marx saw religion as important to social integration, although in a more diabolical way than Durkheim, alienating and even anesthetizing in its influence. Marx, in his rejection of normative, conflict-free social integration as ideal, identified religion as a major agent in the exploitation of the nonpropertied class, the dehumanization of social relationships, and the alienation of the individual from self and others.

More akin to Durkheim, Simmel focused on religion as an integrating and stabilizing force in social life. In his study of "forms," Simmel saw in various levels of social organization and social interaction feelings and relationships that can be characterized as religious. Religion, thus, provides templates for a variety of human relationships both within and outside the religious institutional structure.

Weber, writing from an interactionist perspective and in debate with Marx, was concerned with the internalization of religious perspectives and the operation of ideas, which he saw as crucial to the development of social institutions. Specifically, he saw the Protestant Ethic as conducive to the development of modern capitalism in the West. Weber also offered an analysis of increasing rationalization and bureaucratization in modern society, with a forecast for a declining influence of religion.

Each was concerned with the role of religious beliefs and structures in the larger society; each wrote about the role of these factors in the transition from traditional societies to urbanized and industrialized societies; and each documented the waning influence of religion as societies modernize. As the masters grappled with the problems of social integration, modernization, and authority, each included religion in his equation of influence. Each wrote about the diminishing influence of religion in modern life as other institutions (economics, government, education) develop increasing influence.

112. Victoria L. Erickson, *Speaking in the Dark and Hearing the Voices* (Philadelphia: Fortress Press, 1992) and *Where Silence Speaks: Feminism, Social Theory, and Religion* (Minneapolis: Fortress Press, 1993).

113. Sondra Farganis, "Social Theory and Feminist Theory: The Need for Dialogue," *Sociological Inquiry* 56 (1986): 50–68; Lorber and Farrell, *The Social Construction of Gender;* Erickson, *Where Silence Speaks.*

114. Ruth A. Wallace, "Bringing Women in: The ACSS/ASR Story," *Sociological Analysis* 50, no.4 (1989): 409–413.

5

The Impact of Women's Studies on the Psychology of Religion

Feminist Critique, Gender Analysis, and the Inclusion of Women

DIANE JONTE-PACE

Psychological Studies of Religion

In recent decades two major enterprises have characterized the psychological study of religion.[1] One enterprise, widely known as "the psychology *of* religion" seeks to uncover the origins and trace the effects of religious ideas and practices through the application of the theoretical and methodological perspectives of psychology to the phenomena of religion. Another enterprise, which might be called the "psychology *and* religion movement" emphasizes the historical and cultural connections between psychology and religion. This second enterprise incorporates biographical and cultural studies, often focusing on religious traditions in the lives of formative psychologists. In addition, it incorporates studies of modernization in contemporary culture, analyzing the complex relation of psychology to religion and to secularization, and depicting the rise of psychological ideas as a response to the cultural loss of religious meanings.[2]

In this chapter I'll examine endeavors in both the "psychology *of* religion" proper and the "psychology *and* religion movement," describing the impact of scholarship in Women's Studies on each. I'll focus on four psychological methodologies often utilized in the study of religion: Freudian theory, Jungian theory, object relations theory/self psychology, and poststructuralist psychoanalytic theory. These methodologies do not, of course, exhaust the field: psychological approaches to religion incorporate humanistic theories, experimental theories, behavioral and comparative theories, theories originating within pastoral care and counseling, "dialogic" approaches that seek correlations between theology and psychology, and other approaches as well.[3] But the four methodologies I'll discuss are, in my view, the most significant and influential within the discipline. In addition, these are the areas that have provided the most fertile soil for developments in Women's Studies. Throughout this chapter I will discuss representative and paradigmatic literature to illustrate approaches developed by Women's Studies that have been applied to and within the psychological study of religion. This project is thus consciously and necessarily selective: it will not attempt a comprehensive discussion of the literature in the field.

The Three Tasks of Women's Studies: Critical, Inclusive, and Analytic Projects

Although Women's Studies is a relatively new field, originating in the 1960s, it has already had a significant impact on the academy. In the decades since its inception, new inquiries into women's lives, thoughts, and writings have begun to enrich scholarship in many fields, and new methods and theories formulated within Women's Studies have dramatically challenged foundational assumptions in many disciplines. The psychological study of religion has escaped neither this enrichment nor this challenge: methodological innovations and new interpretive paradigms developed within Women's Studies have been applied to the psychological study of religion. Feminist and Women's Studies methods and approaches[4] in turn have been appropriated by theorists in the psychological study of religion, often leading to innovative perspectives in pedagogy and in research.

The field of Women's Studies "works to bring about an academy that includes what women know," as feminist theorist Jane Gallop notes.[5] In this endeavor Women's Studies has initiated what I'll describe as three tasks or projects: a critical project, an inclusive project, and an analytic project.[6] The critical project maintains a hermeneutic of suspicion toward traditional scholarship, exposing androcentrism in scholarship. Androcentric biases, as historian Ellen Du Bois points out, "might be embedded in assumptions about what subjects are worthy of study, in methods of data collection, or in the conceptualization of questions guiding research."[7] Scholars working within this critical project of Women's Studies have disclosed subtle assumptions about maleness as normative, and about female inferiority in mainstream scholarship; they have also pointed out the absence of women as theorists and as subjects of research. To use the terminology of feminist theorist Peggy McIntosh,[8] the critical project of Women's Studies has uncovered the "womanlessness" of the disciplines. The exposure of a stark androcentrism in virtually all academic disciplines represented a dramatic starting point for Women's Studies more than three decades ago, and continues to be a concern in contemporary feminist scholarship.

The second project initiated by scholars in Women's Studies is the inclusive task of incorporating women into the various academic disciplines. This has involved an attempt to seek out exemplary women overlooked during generations of androcentric scholarship; it has resulted in the addition of women to university curricula, to research agendas, and to publishing lists. This inclusive perspective has inquired into women's "active agency," investigating roles of women and arenas in which women have power, knowledge, and authority.

A third project initiated within Women's Studies has taken a more analytic stance, challenging the methodologies and epistemologies in various disciplines, and investigating how gender shapes both our "ways of knowing"[9] and our disciplinary categories themselves. Scholars working in this area have also investigated why scholarship has remained "womanless" so long, why women have so often been victims of oppressive social structures, and how woman is constructed as "Other" within patriarchal systems.

Emerging from the analytic project is the field of "gender studies," which arose in feminist theory as a way of examining the "fundamentally social quality of distinctions based on sex."[10] Historically rooted in Women's Studies but now to some degree distinct from it, "gender studies" begins with the assumption that it is not primarily the biological differences between men and women that shape our psyches and our bodies. It examines instead the largely unconscious social and cultural constructions of femininity, masculinity, sexuality, and sexual orientation. It inquires into how society constructs maleness and femaleness as different, and how, as theologian Rebecca Chopp puts it, "different categories and structures are marked and constituted through a patriarchal ordering of gender division."[11] The field of gender studies has been a locus of collaboration for feminist scholars, poststructuralist scholars, cultural theorists, gay studies scholars, and ethnic studies scholars. Some inquiries in gender studies have explored ways that gender shapes individual lives, cultures, and ideas; other investigations have attempted to uncover the hegemonic assumptions constructing the gendered hierarchies underlying sexism, racism, and homophobia.

Women's Studies in the Context of Religious Studies

Feminist thealogian Carol Christ has issued a pessimistic assessment of the current status of Women's Studies methodologies within Religious Studies. She cautions that "a great deal of work remains to be done if feminist scholarship is to transform the teaching and study of religion. The challenges posed to the field of Religious Studies are profound and substantive." She notes that "the majority of those who hold power in the field have not changed their world views . . . and they are not likely to do so." Feminists in Religious Studies, she warns, will be "sojourners for a long time to come."[12]

I agree with Carol Christ that the resistance to feminist scholarship in Religious Studies is widespread. The three projects of Women's Studies are a bit like the impossible project of Sisyphus: in spite of the finest efforts of the best scholars, the tasks are constantly in need of repetition. Scholars in Religious Studies are faced with the necessity to demonstrate again and again that traditional scholarship has been androcentric; that women's agency can (and must) be promoted; that the sources of misogyny must be analyzed; that gender is culturally constructed; and that gender shapes both psyche and culture. As the old adage has it, women's work is never done!

And yet, despite widespread mainstream resistance to the methods and projects developed in Women's Studies, feminist work has flourished in some areas of Religious Studies. Within certain scholarly (although perhaps somewhat marginal) territories, a productive and compelling discourse has been generated as new methods for the study of religion have emerged. In my view, the psychological study of religion is one of these territories within which, for a number of reasons, feminist scholarship has flourished.

Women's Studies and the Psychological Study of Religion

The psychological study of religion is somewhat anomalous as an approach within Religious Studies. It is a fairly new field: it originated less than a century ago. It is an interdisciplinary field: it crosses the boundaries of religion and psychology and lacks the kind of unity and systematic focus found in other areas of Religious Studies. Its professional location is ambiguous: publications are more likely to originate from, and to assume an audience of, scholars trained in Religious Studies rather than in psychology, yet much of the discourse relies upon the work of formative psychologists. In addition, the field is often viewed with suspicion by those in more traditional areas of theology and Religious Studies as well as by those in other areas of the academy.[13] For these reasons the psychological study of religion cannot be characterized as a "mainstream" area of Religious Studies—it is, in a sense, a liminal discipline, a discipline at the boundaries of the traditional disciplines, and even at the margins of Religious Studies itself.[14]

How does the liminality of the psychological study of religion influence feminist work in the discipline? My sense is that precisely because the psychology of religion is itself outside of the Religious Studies mainstream, it has offered minimal resistance to Women's Studies. An acceptance of interdisciplinary inquiry in the psychological study of religion has rendered the inevitable disciplinary critique of Women's Studies less threatening. In addition, the relatively recent origins of the psychological study of religion militates against a traditionalism that, in other contexts, leads to the concerted opposition to feminist methodologies. The relative openness to Women's Studies in the psychological study of religion does not, of course, mean that the field is free from androcentrism. Rather, it means that within the psychological study of religion, Women's Studies has been successful in initiating, if not in completing, the three tasks outlined above.

In this chapter, then, I'll describe two "enterprises" (the psychology *of* religion proper and the psychology *and* religion movement), four "methodologies" (Freudian, Jungian, object relations theory, and poststructuralist), and three "projects" of Women's Studies (the critical, the analytic, and the inclusive projects). The projects of Women's Studies, as I'll demonstrate, have shaped all four of the methodologies and both of the enterprises: the kinds of questions asked by scholars in Women's Studies have irreversibly influenced research and teaching in the field. Let us turn first to the psychological study of religion in the work of the theorist who is unquestionably the most significant of the figures we will examine: Sigmund Freud.

Sigmund Freud's Psychoanalytic Approach to Religion

Sigmund Freud's psychoanalytic theory of religion is essentially a projection theory of origins: it seeks the psychological origins of religion in human "projections." Freud argued in the early 1900s that religion is "nothing but psychology projected into the external world" and that "a personal God is psychologically, nothing other than an exalted father."[15] In Freud's view, unconscious structures, images, and desires are projected onto ideas about God, religion, and morality: "[T]he obscure recognition (the endopsychic perception as it were) of psychical factors and relations in the unconscious is mirrored . . . in the construction of a supernatural reality."[16] The psychological study of religion, in Freud's view, is thus the study of the unconscious psyche. Freud's study of religion, it must be noted, represents an atheistic or agnostic critique: from Freud's perspective, religious truth claims are illusions or delusions. He hoped to free human beings from submission to illusory truth claims and authoritarian demands for unthinking obedience.

Freud applied his projection theory of religion to the individual psyche and to culture and history, utilizing the Oedipus complex as the foundational analytic construct for both individual and cultural-historical analyses.[17] Incestuous desire for the mother and parricidal hostility toward the father—the two central elements of the Oedipal fantasy—provide the structure for psychological development, religious ideation, and moral/cultural development in Freud's work. The paradigmatic Oedipal scenario develops in several steps. The child (usually, in Freud's texts, a male child) expresses love for the mother and parricidal wishes against the father. The father forbids the actualization of these incestuous and murderous desires; the son experiences the father's threats as castration anxiety and renounces his fantasies of incest and parricide, submitting to paternal authority. This renunciation and submission sets the pattern for the son's relationships to paternal structures and father figures in the cultural, religious, moral, and political arenas.

Women's Studies and the Psychoanalytic Approach to Religion

All three of the projects and approaches developed in Women's Studies—critical, analytic, and inclusive—have been applied to and appropriated by scholars interested in Freud's theory of religion. While many theorists have attacked the androcentrism characterizing Freud's theory of culture and religion, others have taken a more analytical or interpretive stance, exploring the ways in which Freud's theory is gendered. Still other studies, pursuing the inclusive project of Women's Studies, have begun to explore the contributions and significance of particular women within the psychoanalytic theory of religion.

Much of Freud's own work on religion, and most of the feminist critiques of this work, fall under the rubric of the "psychology of religion" proper. Some "analytic" research, however, as well as some of the "inclusive" projects in the field, contribute to the historical and cultural enterprise of the "psychology and religion movement." In this section I will first describe the feminist critics of Freud's theory of religion, turning subsequently to a discussion of his "analysts," and finally, to some "inclusive" projects investigating historical, biographical, and theoretical work by and about women within the context of the psychoanalytic theory of religion.[18]

The Critical Project of Women's Studies: Exposing Androcentrism in the Psychoanalytic Theory of Religion

Scholars concerned to expose the androcentrism in Freud's theory of religion have focused on the normativity of masculinity in Freud's theory, the "womanlessness" of the theory, and the assumption that only the male is capable of achieving the highest forms of psychological and moral development.[19] As Judith Van Herik notes, in Freud's writing, "masculinity is treated as the general human norm, femininity as a special case or deviation."[20] An essay of Freud's published in 1928 contains a telling example of his sense of the male as the normative or prototypical human being. Describing a short story by Stefan Zwieg, Freud states: "This little masterpiece ostensibly sets out only to show what an irresponsible creature woman is, and to what excesses, surprising even to herself, an unexpected experience may drive her. But the story tells far more than this. If it is subjected to an analytical interpretation, *it will be found to represent . . . something quite different, something universally human, or rather something masculine.*"[21] Thus, a story about a woman, when read psychoanalytically, becomes a universally human story; that is, it becomes a story about men. The universally human or "masculine" story disclosed through analysis is the Oedipal story—the story that for Freud is the foundational story for all (male) human beings and all of culture. Freud's Oedipal subject, thus, is paradigmatically male.[22]

Further, Freud's theory of religion, like his theory in general, is in many ways, "womanless." Women are not *entirely* absent from the Oedipal scenario: in theory, at least, the mother is a significant figure in the Oedipus complex since the child's incestuous desire for the mother is the catalyst for the Oedipal struggle—and the child could be either male or female. But in fact, in many of Freud's analyses of religion, the Oedipal desire for the mother is ignored or de-emphasized, and the child is assumed to be a son, not a daughter. Freud sometimes referred to the Oedipal complex in shorthand terminology as the father-relation or the father-complex. Thus, fathers and sons perform most of the action on the Oedipal stage. The woman, the mother, and the female child are rarely the *subjects* of desire: the position of the maternal *object* of filial desire is the major role available to women, and this role itself is frequently eliminated. As psychologist of religion David Wulff notes, "[A]lthough both sexes experience infantile helplessness, Freud's psychology of religion is otherwise clearly centered in masculine reactivity. It is the male's ambivalent relationship with his father, both in his own and in the race's childhood that lies at the core of religion as Freud views it."[23]

In an additional type of androcentrism in Freud's theory of religion, the male alone is viewed as capable of achieving the highest forms of moral development: "[O]nly masculinity has the potentiality to realize the human ideal, understood both as ideal type and as best."[24] Renunciatory morality and detached rationality, the psychoanalytic ideals, are male preserves. In a short essay entitled "Some Psychical Consequences of the Anatomical Distinction between the Sexes," for example, Freud describes the obstacles to the development of morality in females, explaining that moral development is based on the castration complex: male castration anxiety makes possible the renunciation of incestuous and parricidal desires—a renunciation that provides the foundation for morality. Girls experience the castration complex as penis envy rather than castration anxiety, and thus are less capable than boys of the renunciation of desires, fantasies, and illusions, and less capable of developing a strong, internalized moral sense, that is, a "superego." In this essay Freud reluctantly presented the conclusions he knew were unpalatable: "I cannot evade the notion (though I hesitate to give it expression) that for women the level of what is ethically normal is different from what it is in men. Their superego is never so inexorable, so impersonal, so independent of its emotional origins as we require it to be in men. . . . Women . . . show less sense of justice. . . . [T]hey are less ready to submit to the great exigencies of life, they are more often influenced in their judgments by feelings of affection or hostility."[25] Freud softens his argument with the assurance that "we shall of course willingly agree that the majority of men are also far behind the masculine ideal"—but the impact of his statement cannot be mitigated. Only males, in Freud's view, are capable of true morality.[26]

He extends this to the cultural context in *The Ego and the Id:* "Religion, morality, and a social sense—the chief elements in the higher side of man— were . . . acquired phylogenetically out of the father-complex. . . . [T]he male sex seems to have taken the lead in all these moral acquisitions."[27] In both individual development and cultural development, in other words, women are incapable of the renunciations and sublimations required for the production and maintenance of culture, religion, and morality. Freud's theory thus privileges the male and assumes female deficiency.

Scholars in Women's Studies, then, have pointed out three kinds of androcentrism in Freud's work on religion: a premise that the male is the human norm; a "womanlessness" evident in the notion that the definitive cultural and psychological relation is between father and son; and an insistence on female moral and intellectual inferiority.

The Analytic Project of Women's Studies and the Psychoanalytic Theory of Religion

Some theorists in Women's Studies have found Freud's androcentrism sufficient grounds for dismissing his theory entirely. Others, however, have attempted to analyze and interpret his work rather than dismiss it, pursuing Philip Rieff's provocative insight that "Freud's misogyny is more than prejudice; it has a vital intellectual function in his system."[28] These scholars seek to understand how, as Rieff puts it, "the pejorative image of woman serves as a measure of the general critical component in Western philosophies."[29] Also significant in the feminist reevaluation of Freud is the work of feminist psychoanalyst Juliet Mitchell who argued in 1974 that psychoanalysis may provide an accurate description of the construction of gender within phallocentric and patriarchal culture.[30]

Foremost among these analytic theorists is Judith Van Herik, whose *Freud on Femininity and Faith* analyzes the asymmetry of gender in Freud's theory of culture and religion. Without dismissing Freud as simply a misogynist, Van Herik shows that Freud associates illusion, wish fulfillment, and religious belief with femininity, while, by contrast, he associates renunciation of illusion, rationality, the reality principle, and morality with masculinity. Van

Herik is concerned with the internal structure of the "gender asymmetry" in Freud's texts, that is, with the functions of the concepts of masculinity and femininity within his theory of religion and culture. She is less concerned with whether Freud's view of culture is correct: "[W]hether one should locate consistencies between Freud's critiques of gender and religion in his accuracy about the deep structure of mental life in culture or in Freud's own critical consistency is not an issue which [her] study decides."[31] She does, however, acknowledge the necessity to consider carefully the possibility that Freud's gendering of illusion and belief corresponds to a broad cultural pattern, and urges a serious consideration of Freud's claims "about how gender works in our moral economy and about how gender and uses of God are thereby intertwined."[32]

Van Herik's analysis of Freud's theory of religion has shaped many subsequent studies. Utilizing Van Herik's analytic approach and Mitchell's feminist reevaluation of Freud, I have undertaken, in an essay on psychoanalytic readings of woman and religion, a gender analysis focusing on Freud's writings on religion, death, and absence. I've argued that underlying Freud's texts are gendered assumptions about absence and presence, life and death: "Woman as absence, man as presence, feminine religion as the denial of absence, masculine reason as the renunciation of false presence. . . . Freud's texts are full of these linkages."[33] Through an inquiry into Freud's ideas about maternal absence, the death instinct, and castration anxiety, I uncovered Freudian insights (not fully articulated in psychoanalytic theory, but present in the texts nevertheless) into the sources of misogyny in the fear of death. The experiences of maternal absence and castration anxiety establish unconscious links between absence and the feminine; the fear of death and non-being (absence of a different sort) is displaced onto the fear of women. Misogyny displaces death anxiety, I argued, as the difference of gender stands in for the absence of death.

Other scholars have initiated gender analyses of a different sort by examining contradictions within Freud's theory of religion. Howard Eilberg-Schwartz, for example, exposes gaps in Freud's constructions of the origins of monotheism.[34] In a provocative analysis of *Moses and Monotheism*, he demonstrates that, on the one hand, Freud "asserts that in monotheism the father is rediscovered behind the image of God." On the other hand, Freud insists that "what is discovered is a conceptual idea of God with no imaged content."[35] Inquiring into the "disappearance of God's body" in these texts, Eilberg-Schwartz suggests that the Jewish prohibition of images is a means of "veiling the body of the father God," which in turn is a veiling of male erotic desires for the father, a veiling Freud was able to perceive in his case studies but not in his cultural analyses. In case studies such as the famous analysis of Daniel Paul Schreber, Freud exposed homoerotic desire underlying religious imagery. But in his analysis of monotheism and the history of Judaism he "could not or would not think about why the image/body of the Father God had to be veiled and hence did not face the issue of the male's erotic desires for the father."[36] This refusal to consider homoeroticism, Eilberg-Schwartz believes, was a defensive posture on Freud's part, "an attempt to deny the association between femininity, passivity, and Jewishness that plagued Freud's own identity."[37]

Other scholars as well have initiated gender analyses through examinations of the question of Freud's Jewish background, the Jewish origins of psychoanalysis, and the relationship of Judaism and gender.[38] Some of this scholarship illustrates the concerns of the "psychology and religion movement" in its inquiry into the impact of modernization upon Freud's world and work. One important theorist utilizing the methodologies developed in Women's Studies and gender studies is Jay Geller.[39] Geller's research has been instrumental in demonstrating the "feminization" of Judaism in *fin de siècle* Europe. His writings on circumcision, on ideas about the Jewish body, and on nosological concepts have revealed widespread cultural symbol systems—symbol systems that Freud himself, to some degree, shared—within which male Jews were perceived as emasculated or effeminate. Geller's research, I have argued elsewhere, provides an important context within which to understand Van Herik's thesis about Freud's feminization of religion: as a Jewish male in a world that feminized Jewish males, Freud found it useful to "turn the tables" by subtly underscoring the psychological femininity of Christian belief and the psychological masculinity of renunciatory (Jewish) morality and intellect.[40]

Another scholar of gender and Judaism is British psychoanalyst Estelle Roith who examines Jewish influences on psychoanalysis, arguing that the Eastern European Jewish background of Freud's parents and family constellation had a significant influence on his theory of female sexuality. She emphasizes his origins as the "son of Jewish parents, both of whom were born in the kind of provincial ghetto or hamlet of Eastern Europe where Jews had lived, in the main, in isolated communities and in a state of strict religious orthodoxy for hundreds of years."[41] Eastern European rabbinic sexual doctrines and the family structure of the *shtetl* are crucial in her analysis of Freud's theory. She traces a number of Freud's concepts of female sexuality directly to traditional rabbinic teachings. The rabbinic tradition, in her view, encompassed a "curious mix of hostility, aversion, and respect" toward sex.[42] She characterizes this attitude as a joyless sexual realism or sexual utilitarianism accompanied by a rigid, self-imposed discipline of sexual restraint.

Roith's emphasis on Freud's Eastern European Jewish origins is challenged by historian and cultural theorist Sander Gilman who develops a more nuanced perspective on Freud, Judaism, and gender. In Gilman's view Freud's identity was shaped by the tension *between* the unassimilated Eastern European *shtetl* Judaism of his parentage, and the assimilated, Westernized, nonreligious Judaism of Viennese Jewish scientists; the tension, that is, between the religious Judaism of his ancestry and the ethnic or racial Judaism of the dispassionate Jewish scientist. Gilman identifies Freud as a highly acculturated Western Jewish physician/scientist with Eastern Jewish roots. He insists, contra Roith, that the "complex questions that Freud's new science of psychoanalysis proposed in regard to human sexuality certainly had more to do with Freud's understanding of science than with Rabbinic lore."[43]

Gilman's central concern, however, is not the influence of Freud's religious background on his theory of female sexuality. Rather, he is concerned with the relationship between representations of race and gender in Freud's work and his world. Gilman brings to this inquiry the kind of methodological approach often utilized in Women's Studies and gender studies. His project is not only an account of the gendering of Judaism, but also of the problematizing of gender—of masculinity as well as femininity, of homosexuality as well as heterosexuality. He aims to show "how the masculine and the feminine as well as the homosexual (gay/lesbian) categories of identity are structured by the rhetoric of race."[44] He points out the complex ways in which the image of the male Jew was constructed as feminine and homosexual in the cultural imagination of nineteenth- and early twentieth-century Europe.

In Gilman's analysis, the Aryan equation of the Jewish male with the feminine and the homosexual was subtly challenged by Western acculturated Jews of Eastern European descent such as Freud. Through rejection of "religious" elements of Eastern European Jewish belief and practice, these Jews became less "feminized." If, in the symbol systems of the culture, Eastern European Jewish males were feminized in relation to Aryan males, they could be "masculinized" through acculturation into Western scientific Aryan culture: "In acquiring the professional mantle of the scientist the Jew became 'masculine'. . . . [T]he exclusionary category of the Jew was abrogated and the Jew became in his own estimation a scientist equivalent to every other scientist . . . the question of racial identity was suspended."[45]

It may be useful to point out at this juncture that the analysis of race and gender by such scholars as Gilman and Geller not only illustrates the concerns of the "psychology and religion movement," but also resonates with the innovative research now emerging in Women's Studies on race, racism, and ethnicity. In recent years, theorists in Women's Studies such as bell hooks, Cherrie Moraga, and Gloria Anzaldua have begun to analyze and interrogate the social and cultural structures of exclusion and marginalization that have led not only to sexism but also to racism.[46] This important endeavor, so visible now in Women's Studies, has barely begun to influence the psychological study of religion. Geller and Gilman are among the first to explore this area.

Their projects differ from the projects within Women's Studies in that their conclusions are specific to Freud's cultural context, and that race and ethnicity are discussed solely with reference to Judaism. However, their work represents an important step for the psychological study of religion.

The Inclusive Project of Women's Studies: The Influence of Women on the Psychoanalytic Theory of Religion

An additional area of promising research for the "psychology and religion movement" lies in the investigation of the lives and ideas of the women who were disciples of Freud and members of the Vienna psychoanalytic community.[47] Particularly notable among these was Lou Andreas-Salomé, mistress of the poet Rilke, beloved of Nietzsche, and friend and confidante of Freud from 1912 until her death in 1937. One of the most dynamic and significant of Freud's female disciples, she was a prolific writer, publishing several psychoanalytic essays as well as a number of fictional, dramatic, critical, and autobiographical texts. She is said to have been the inspiration for Freud's description of the self-contained woman in "On Narcissism." With a strong sense of spirituality and the "presentness of the natural world," she often engaged in open and friendly disagreement with Freud regarding religion. Recent discussions of the significance of this woman and her ideas—and of others such as Melanie Klein, Karen Horney, and Marie Bonaparte—in the development of Freud's theory are now beginning to uncover important new materials that may prove productive for the psychological study of religion.

Two other women particularly important in influencing Freud's ideas about religion are his "two mothers," that is, his own mother Amalie Freud, and the Roman Catholic nanny who cared for him during the first two and a half years of his life. The nanny, who frequently took the young Freud to Mass, was abruptly dismissed from the employ of the household. Her sudden departure was experienced by the young Freud as a traumatic loss. Many have argued that this loss may have shaped Freud's critical stance toward religion.[48] Several studies, a few of which have addressed his theory of religion, have inquired into Freud's relationship with his mother. Cultural theorist Peter Homans has commented that the Jewishness of Freud's mother is "a possible source of Freud's affirmation of a non-doctrinal religious identity." He also suggests that Freud's "gentle and rational brand of Jewishness (and) his lack of illusions about immortality . . . may have been all that he cared to retain from his identification with (his mother)."[49] I agree with Homans that Freud's mother played an important role in molding his view of religion and his view of death—and that this connection might be profitably pursued in future research.[50]

Assessment: Freud, Religion, and Women's Studies

We've seen that Freud's "psychology of religion" has been subjected to a thorough critique by scholars in Women's Studies. Focusing on his androcentrism, scholars initially attacked Freud for privileging the "father relation," for assuming male normativity, and for constructing a theory of culture, religion, and morality in which women appear biologically, intellectually, and ethically deficient. We also noted that this critical stance has given way to a feminist reassessment of Freud: in the last two decades feminist scholars have argued that Freud's theory might represent a useful, valuable, and perhaps accurate analysis of the construction of gender within patriarchal culture. Thus, feminists engaged in the "psychology of religion" have begun to adopt, incorporate, and analyze, rather than to critique and reject psychoanalytic theory.

In addition, we have noted that within the "psychology and religion movement," the analytic project of Women's Studies has flourished as scholars have directed attention to the gendering of religion and race in Freud's cultural context. And, although the inclusive project of Women's Studies—the rediscovery of women's lives and thoughts—remains, for the most part, still unexplored, some recent scholarship in this area appears promising. We turn now to an examination of the work of C. G. Jung, a theorist who has elicited a rather different response from scholars in Women's Studies.[51]

C. G. Jung's Approach to Religion

Swiss psychologist Carl Gustav Jung devoted a great deal of his voluminous oeuvre to religion. His theories have generated an ongoing discourse about myth, religion, healing, and spirituality. Although his work is often contrasted with Freud's, the two figures share many common assumptions about religion and psychology. Both Jung's "analytical psychology" and Freud's "psychoanalysis" seek to trace the origins of religion, both develop "projection theories" in their quests for origins, and both assume that the contents of the unconscious are the primary force shaping religious ideas, images, and symbols. In addition, they share a common understanding of the significance of dreams and of the dynamics of the unconscious.

Unlike Freud, however, Jung does not argue for the abandonment of religion. Jung feels that contemporary culture accords insufficient attention to religion and religious imagery. He urges greater respect for the contents of the unconscious—especially for its religious and mythic projections. Nor is Jung's projection theory atheistic in its approach. Jung's analysis of the source of the "imago dei" in the unconscious does not constitute a claim that God is *only* an unconscious projection. His project is psychological, not ontological, he insists. But Jung's affirmation of religion is not uncritical. He urges a substantial transformation of Christianity,[52] offering a diagnosis of its pathology and a program for its cure. Most important, he argues, contemporary religion has lost contact with its unconscious, collective, and "archetypal" components.

In Jung's view the personal unconscious and the collective unconscious must be differentiated. While the personal unconscious is the repository of *individual* memories, fantasies, and desires, the collective unconscious is shared by all human beings. Structured by the "archetypes" rather than by Oedipal desires and conflicts, the Jungian collective unconscious is the carrier of archetypal "forms without content," symbols *in potentia,* which are manifested in dreams and myths. These archetypes can be described as a cross-cultural and transhistorical propensity to produce similar mythic and symbolic ideas.[53] Generated during the many centuries of human history and prehistory the archetypes, Jung asserts, cannot be traced to individual experiences or memories. These collective images continue to influence our lives and our psyches: we ignore them at our peril.

A great deal of Jung's writing was devoted to categorizing these archetypes, describing their manifestations, and demonstrating their relations to individual and cultural health and pathology. In Jung's archetypal theory, individuals and cultures typically progress along a continuum toward greater "individuation" (wholeness or self-realization); although imbalance and regression sometimes prevent individuation and result in pathology. This journey toward individuation involves a predictable sequence of encounters with the archetypes followed by their "integration" into consciousness. First one encounters the "shadow," the darker side of the personality, portrayed in Western religious imagery as the devil. Then one encounters the "contrasexual archetype"—the anima (the feminine, relational, "Eros" side of the male unconscious) or the animus (the masculine, rational, "Logos" side of the female unconscious). The anima, according to Jung, appears in religious discourse as the soul, while the animus may appear as a spiritual guide. After integrating the anima or animus, one typically encounters the archetype of the Great Mother and the Wise Old Man. Other archetypes such as the trickster, the hero, or the child may emerge as well. Finally, one confronts, and, ideally, integrates the archetype of the Self which often takes the form of a deity, a four-sided "quaternity," or a "mandala."[54]

Jung constructs a critique of contemporary culture and religion, and, especially, the Western God-image, based on his understanding of the archetypes, individuation, and the collective unconscious. Contemporary Western religion has become excessively rational and masculine, losing touch with the collective unconscious in general and with the feminine archetypes in particular. Christianity's God-image, in Jung's view, is imbalanced: rather than offering a divine representation of wholeness incorporating male and female, good and evil, spirit and matter, the Christian God-image is excessively masculine, good, and spiritual. Jung calls for a cultural and religious rebalancing through a reincorporation of the missing archetypal elements.

Jung's view of the problem of the repression of the "feminine archetype" in religion and culture is illustrated clearly in his analysis of the doctrine of the Trinity. In a 1938 essay Jung argued that as an image of the Godhead, the Holy Trinity was incomplete. Through historical and cross-cultural studies he had learned that God-images typically (or "archetypically") contain four parts: the "quaternity" is culturally and historically a more frequent God-image than the Trinity. In addition, he noted, while God-images usually contain male and female components, the Trinity is entirely masculine: the Trinitarian "persons," Father, Son, and Holy Spirit, constitute a purely masculine Godhead. In the doctrine of the Trinity, the "missing fourth" was the feminine.[55] When the dogma of the Assumption of the Blessed Virgin was proclaimed by Pope Pius XII a few years later, Jung felt that his assessment of the "missing fourth" in Trinitarian doctrine had been corroborated. He asserted that the dogma of the Assumption was "the most important religious event since the Reformation."[56] The feminine archetype, after centuries of repression or exclusion, was now, in Jung's view, incorporated into the Godhead. Jung found the notion of Mary's *bodily* assumption into heaven to be especially significant: the physical was integrated into the spiritual. With this new dogma, Jung argued, the Trinity was becoming a quaternity.[57] Christianity—at least Roman Catholic Christianity—was progressing toward wholeness or individuation, an individuation that was, in a sense, a subversion of male dominance or of an exclusively masculine God-image.

Women's Studies and C. G. Jung's Psychology of Religion

Scholars in Women's Studies have had a different relationship to the work of Jung than to the work of Freud. If feminists first rejected Freud and only later began to interpret, analyze, and adopt Freudian insights, the opposite is the case with Jung. Prior to the 1980s, Jung's approach was often enlisted as a methodology compatible with Women's Studies. His critique of the cultural repression of the feminine was seen as an aid in the critical project of Women's Studies, the discovery of cultural androcentrism. And his attention to the feminine archetypes was viewed as part of the inclusive project of Women's Studies, the incorporation of women's lives into contemporary scholarship. However, this initial enthusiasm was followed by a more cautious stance as feminists began to discover problematic forms of androcentrism within Jung's own work and began to express concern about exploiting Jungian methodologies in their inclusive efforts.

I'll describe fairly briefly and selectively the feminist acclaim and critique for Jung's "psychology *of* religion." Then I'll turn to the endeavors of the "psychology *and* religion movement" and examine some recent "inclusive" literature on women in Jung's life and thought.

Feminist Acclaim for Jung's Psychology of Religion:
The Inclusive Project in Women's Studies

Jung's psychology of religion has been acclaimed as feminist or proto-feminist for a number of reasons. First, in its foundational principles, the theory is not "womanless." Jung directed unprecedented attention to religious images, symbols and archetypes of the feminine such as the "Great Mother Goddess" and the "Divine Bride" who constitute one axis of the quaternary formulation of the God-image.[58] Second, Jung's notion of the "contra-sexual archetypes" of anima and animus and his insistence that men must integrate their unconscious femininity, and women their unconscious masculinity, have been seen as challenges to stereotyped and essentialist understandings of gender. Third, his critique of culture and religion as excessively masculine resonates with feminist critiques of patriarchal culture and exclusively male God-imagery. The Jungian theoretical framework affirms the salvific or healing qualities of the feminine archetype for culture and for individuals. An encounter with goddess images and feminine religious symbols excluded from our historical tradition can revivify our lives and our cultures, functioning as a kind of cultural therapy. Renewed contact with heretical, repressed, or forgotten feminine images connects us with unconscious archetypal processes in a way that is "meaning-making" and healing. Jungian scholar Joan Chamberlain Engelsman, for example, in a classic expression of this view, articulates the dangers of the repression of the feminine archetype and the salvific possibilities in its recovery. "[I]f the feminine is not restored to its archetypal place in Western religion, the results might be catastrophic. Although the repression of the feminine dimension of the divine creates especially poignant problems for women, its restoration may be necessary for the psychic health of all people."[59]

An immense body of Jungian literature—some of it predating the origins of Women's Studies in the 1960s—examines "the feminine archetype" in religion.[60] I'll describe just one example of this literature: Engelsman's historical analysis of Christian doctrine in *The Feminine Dimension of the Divine*. Engelsman describes representations of the archetypal feminine in the goddess religions of the Hellenistic world; she examines the repression of the feminine in early Christianity; and she explores the return of the feminine in distorted and disguised forms in the theology of the early church. In each case, she assumes a link between archetype, God-image, and social structure: she argues that female God-images were accompanied by egalitarian and democratic social structures, and that the repression of the female God-image and the reemergence of the feminine in distorted forms was accompanied by social structures promoting female inferiority.

In Engelsman's view, the "return of the repressed feminine" is manifested in early Christianity in disguised and distorted forms in Mariology, Christology, and Ecclesiology. In spite of the strength and power of Marian doctrine and iconography, the Virgin Mary remains, from a Jungian perspective, a "one dimensional figure": Mary is "always good, merciful and supportive. She has no dark side . . . her theology is fraught with conflicting messages and the image that results is confused." From this perspective, Mary represents an incomplete form of the archetype: "She is, and is not, a goddess or a representation of the feminine dimension of the divine."[61]

Christology, in Engelsman's reading, embodies another distorted expression of the feminine archetype. The historical origins of Christology lie in a tradition in which "Sophia" or "Wisdom" is envisioned as a feminine dimension of the divine. This authentic expression of the feminine archetype, in Engelsman's view, is contained in the Wisdom literature of the Hebrew Bible. The Christology developing in the early Christian church absorbed the feminine Sophia tradition, replacing it with a masculinized Logos theology, thereby repressing the feminine archetype. Similarly, ecclesiological literature simultaneously expresses and represses the archetypal feminine by speaking of church as mother, as bride of Christ, and as Wisdom. In Engelsman's view the archetypal feminine in these doctrines, while present in distorted form, is not beneficial or "individuating" because it cannot be openly, consciously, and explicitly acknowledged.

Engelsman stresses the desiccation of Christianity in its current form, and the rejuvenating transformation that might occur with the integration of feminine images for the divine. She argues that "our prior dependency on a relatively narrow image of the divine as male, particularly as male parent, may have stifled our faith and limited our experience of God. . . . When the ikon of God as father is replaced by a multiplicity of images, including the feminine, Christianity may undergo a rebirth which might expand, rather than diminish, its appeal."[62]

Thus, the work of Jungian feminists like Engelsman illustrates the use of archetypal theory as a tool for assessing religion by constructing a diagnosis of a cultural malady and offering a cure. Engelsman discovers a repressed and distorted form of the feminine archetype within church history and doctrine, and recommends a program of treatment for the malaise of contemporary Western religion. The recovery of the feminine, she argues, will rejuvenate Christianity in its God-imagery, in its religious and spiritual life, and in its theology.

The Critical Project: Androcentrism in Jung's Theory

Although many feminists like Engelsman have enthusiastically embraced Jung's psychology of religion, others have been more cautious, arguing that, in spite of the inclusion of Great Mothers, anima figures, and goddesses, Jung's theory of religion, like his psychology more generally, remains androcentric or misogynist. Devoting attention to female imagery—even female God-imagery—need not enact a feminist move. Female imagery can convey sexist or misogynist perspectives: androcentrism is sometimes expressed in subtle and unconscious notions of female inferiority or male normativity, rather than simply in the absence of women.

Jung's psychology of religion, and its development in the work of such theorists as Engelsman, has been criticized for its ahistorical, universalist, and broadly cross-cultural approach: by seeking universal archetypal forms, critics complain, Jungian analyses of culture and religion ignore cultural and historical specificity. In addition, Jung's thought has been accused of a certain arbitrariness. At times the selections of mythological materials to demonstrate or illustrate archetypes seem predetermined to fit the conclusions—thus all trinities, three-sided figures, and triads are culturally, developmentally, and spiritually inferior to all four-sided figures and quaternities. The assumption evident in the work of Engelsman and other Jungians that God-imagery recapitulates social structure is also problematic. There's no clear evidence that cultures with female deities are socially egalitarian. While religious cosmologies do provide complex charters for social organization, goddess religions are not incompatible with social structures ensuring female subordination.

Most problematic, however, is the subtle androcentrism in Jungian thought. Several scholars have mounted a critique of Jungian theory, arguing that the notion of the archetypal feminine is rife with stereotyped and essentialist assumptions about gender and female inferiority. One of the most significant of these scholars is Naomi Goldenberg, whose work on Jung illustrates well the critical project of Women's Studies. Goldenberg's early work was sympathetic to Jung. In her first book, *The Changing of the Gods,* she argued that Jung's theory constituted a useful tool for dismantling the Father-God traditions, eliminating the need for eternal, transcendent, authoritarian deities, and making possible the emergence of "feminist religions" in which the authority and divinity of the self are valued. Her early enthusiasm for Jung notwithstanding, Goldenberg soon initiated a rigorous feminist critique of his work, uncovering androcentric aspects of his thought. Although Jung valued the feminine, she showed, he did not value women. Jung defined woman in terms of "her remarkable and all too often overlooked 'Eros.' But . . . he wanted her to stay in the sphere of that 'Eros.' Once she moved into a 'Logos' arena she was not only at a great disadvantage, but extremely annoying as well."[63]

Goldenberg also notes that in Jung's work the subject is typically male: the integration of the contents of the male unconscious provides the essential paradigm for individuation. In addition, Goldenberg expresses concern over Jung's theory of archetypes: "If we set up these images as archetypes we are in danger of setting bounds to experience, defining what the 'proper' experience of woman is. I see this as a new version of the Eternal Feminine enterprise which could be just as restrictive as the old Eternal Feminine ever was."[64] Jung's theory, in other words, is androcentric in its assumption of the male psyche as the human norm and in its notion of female inferiority.

Goldenberg also argues that Jung's archetypal theory contributes to one of the pathologies of our culture: a tendency toward dualism that values eternal, transcendent, disembodied, archetypal "truths," and devalues embodiment, life, and physicality. In this dualistic ideology, bodies—especially female bodies—are devalued. Jungian archetypal theory and theistic religions, both based on "fantasies of independence from matter,"[65] are expressions of this anti-body dualism wherein mind, soul, and God are "seen as qualitatively different from physical existence, as separable from the physical world and definitely superior to it."[66]

Even more damning is Jung's troubling denigration of Jews. In racist, antisemitic, and misogynist statements made during the era of National Socialism, Jung described Jews as weak, inferior, and "effeminate," arguing that they have "never produced and presumably never will produce a culture of [their] own."[67] Jung was, in a sense, a perpetrator of the ideology of the feminized, effeminate, and inferior Jew which marked Freud's milieu. This material deserves further investigation.

A Postcritical Defense of Jung

In *Jung and Feminism: Liberating Archetypes,* Demaris Wehr approaches Jung's theories from a feminist perspective that is both critical and inclusive. She finds Jung's work particularly valuable for feminist thought and feminist theology but argues for the necessity of a reconstruction of Jungian theory. Wehr acknowledges that Jung's concept of femininity serves to keep women subdued and out of the public sphere.[68] Like Goldenberg, she criticizes Jung for giving the archetypes a sacred and unchangeable quality by connecting them with the immutable categories of the collective unconscious.

However, Wehr does not abandon Jung's ideas. She finds value in Jung's insights about the way the mind works, about the religious dimensions of the psyche, and about the function (if not the structure) of the personal and collective unconscious. The Jungian emphasis upon "making the unconscious conscious" must be used in "making unconscious androcentrism conscious."[69] Jung's theory of the psyche, she suggests, can even function as a self-reflexive mirror capable of critiquing its own premises regarding gender. Jung's theory, in Wehr's view, can serve as a tool in deconstructing its own internalized and institutionalized categories of oppression and in deconstructing religious and cultural misogyny.

Assessment: Jung, Women's Studies, and the Two Enterprises Within the Psychological Study of Religion

Thus, from the perspective of Women's Studies the initial response to Jung's psychology of religion was positive; Jungian thought seemed to provide methodologies that aided in accomplishing one of the primary tasks of Women's Studies: the inclusion of women in scholarship. Utilizing a Jungian methodology, inclusive projects were initiated uncovering the repressed feminine in heretical religious texts and obscure iconography, projects that discovered distorted representations of the feminine just below the surface of orthodox doctrines. Jungian theory also seemed to offer a method useful for a critique of the womanlessness of Western religion and culture.

Subsequent reactions to Jungian thought have been more cautious: rather than exploiting Jung's thought in a feminist critique of culture, scholars have begun to subject Jung's psychology of religion itself to a feminist critique. From this perspective his theory appears to promote androcentrism, gender essentialism, and female inferiority. Some feminists have dismissed him on these grounds; others continue to find his work valuable. These two projects of Women's Studies, the inclusive project and the critical project, have constituted the bulk of feminist research on Jung's psychology of religion. The analytic project of Women's Studies has been less clearly represented in this literature.[70]

Most of the aforementioned research by Jung, Jungians, and critics of Jung has reflected the concerns of the psychology of religion proper. Other research, primarily biographical, illustrates the concerns of the psychology and religion movement. Many biographical studies have devoted attention to the role of religion in Jung's life and theory. However, with the exception of a few works such as Peter Homans's *Jung in Context,* the historical and cultural background of Jung's thought has not received the kind of intense scrutiny one finds in the literature on Freud.[71] Some recent scholarship, however, has begun to examine the role of particular women in the development of Jung's theory of religion. These include Toni Wolff and Sabina Spielrein.

Jung's relationship with patient, disciple, and lover, Toni Wolff, is well known and widely discussed in biographical literature on Jung.[72] Often invoked as Jung's inspiratrice and muse, Wolff wrote an important article on the archetypal psychology of women which has been influential in shaping later Jungian thought on the feminine archetype.[73] She established a Jungian practice and took a leading role, along with Jung's wife Emma, in the administration of Jungian programs in Zurich.

The discovery of a cache of letters documenting Jung's relationship with Sabina Spielrein, a Russian woman who was his patient, disciple, lover, and colleague during the early years of the twentieth century, has provided new insight into the formation of Jung's ideas.[74] John Kerr's recent study, *A Most Dangerous Method: The Story of Jung, Freud, and Sabina Spielrein,* while not specifically devoted to the psychology of religion, does not neglect Spielrein's Jewish background, her attitude toward religion, or her participation in the new discourse initiated by Freud and Jung. A study focusing in particular on religion and psychology in Spielrein's life might provide a productive case study, significant both for the "psychology and religion movement" and for the inclusive project of Women's Studies as well. Further cultural, biographical, and historical studies may prove fruitful in developing new understandings of the significance of gender in Jung's theory, the roles of particular women in the development of psychological ideas about religion, and the problematic relationship between Jung's ideas and his tendency to develop sexual relationships with his disciples. How, for example, are Jung's theories of religion, culture, and psyche intertwined with his sexual/analytical relationships of power over and knowledge of his female patients? Such issues demand further attention from theorists in this field.

We turn now to psychoanalytic object relations theory, which, like the work of Jung, begins in dissatisfaction with Freud's failure to attend to the mother, the feminine, or the female.

Psychoanalytic Object Relations Theory and Religion

Object relations theory brings a new perspective to the psychological study of religion. With roots in psychoanalysis, object relations theory shares many of the assumptions and methods of classical Freudian theory, but differs from psychoanalysis in a number of ways. Most significantly, it devotes attention to the pre-Oedipal period of human development, the period of mother-infant relationship in the earliest months and years of life, focusing on the interrelatedness of human beings and on the significance of "objects" (people and internal images of those people) in human development.

Freud devoted only minimal attention to the pre-Oedipal period, arguing that it was like the impenetrable "Minoan-Mycenean civilization behind the civilization of Greece . . . grey with age and shadowy and almost impossible to revivify."[75] Instead, as we've seen, he emphasized the Oedipal relationship or "father-relation" as the source of personal, cultural, and religious structures. Object relations theorists such as D. W. Winnicott, Melanie Klein, W. D. R. Fairbairn, Margaret Mahler, Harry Guntrip, and Heinz Kohut,[76] however, have found the pre-Oedipal period less obscure than Freud had suggested. Rather, they have argued, it is accessible to analytic recovery, and it is crucial in the development of a sense of self, a sense of the other, and an ability to be in relationship. Some object relations theorists have developed suggestive analyses of religion, arguing that the pre-Oedipal relationship is the definitive matrix of religion and culture. Other theorists, often trained in Religious Studies,[77] have extended this approach into more fully developed analyses focusing on the psychological sources an·! effects of religious ideas, beliefs, and practices. Object relations theory thus makes a significant contribution to the "psychology of religion proper"—and, as we shall see, to Women's Studies. However, the import of object relations theory for the cultural and historical endeavors of the "psychology and religion movement" has been less fully explored.

Object Relations Theory, Religion, and Women's Studies

The concerns of object relations theory coincide in many ways with the concerns of Women's Studies, making possible new forays both into inclusive projects devoted to rediscovering women's subjectivity and into analytic projects devoted to the understanding of gender and misogyny. The study of religion from an object relations perspective has not been characterized by the androcentrism that has marked other psychological theories of religion. Even in its earliest phases, some of its major theorists were women—Margaret Mahler and Melanie Klein, for example. Many of the earliest theorists held explicitly feminist views, having developed their ideas in reaction against Freud's insistence on the centrality of penis envy, castration anxiety, and biological determinism.[78] Nor are contemporary object relations theorists androcentric in their analyses of religion. Not only is the early relationship to the mother considered a crucial foundation for religious and cultural experience, but the subject of object relations theory is as likely to be female as male. The potential of this perspective to develop a feminist approach within the psychology of religion has been an explicit focus of attention in much of this work.[79]

The critical project of Women's Studies has taken a different form in this context. Rather than critiquing androcentrism, some theorists have mounted critiques of "pre-Oedipalism," essentialism, and biologism in object relations theory. Judith Butler, for example, attacks the emphasis on the pre-Oedipal mother, arguing that this focus "has come to occupy a hegemonic position within the emerging canon of feminist theory."[80] According to Butler, object relations theory also fails to unmask the presumptive heterosexism shaping gender categories, and attends insufficiently to social and cultural structures of power. Similarly, Jane Flax cautions against the tendency in object relations theory to idealize women as uniquely capable of relationality and nurturance. Although Butler's and Flax's critiques have been very influential within some arenas of feminist discourse, their work has only recently begun to affect the study of religion.[81]

Object relations theory takes two different approaches, both of which I'll discuss briefly below, to the interpretations of religion. One approach assumes that religion is valuable and benign, and that a loving relationship with a good or "good enough" mother[82] provides the psychological foundations of faith, mysticism, ritual, and God representations. This approach thus takes a critical stance toward Freud's attack on religion: from this perspective, object relations theory contributes to an understanding of the developmental sources of religious experience without participating in the antireligious animus of orthodox psychoanalysis. This approach exemplifies the "inclusive" project of Women's Studies in the hermeneutic centrality of the mother.

Another object relational approach assumes that religion sometimes functions as a carrier for psychological and cultural fears of destructive and vengeful women, and that the psychological source of these fears and fantasies is fear of the mother or matriphobia. Scholars in this tradition have examined religious asceticism, sacrificial ritual, and other religious phenomena as manifestations of matriphobia. These approaches support Freud's hermeneutic of suspicion by taking a position critical of certain religious ideas and practices and extending that hermeneutic to a critique of cultural and religious misogyny. This approach exemplifies the analytic project of Women's Studies. I would like to illustrate these developments by describing a few studies representative of each approach.

The Inclusive Project: The Good Enough Mother and Religion

Particularly significant in the object relational approach to religion is a concern with the "God representation"—the image of God in individual and cultural symbols. While Freud, as we have seen, insisted "God is . . . an exalted father,"[83] object relations theorists have argued that God is also a beloved mother. Ana-Maria Rizzuto and John McDargh have shown that even the traditionally patriarchal Judeo-Christian deity has a maternal component in the unconscious. Similarly, James Jones, utilizing object relations theory, has directed attention to the emerging goddess imagery and goddess worship in contemporary American neopaganism.[84]

Also important in the object relational approach to religion is a concern with the experience of mysticism, the sacred, or what Freud called the "oceanic feeling." In *Civilization and its Discontents*, Freud described the "oceanic feeling" as the feeling of "an indissoluble bond; of being one with the external world as a whole." He acknowledged that this feeling may arise in "an early phase of ego feeling" originating in the infant's experience at the mother's breast. However, he argued, this feeling is essentially unrelated to religion. Instead, he located the source of religion in "the infant's helplessness and the longing for the father aroused by it."[85] In Freud's thought, alienation, the father relation, and religion are connected. The "oceanic feeling," on the other hand, is related to the mother, but it is not associated with the psychological origins of religion. While the psychological source of mysticism, in other words, may reside in the relationship to the mother, mysticism, in Freud's view, is unrelated to the essence of religion.

Object relations theorists, dissatisfied with Freud's formulation of the "oceanic feeling" have pursued this question farther, arguing that the sense of faith, the sense of the sacred, the sense of being united with God in mystical union, and the sense of being connected to and in relationship with the world, are all religious experiences, and can all be traced to the earliest phases of the child's life, prior to separation from the "maternal environment." Harry Guntrip, for example, describes religion as an "expression of our fundamentally dependent nature, in a relationship of emotional rapport with and reverence for external reality as a whole, immediate and universal,"[86] locating the origins of this religious sense in the child's earliest relationship with the mother.

In a related argument, Harriet Lutzky draws upon the work of object relations theorists to argue that the distinction between the sacred and the profane emerges from the "dual nature of the primary experience of the maternal object."[87] She also finds parallels between Melanie Klein's notion of "reparation" through reincorporation of the maternal object and the Kabbalistic myth of the re-creation of the cosmos or "Tikkun" in which humankind is assigned the responsibility for reuniting the exiled, separated aspects of God. Lutzky points out that "fragmentation and loss are overcome in the Kabbalah just as in Kleinian thinking, mainly through the process of unification/integration and containment /idealization. And, most dramatically, in the Kabbalah these processes are symbolized essentially by a maternal image, as they are in Klein's concept of the reparation of the internal object."[88]

These theorists thus address forms of experience Freud hesitated to consider religious—the "oceanic feeling," "reverence for external reality," and "reparation"—constructing projects that locate the psychological origins of these experiences in the child's earliest relationships with the mother. Many feminist theorists have found this approach promising because of its explicit attention to the significance of the mother in culture and psyche, and its inquiry into the dynamics of human relationality.[89] These scholars tend to find the maternal relationship benign and religion a positive force in human experience.

The Analytic Project: Matriphobia and Religion

A second group of scholars working with object relations theory also examines the maternal relation as the psychological source of religion, but, in contrast, finds fear and anxiety toward the mother at the core of religious phenomena, and discovers pathological or negative forms of religiosity. Naomi Goldenberg, for example, has developed a critical analysis of the psychological origins of religious asceticism in what Melanie Klein called "splitting." Klein had argued that the child experiences the world as a set of positive or negative sensations: when associated with pleasure these sensations are perceived as good and idealized as perfect; when accompanied by pain or discomfort, they are perceived as bad. Under stress, these sensations are separated from each other through fantasies of "splitting." In the child's fantasy the mother's breast is split into an idealized "good (nourishing) breast" and a "bad (withholding) breast." In Klein's analysis, the child, in fear and rage, launches sadistic attacks on "bad" objects such as the mother's withholding breast. Having projected its own sadistic feelings onto the mother, the child expects a reciprocal assault from the mother. Thus "the mother's body becomes a place filled with dangers which give rise to all sorts of terrors."[90] Drawing upon Klein's concepts of aggression, splitting, and fear of the maternal body, Goldenberg suggests, "Children tend to idealize parents in order to control their fear of them and anger toward them."[91] She links fear of parents and idealization of parents with the idealization of deities. In her view, "[H]ostility is often held at bay by more generalized forms of idealization of gods and goddesses . . . extreme idealization, such as insistence on the goodness of God, always masks a physical terror of a parent."[92]

In Goldenberg's Kleinian analysis, the notion of the distinction between body and soul is another manifestation of the dualism originating in splitting and idealization. If the domain of the spiritual, the soul, must remain pure, loving, and immortal, the body becomes the container for the contaminated, mortal, "sinful qualities of being human."[93] She argues, as we saw in her comments on Jung, that the theological consequence of this separation is that theistic religions have exacerbated the psychological consequences of splitting, promoting a hostility to life, to the body, and to women.

Inclusive and Analytic Projects in Tension: The Question of the Eucharist

These radically different object relational perspectives, one focusing on loving mothers and positive forms of religion; the other on terrifying maternal objects and religious pathologies, can be thrown into relief by an examination of three studies focusing on the same religious phenomenon: the Christian Eucharist. Utilizing different perspectives within object relations theory and the related methodology of self psychology, three groups of feminist scholars have developed contrasting interpretations of the psychological, cultural, and gender dynamics underlying the Mass.

In the first study, Mary Ellen Ross and Cheryl Lynn Ross, drawing upon Winnicott's notion of "transitional space" and anthropologist Victor Turner's notion of ritual liminality, have developed a theory of the Eucharist as an expression of themes involving nurturance, unification, and ludic liminality. Ross and Ross emphasize the playful, creative dimensions of ritual, suggesting that the Winnicottian "transitional space," the "potential space" between baby and mother, provides the psychological locus for the kind of experience offered by participation in the Eucharist.[94] Arguing that many aspects of ritual can be "comprehended within a psychoanalytic interpretation if such interpretation is extended to include the pre-Oedipal period of life, the period when the mother, not the father, is the critical figure,"[95] they show that the characteristics of the Mass "flow from what is essentially an experience of God as mother."[96]

If Ross and Ross expose the pre-Oedipal themes of nourishment and unification, William Beers, in the second study, offers a rather different analysis. Emphasizing the "sacrificial" nature of Eucharistic ritual, Beers draws upon Nancy Jay's sociological perspective, arguing that sacrifice functions both socially and psychologically to affirm male power and control over women.[97] The social context of sacrifice is patriliny: it is performed primarily by men, and it serves to maintain patrilineal kinship structures and to deny the value of maternal descent. Psychologically, Beers argues, sacrifice expresses male narcissistic anxiety originating in the earliest phases of mother-son interaction. Mothers treat sons as "others" or "objects" while they treat daughters as extensions of themselves. As a result, male infants experience the "omnipotent maternal self" as "other." They simultaneously desire and dread a merger with the mother; they develop rigid ego boundaries to differentiate themselves from the mother; and they are likely to feel anxiety or rage later in life when boundaries are threatened.

Sacrifice, in Beers's Kohutian analysis, provides a socially structured context in which archaic male rage and anxiety can be expressed in controlled performances of ritualized bloodshed, and in which male power and control over women is symbolically affirmed: "[T]he complex ritual violence performed by men is an ancient way for men to identify with each other as men and to separate from women."[98] The contemporary Christian Eucharistic sacrifice, in Beers's reading, functions psychologically and socially in the same way.

Kelley Raab, in the third study, finds feminist object relations theory useful in examining gender reversal in the Eucharist, especially in the role of the officiating priest. She argues that "in the case of the Eucharist we have a 'gender masquerade' or 'gender reversal' taking place in which men appropriate women's functions while prohibiting them from performing those functions."[99] She situates this gender reversal within the context of men's unconscious identification with women. Karen Horney's thesis that men feel envy toward women's capacity for pregnancy, childbirth, and lactation, and Melanie Klein's thesis that infants fear maternal functions, provide the foundations of her argument that "envy and fear of maternal capacities . . . provide primordial motivations for men's co-optation of female functions in the Eucharist and other blood sacrificial rituals."[100]

Raab develops an argument supportive of the ordination of women as priests, suggesting that when women function as priests officiating at the Eucharistic sacrifice they perform a radically transformative function for religion and for culture, deconstructing social structures and altering the symbolism of the liturgy. When women are celebrants, "pre-Oedipal themes, through a process of symbolic association, become more prominent . . . reestablish[ing] female genealogical structures through the mother and giv[ing] back to women their reproductive powers."[101]

These very different analyses illustrate clearly the major feminist approaches to the psychology of religion found in object relations theory Ross and Ross enact the affirmative, inclusive project of Women's Studies, uncovering benign maternal foundations for benign religious experience. Beers, in contrast, pursues the analytic project of Women's Studies through the exposure of terrifying maternal imagery beneath matriphobic religious experience. Ross and Ross discover a comforting mother at the source of the sense of a loving, nourishing God and a unitive Eucharistic ritual. Raab and Beers, on the other hand, assume an ambivalent relationship to the mother—especially for males. Raab's analysis focuses more specifically on male *envy* of maternal functions as a source of rituals of gender reversal, while Beers focuses on male *anxiety* over separation from and merger with a terrifying mother as a source of the exclusion of women from rituals of blood sacrifice.

For Ross and Ross, the Eucharist is something positive—its maternal origins redeem it. For Raab, the Eucharist can be positive—even transformative—but only when the celebrants include women. For Beers, on the other hand, the Eucharist is a pathological expression of deep cultural and psychological misogyny, even in the exceptional cases when women are the celebrants.[102]

In concluding this discussion of object relations theory in the study of religion, we can affirm that object relations theory has incorporated the methods and concerns developed within Women's Studies, applying those concerns to the study of religion and culture. The androcentrism of earlier theoretical perspectives is countered through inclusive projects in which, for example, God as mother is discovered as a subversive figure in the Mass and mysticism is found to have a maternal foundation. And analytic projects expose the misogynist foundations of cultural phenomena when, on the other hand, matriphobia is discovered as a dominant paradigm in the Mass and in ascetic practices and beliefs.[103] While the cultural and historical inquiry of the "psychology and religion movement" is not well represented in the literature within object relations theory,[104] the interpretive enterprise of the "psychology of religion proper" as we have seen, has flourished.

Poststructuralism, French Feminism, and the Psychological Study of Religion

In the 1970s, '80s, and '90s a group of methodologies, which can broadly be described as "poststructuralist," began to influence intellectual discourse— including Women's Studies and feminist studies—in the West. Rejecting claims to universal truths, the discourse of poststructuralism maintains a hermeneutic suspicious of "meta-narratives" or "master narratives."[105] It throws into question the notion of scholarly objectivity, the ideology of progress, and the search for origins characterizing much of intellectual discourse (including, of course, the psychological study of religion). It is critical and self-reflexive even about its own intellectual and analytic claims. Poststructuralism emphasizes the effects of power on knowledge, and, most important, it foregrounds the significance of language in shaping thought, gender, and culture. This approach thus constitutes a radical challenge to the foundational assumptions of scholarship in the twentieth century.

The writings of philosopher Jacques Derrida, historian Michel Foucault, and psychoanalyst Jacques Lacan have been particularly significant in shaping poststructuralist thought. Derrida's "deconstructive" project has critiqued the assumptions underlying the entire tradition of Western metaphysics, arguing that the metaphysical tradition is the prisoner of the idea of "being as presence," that is, the notion of "some anchor of being behind language which was its ultimate truth or referent." Everything, he argued, is "always already in the web of language."[106] In the work of Foucault, a new set of provocative questions were posed regarding the relations of power and knowledge in the construction of subjectivity and sexuality.[107] And Lacan brought a poststructuralist perspective to psychoanalysis, reading Freud through the lens of the linguistic theories of Ferdinand de Saussure. For Lacan the unconscious is "structured like a language"; gender is linguistically and culturally constructed; and lack, absence, or "otherness" structure the core of both subjectivity and the unconscious.[108]

The work of Lacan, Foucault, Derrida, and other poststructuralists has generated an immense quantity of discussion and debate within feminist theory, as within many other disciplines. Particularly significant in bringing poststructuralist concerns into feminist thought are three "French feminists," Julia Kristeva, Luce Irigaray, and Hélène Cixous.[109] These theorists, strongly influenced by Lacan, Foucault, and Derrida, are nevertheless critical of their perspectives in a number of ways.

In the last decade, "French feminist" and poststructuralist discourse has begun to influence Religious Studies, first through developments in theology, and more recently through developments in the psychological study of religion. While theological discourse has drawn upon, in particular Foucault, Lacan, Derrida, Kristeva, and Irigaray,[110] the psychological study of religion, to date, has drawn primarily, although not exclusively, upon the work of Julia Kristeva. I will discuss briefly some of Kristeva's contributions to the psychology of religion and some recent research in the field utilizing a Kristevan methodology. Again I have been selective: I've chosen a set of representative texts rather than attempting a comprehensive analysis of the literature.

Kristeva and the Inclusive Project of Women's Studies

A practicing analyst since 1979, Kristeva often writes from a psychoanalytic perspective, frequently addressing religious issues, images and documents without attempting to construct a systematic psychology of religion. Her texts "Stabat Mater," *Powers of Horror, In the Beginning Was Love, Tales of Love, Black Sun, Desire in Language, On Chinese Women,* and *Strangers to Ourselves* explore religion—primarily Christianity and Judaism—from a psychoanalytic perspective informed to a large degree, by poststructuralist feminism.

Her approach differs in subtle ways from the "origin theories" of Freud, Jung, and the object relations theorists. When she does seek the sources of religious ideas and practices in psychological experiences, she acknowledges the embeddedness of the psychological experiences themselves in language and culture: there is no absolute origin or source in Kristeva's analyses. Much of her work, rather than exploring origins, examines the *effects* of religion on the psyche. Her essay "Stabat Mater," for example, examines the efficacy of the symbolism of the Virgin Mary in providing a unified vision of meaning, ethics, and aesthetics for Christianity.[111] She analyzes religious discourse on motherhood and assesses the effect of this discourse on women and men in the West. She is fully aware of the problematic dimensions of this endeavor for feminism: she acknowledges the splitting or division of the figure of woman in Marian doctrine wherein the Virgin Mary is split into a maternal figure and a virginal figure, and sex is separated from both the maternal and from death. But her texts do not mount an indictment of Christianity or Mariology. Rather, they enact an analysis of the psychological and cultural significance of these split images of woman.

Kristeva's work constitutes an important inquiry into the possibilities for human ethics and relationality through the investigation of the category of otherness. Some of her work seems to locate the possibility of relationality in the connection to the mother—or in the "maternal metaphor." *In the Beginning was Love: Psychoanalysis and Faith,* for example, explores the source of both religious faith and psychoanalytic healing in the pre-Oedipal relationality of the mother-child dyad, and "Stabat Mater" seeks a "heretical ethics" in the maternal relation.[112] Other writings, however, seem to locate the possibility for an ethics of otherness and relationality within psychoanalysis itself. Kristeva finds psychoanalysis invaluable—even salvific—not only as a method of cultural analysis, but also as a therapeutic technique and as a tool for cultural transmutation. By offering a praxis whereby the internal Otherness of the self is encountered (although never fully known), psychoanalysis makes possible a form of relationality within which new possibilities unfold for the recognition of the "otherness" of *l'étranger*—the stranger or the foreigner.[113]

Although Kristeva's relational concerns link her work to that of the object relations theorists, her linguistic emphasis differentiates her from them and situates her among the poststructuralists. While she seeks the raw material of religious faith and the potential for psychoanalytic cure through the transference relationship in the earliest human experiences of love "close to the maternal container," she underscores the fact that this "originary" maternal love is "always already" in language. Language and culture precede us.[114]

Kristeva and the Analytic Project of Women's Studies

If the aforementioned Kristevan texts contribute to the inclusive project of Women's Studies, the analytic project of feminism is also well represented in Kristeva's work. Her *Powers of Horror,* for example, undertakes an analysis of the maternal mytheme underlying the sense of the sacred and informing the structure of religious ritual. Kristeva argues, in an inversion of Freud's classic formulation in *Totem and Taboo,* that what religion represses is not a primal parricide but a primal abhorrence of the mother. She examines the confrontation with the maternal, the "coming face to face with the unnamable,"[115] the "abject" at the base of all religions. She discovers this sense of the abject in religious rituals of defilement and purification and in notions of the sacred: "the function of these religious rituals is to ward off the subject's fear of his very own identity sinking irretrievably into the mother . . . risking the loss not of a part (castration) but of the totality of his living being."[116] Thus, Kristeva, in an analysis parallel to Beers's and Goldenberg's, discovers the "matriphobia" underlying certain religious ideologies, and interrogates religious practices and ideas, finding abjection, abhorrence of the maternal, and fear of the generative and destructive powers of the mother underlying conceptions of sacrality, ritual purification, and sin.

Kristeva pursues a similar analytic project in *Black Sun: Depression and Melancholia,* which contains a discussion of the power and ubiquity of religious images of death as feminine. Rather than a hermeneutic of suspicion or critique, however, she maintains toward this image simply a hermeneutic of analysis, arguing that "the feminine as an image of death is an imaginary safety catch for the matricidal drive that, without such a representation, would pulverize me into melancholia if it did not drive me to crime."[117] Thus, she seeks to analyze and understand, not to challenge and critique.

Kristeva's relationship to religion, to feminism, and to psychoanalysis is often debated.[118] Some have seen her as an apologist for Christianity; others see her as a critic of Christianity. Some have accused her of being an opponent of feminism; others see her as unambiguously feminist. Some claim she stands outside of psychoanalysis; others see her as an uncritical proselyte for psychoanalytic therapy. These critiques need to be taken seriously by scholars who seek to utilize her work in the psychological study of religion. Nevertheless, I think her theories offer productive new paths for the field.[119]

Perspectives on Kristeva from within the Psychology of Religion

Kristeva's thought has inspired several recent studies within the psychology of religion. One collection of essays on her work, *Body/Text in Julia Kristeva: Religion, Women, and Psychoanalysis,* contains provocative new perspectives on Kristeva's feminist psychoanalytic approach to religion. These essays investigate a number of themes within Kristeva's work: metaphor and the figure of the mother in "Stabat Mater" is analyzed in one text;[120] another describes Kristeva's account of narcissism, the triadic foundation of subjectivity, and the implications of this triadic structure for an explication of Christianity.[121] A Kristevan analysis of sacrifice, violence, and the sacred is contrasted with René Girard's formulation;[122] and Kristeva's notion of the "chora" is taken up from the perspective of postmodern ethics.[123] Other essays deal with the role of the imagination in religious discourse and in prayer in Kristeva and Aquinas,[124] with Kristevan *jouissance* in the religious practices of Voodoo,[125] and with parallels in Kristeva's, Freud's, Winnicott's, and Lacan's associations of the feminine with otherness and with death.[126]

If these Kristevan forays into "Religion, Women, and Psychoanalysis" exemplify the impact of new methodologies in Women's Studies on the psychology of religion, they also exemplify the impact of poststructuralist thinking on feminism and on the study of religion. In these essays, and in Kristeva's work, the subject is as likely to be female as male, and at the same time, the notion of subjectivity itself is thrown into question. The gendering of epistemological and cultural categories is explicitly investigated, while the construction of gender is questioned. The significance of the mother—both as feared object and as loved object—is foregrounded; the devaluation of the mother is continually interrogated; and the cultural and religious construction of the notion of motherhood is brought to the surface. Religious ideas and practices are examined for their psychological sources and for their psychological effects upon women and men, and upon culture and society. At the same time, the obsession with origins—both individual and historical—is thrown into question.[127] Feminism itself is interrogated; while misogyny is critiqued and an egalitarian vision is maintained as an ideal, the tendency of feminism to make universal claims to truth and knowledge and to frame itself as an unassailable ideology with "religious dimensions"[128] is exposed. These Kristevan projects pursue the inclusive and analytic projects initiated by Women's Studies, asking new kinds of questions—questions shaped by poststructuralism as well as by feminism—about the paradoxes of gender, culture, religion, and the unconscious.

Possibilities for Poststructuralist Inquiries into the "Psychology and Religion" Movement

These promising inquiries represent provocative new approaches for the "psychology *of* religion." While most of the research in this area has neglected the cultural and historical emphasis of the "psychology *and* religion movement" in favor of the "psychology *of* religion proper," it seems to me that Kristeva's work, and the work of other poststructuralist feminists, may provide rich material for cultural and historical analyses of modernity, "postmodernity," and secularization. Kristeva's *Strangers to Ourselves*, for example, takes a broad view of politics and society, examining, in the context of an inquiry into Western attitudes toward foreigners, the influence of psychoanalysis upon culture. I anticipate that new studies in the field will continue to draw upon the work of Kristeva, and will find rich resources in the writings of other poststructuralist feminists as well.[129] I anticipate, in addition, studies developing the insights of Lacan and Foucault in the service of feminist analytic projects in both the fields of the "psychology *of* religion" and "psychology *and* religion." In my view this area represents a vibrant new direction for the psychological study of religion, a direction which integrates this discipline into the dynamic conversations taking place throughout the academy.

Conclusion

In this discussion of the influence of Women's Studies on the psychological approaches to religion, we've examined two "enterprises," four "methodologies," and three "projects." The two enterprises we've referred to as the "psychology *of* religion proper" and the "psychology *and* religion movement." The first pursues interpretations of religious phenomena utilizing the methodological perspectives of psychology; the second emphasizes historical and cultural connections between psychology and religion, and inquires into the process of modernization and secularization. The four psychological methodologies described here—Freudian, Jungian, object relational, and poststructuralist psychoanalytic—have been the sites upon which or the tools with which these enterprises have been pursued. The three "projects" include the critical, the inclusive, and the analytic projects of Women's Studies. Both of the enterprises in the psychological approach to religion (and all four methodologies) have been shaped by the projects of Women's Studies.

One caveat is appropriate here. Framing our question in terms of the impact of Women's Studies upon the psychological study of religion implies that forces and influences have unidirectional effects; that is, that Women's Studies has enacted the impacting while the psychological study of religion has experienced the impact. It is important to note that this formulation of the issue constructs a simplified version of impact and influence. What is lost in this construction is its reversal: the question of the impact or influence of psychological methodologies upon Women's Studies. Reframing the issue to allow the emergence of multidirectional influences, one discovers, as we saw in the case of poststructuralist feminism, that the kinds of questions asked by scholars within Women's Studies have been shaped to a significant degree by psychoanalytic inquiries into gender, culture, and psyche. If the psychological study of religion has developed new methodologies, approaches and projects under the influence of Women's Studies, Women's Studies has, in turn, developed new methodologies, approaches, and projects under the influence of psychoanalysis, object relations theory, poststructuralist theory, and arguably Jungian theory. Two brief examples will suffice: the gender analyses so productive for Women's Studies research in the psychological study of religion are, in a sense, a product of the influence of psychoanalytic theories of gender and gender development upon Women's Studies. Similarly, the critical project of Women's Studies has developed, under the influence of psychoanalytic attention to subtle cultural forces and unconscious symbol systems, a sharper acuity, capable of perceiving subtle and unconscious forms of androcentrism, and a vocabulary with which to enter the debate.

The Projects of Women's Studies in the "Psychology of Religion"

We've seen that the "psychology of religion proper," especially in its Freudian variant, was initially subjected to a thorough critique by scholars in Women's Studies. Focusing on his androcentrism, scholars attacked Freud for writing women out of culture by privileging the "father relation," for assuming male normativity, and for constructing a theory of culture, religion, and morality in which women are biologically, intellectually, and morally deficient. Jung was attacked as well for constructing an archetypal theory of religion that subtly promoted female inferiority and assumed male normativity. While object relations theory and poststructuralist psychoanalytic theory have not escaped feminist critique, they do seem to offer alternatives to the androcentrism of Freud and Jung. These approaches have been particularly open to the inclusive project of Women's Studies. Object relations theorists, for example, have examined the pre-Oedipal, maternal matrix of religious experience and religious phenomena, while feminist poststructuralist psychoanalytic theorists have problematized gender and motherhood in religious discourse.

Other studies in the psychology of religion, examining the sources of misogyny and the construction of gender, clearly exemplify the analytic project of Women's Studies. Representative of this analytic project are, for example, gender analyses focusing on concepts of death and homoeroticism in Freud's theory of religion; object relational studies of matriphobia underlying rituals of sacrifice; and poststructuralist studies of matricide within concepts of the sacred. Thus, Freudian, Jungian, object relational, and poststructuralist psychologies of religion have all adopted the critical, inclusive, and analytic projects of Women's Studies, becoming, in a sense, feminist psychologies of religion.

It is important to note at this juncture an absence or bias in the literature of Women's Studies and the psychology of religion: the focus of research remains predominantly Western. Most of the literature examines Christianity. While Judaism receives some attention, other religions are virtually ignored. Ironically, a rich discourse on religion, gender, and psychology in the context of Islam, Hinduism, and other religions has been developed within the field of Psychological Anthropology—yet this literature, much of which is feminist in orientation, is relatively unknown to scholars in Religious Studies. Katherine Ewing's psychoanalytic inquiry into Pakistani women's lives in "Can Psychoanalytic Theories Explain the Pakistani Woman? Intrapsychic Autonomy and Interpersonal Engagement in the Extended Family," and Fatna Sabbah's *Woman in the Muslim Unconscious* are just two examples of this important literature, which could greatly enrich the perspective of feminists within the psychology of religion by enacting a turn away from the traditional Eurocentrism of the field.[130]

The Projects of Women's Studies and the "Psychology and Religion Movement"

The second major enterprise in the discipline, the analysis of culture, secularization, and religion in the "psychology and religion movement," shows the effects of Women's Studies to a lesser degree than the first enterprise, the "psychology of religion." The possibilities for such a critique, however, are manifold.[131] And, with certain notable exceptions, this enterprise as well remains inattentive to non-Western cultures and religions.[132]

Some recent work in the "psychology and religion movement" is moving in the direction of the inclusive project of Women's Studies. One of the ways the psychology and religion movement has pursued an analysis of secularization is by examining the religious backgrounds of major thinkers. Several studies suggest that many of the early psychologists developed their theories as replacements for the religious world views they had lost or abandoned.[133] Although most of the formative thinkers in the development of psychology were male, there were a number of significant women in the movement: Melanie Klein, Karen Horney, Lou Andreas-Salomé, and Sabina Spielrein, for example. An examination of these women's lives, ideas, and religious backgrounds may well represent a significant contribution to the area of psychology and religion in its formulation of a theory of secularization. This sort of project may represent an important contribution to the inclusive project of Women's Studies as well. Kerr's recent discussion of Jung, Freud, and Sabina Spielrein is a major step in this "inclusive" direction.

The analytic project of Women's Studies has flourished within the "psychology and religion movement" by posing important questions about secularization and the gendering of Judaism. Gilman and Geller explore Freud's attempt to "masculinize" secular (scientific) Judaism and to renounce "feminized" (religious) Judaism; Van Herik explores Freud's rejection of "feminine" religion, his attempt to construct a secular "masculine" rationality, and his location of the ethics of Judaism within the territory of renunciatory "masculinity." This sort of gender analysis, best articulated in studies of Freud, might be pursued farther in studies of originative psychologists working within other methodologies and traditions, in efforts to bring together in new ways the analytic project of Women's Studies and the hermeneutic project of the psychology and religion movement. In addition, as noted above, the work of the poststructuralist thinkers may provide rich material for cultural and historical analyses of modernity and "postmodernity" from a feminist perspective.

Earlier in this chapter I noted that the three projects of Women's Studies are constantly in need of repetition. Let me reiterate this point: we cannot assume that the tasks of critique (the naming of androcentrism), inclusion (the rediscovery of women's lives and experiences), or analysis (the interpretation of gender and misogyny in culture) are ever completed. Like the interminable task of Sisyphus, the projects of Women's Studies need to be constantly reinitiated in classrooms, curricula, and research. Even the flourishing of feminist scholarship within the psychological study of religion is, in a sense, only a beginning. The two major enterprises within the psychological approach to religion have both embraced the methods and concerns of Women's Studies. But as long as androcentrism, misogyny, and the exclusion of women still characterize culture, religion, and the academy, the Sisyphean efforts of scholars in Women's Studies must and will continue.

Notes

1. An earlier version of this chapter appeared in "Analysts, Critics and Inclusivists: Feminist Voices in the Psychology of Religion," in *Religion*

and Psychology: Mapping the Terrain, eds. Diane Jonte-Pace and William Parsons (New York: Routledge Press, 2001), 129–146. I thank the publisher for permission to revise and reprint material from the chapter. I am greatly indebted to my research assistants Stephanie Shindler and Alexis Strachan whose efficient, thorough, and clear-sighted efforts aided immeasurably in the completion of this project. I am grateful to my colleagues Marilyn Edelstein and Mary Hegland of Santa Clara University for commenting on an earlier draft. Thanks are due as well to Mary Ellen Ross, Roy Steinhoff Smith, and Kelley Raab for their comments. I would also like to thank Santa Clara University for providing funding in the form of Presidential Research Grants in 1993 and 1994.

2. See Peter Homans, "The Psychology and Religion Movement," *Encyclopedia of Religion* 12 (1987): 66–74. Homans describes three sorts of interactions between religion and psychology: the psychology of religion, the dialogue between theology and psychology, and psychology and religion proper. I've modified Homans's categories and terminology slightly. For the sake of simplicity, I will usually refer to the entire field as "the psychological study of religion." The two major branches or "enterprises" will be referred to as "the psychology of religion proper" and "the psychology and religion movement."

Peter Homans is a major thinker in the "psychology and religion movement." As Susan Henking notes, Homans "provides a framework for understanding secularization and modernization—a framework rooted in the notions of deidealization and the creation of meaning. The making of psychoanalysis for Homans models a much broader human phenomenon: it refers to mourning and memorialization, the loss of ideals and cultural values, the ways in which all change is rooted in and builds upon loss" (Susan Henking, "Placing the Social Sciences: Cases at the Intersection of the Histories of Disciplines and Religions," *Religious Studies Review* 19 [1993]: 116–126).

3. See, for example, Donald Capps, Lewis Rambo, and Paul Ransohoff, *The Psychology of Religion: A Guide to Information Sources* (Detroit: Gale Research Co., 1976); Hendrika Vande Kemp, with H. Newton Malony, *Psychology and Theology in Western Thought 1672–1965: A Historical and Annotated Bibliography* (Millwood, N.Y.: Kraus International Publications, 1984); David Wulff, *Psychology of Religion: Classic and Contemporary Views* (New York: Wiley, 1991). Wulff's textbook includes chapters not only on Freud, Jung, and Object Relations Theory, but also on Biological Foundations of Religion, Behavioral and Comparative Theories, Religion in the Laboratory, The Correlation Study of Religion, The German Descriptive Tradition, The American Humanistic Synthesis, William James, and Erik Erikson. These "subfields" of religious studies have been only minimally impacted by Women's Studies, although Erikson shares a great deal with the inclusivist object relations theorists in his attention to the child's relation to the mother. See also

Bonnie Miller-McLemore, "Shaping the Future of Religion and Psychology: Feminist Transformations in Pastoral Theology," in *Religion and Psychology,* eds. Diane Jonte-Pace and William Parsons (New York: Routledge, 2001), 181–201.

4. In my use of these terms, "feminist" methodologies and "Women's Studies" methodologies are roughly equivalent.

5. Jane Gallop, "Feminism and Harassment Policy," *Academe* (Sept.-Oct. 1994): 16.

6. I'm drawing upon Peggy McIntosh, "Interactive Phases of Curricular Revision: A Feminist Perspective" (Working Paper 124) Wellesley College, Wellesley, Mass., 1983; Margaret L. Anderson, "Changing the Curriculum in Higher Education," *Signs* (1987): 222–254, Ellen Carol Du Bois et al., *Feminist Scholarship: Kindling in the Groves of Academe* (Urbana: University of Illinois Press, 1985); bell hooks, *Talking Back: Thinking Feminist Thinking Black* (Boston: South End Press, 1989) and *Yearning: Race, Gender, and Cultural Politics* (Boston: South End Press, 1990); Vivian P. Makosky and Michele A. Paludi, "Feminism and Women's Studies in the Academy," in *Foundations for a Feminist Restructuring of the Academic Disciplines,* ed. Michele A. Paludi and Gertrude A. Steuernagel (New York: Harrington Park Press, 1990), 1–37; and others in this discussion. See McIntosh for a five-phase model of curriculum change; see Anderson for a discussion of curricular change in higher education; see Du Bois et al. for a discussion of the tensions between feminist scholarship emphasizing women as victims and feminist scholarship emphasizing women as active agents; see bell hooks for a discussion of racism, feminism, and pedagogy.

7. Du Bois et al., 15–16.

8. McIntosh, 3.

9. Mary F. Belenky et al., *Women's Ways of Knowing: The Development of Self, Voice, and Mind* (New York: Basic Books, 1986).

10. Cited in Rebecca Chopp, "From Patriarchy into Freedom: A Conversation between American Feminist Theology and French Feminism," in *Transfigurations: Theology and the French Feminists,* ed. C. W. Maggie Kim, Susan M. St. Ville, and Susan M. Simonaitis (Minneapolis: Fortress, 1993), 38.

11. Ibid.

12. Carol P. Christ, "Feminists—Sojourners in the Field of Religious Studies," in *The Knowledge Explosion,* ed. Cheris Kramarae and Dale Spender (New York: Teachers' College Press, 1992), 87.

13. Psychological approaches to religion are seen, on the one hand, as suspect, hostile toward religion, and potentially destructive to faith. On the other hand, they are seen as excessively faith-oriented, "soft," and unscholarly. Among academic psychologists the psychological study of religion is often seen as a fairly marginal branch of the field.

14. See Randi R. Warne, "Toward a Brave New Paradigm: The Impact of Women's Studies in Religious Studies," *Religious Studies and Theology* (1989): 35–46, who points out that Religious Studies has always had its own insider/outsider debate and thus is uniquely disposed toward a resonance with some of the concerns of Women's Studies, including the critique of false objectivity and the acknowledgment of subjective positionality as a hermeneutical stance.

15. Sigmund Freud, *The Standard Edition (SE) of the Complete Psychological Works of Sigmund Freud*, trans. J. Strachey. Vol. 6 (London: Hogarth Press, 1953–1964), 258 and Vol. 11, 123. Hereafter cited as SE followed by volume and page numbers.

16. *SE* 6, 258–259.

17. His cultural writings are well known: *Totem and Taboo, The Future of an Illusion, Civilization and Its Discontents,* and *Moses and Monotheism* are considered classics in the psychoanalytic theory of religion. But the lesser-known writing on individual religious experience also comprise a rich body of literature. These include essays on Leonardo da Vinci and on Dostoevsky, a case history of one of Freud's patients, the "Wolf Man," a short analysis of a crisis of faith of an American doctor, and two analyses of texts recounting religious visions: *Psychoanalytic Notes on an Autobiographical Account of Paranoia* (the "Schreber Case") and *A Seventeenth Century Demonological Neurosis.*

18. Because Freud's work has evoked such an immense response from scholars in Women's Studies, I will devote more attention to this section of the chapter than to other sections. A great deal of debate over the legacy of Freud has occurred in feminist theory, literary theory, critical theory, political theory, philosophy, psychology, and other fields. Much of this literature has been influential for scholars within the psychological study of religion. While I will not discuss this larger body of literature, I do want to emphasize the fact that interdisciplinary dialogue and debate characterizes this field. Because research in Women's Studies crosses the boundaries of traditional disciplines, the fields influenced by Women's Studies have likewise become more fluid.

19. I am indebted to Judith Van Herik for this triadic formulation of Freud's androcentrism. See Judith Van Herik, *Freud on Femininity and Faith* (Berkeley: University of California Press, 1982), 29–39.

20. Ibid., 31.

21. *SE* 21, 191, emphasis mine.

22. Although some of his later work inquired into the differences between the girl's and the boy's experience of the Oedipus complex, in most of his writing Freud focused on the unconscious fantasies and desires of the male child.

23. Wulff, *Psychology of Religion,* 280. In addition, Freud's inattention to the pre-Oedipal period, and particularly to the pre-Oedipal mother, is

well known. (See however the discussion below of Object Relations Theory for a depiction of feminist work on pre-Oedipal issues in religion.)

24. Van Herik, *Freud on Femininity and Faith*, 31.

25. *SE* 19, 257.

26. The "phallocentrism" of this argument has been widely noted by critics of Freud. The penis, in Freud's view, is crucial in cultural and moral development. Women's relationship to this organ is formulated in terms of lack or absence: the female experiences "penis envy" and the male, when he realizes the girl's lack of a penis, experiences castration anxiety. Some of the earliest debates over Freud's theory of gender emerged over these issues.

27. *SE* 19, 37. See also *Civilization and Its Discontents* where women appear as the enemies of culture. Less capable of renunciation and sublimation, women "come into opposition to civilization and display their retarding and restraining influence. . . . [T]he work of civilization has become increasingly the business of men, it confronts them with ever more difficult tasks and compels them to carry out instinctual sublimations of which women are little capable." *SE* 21, 103.

28. Philip Rieff, *Freud: The Mind of the Moralist* (Chicago: University of Chicago Press, 1979), 181.

29. Ibid., 182.

30. Juliet Mitchell, *Psychoanalysis and Feminism* (New York: Random House, 1974).

31. Van Herik, *Freud on Femininity and Faith*, 16.

32. Ibid., 200. Among the scholars who have developed gender analyses grounded in Freud's theory of religion are Howard Eilberg-Schwartz (*God's Phallus and Other Problems for Men and Monotheism* [Boston: Beacon Press, 1994]); Naomi Goldenberg (*Returning Words to Flesh: Feminism, Psychoanalysis, and the Resurrection of the Body* [Boston: Beacon Press, 1990]); Diane Jonte-Pace ("Maternal Absence, Castration, and the End of the World: A Freudian Reading of the Notion of Self as Endangered Species," in *The Endangered Self*, ed. D. Capps and R. Fenn [Princeton: Center for Religion, Self, and Society, Monograph 2, 1992], 115–128); Jay Geller ("[G]nos[e]ology: The Cultural Construction of the Other," in *People of the Body: Jews and Judaism from an Embodied Perspective*, ed. Howard Eilberg-Schwartz [Albany: State University of New York Press, 1992] and "A Paleontological View of Freud's Study of Religion: Unearthing the Leitfossil Circumcision," *Modern Judaism* 13 [1993]: 49–70); Marianna Torgovnick (*Gone Primitive: Savage Intellects, Modern Lives* [Chicago: University of Chicago Press, 1990]); and Sander Gilman (*Freud, Race, and Gender* [Princeton: Princeton University Press, 1993]).

33. Diane Jonte-Pace, "Situating Kristeva Differently: Psychoanalytic Readings of Woman and Religion," in *Body/Text in Julia Kristeva: Religion,*

Women, Psychoanalysis, ed. David Crownfield (Albany: State University of New York Press, 1992), 15. See also Diane Jonte-Pace, "At Home in the Uncanny: Freudian Representations of Death, Mothers, and the Afterlife," *Journal of the American Academy of Religion* 64 (1996): 61–88, and *Speaking the Unspeakable: Religion, Misogyny, and the Uncanny Mother in Freud's Cultural Texts* (Berkeley: University of California Press, 2001).

34. Howard Eilberg-Schwartz, "Homoeroticism and the Father God: An Unthought in Freud's *Moses and Monotheism,*" *American Imago* 51 (1994): 127–159. See also Eli Sagan, *Freud, Women, and Morality* (New York: Basic Books, 1988), in which Sagan reveals contradictory formulations of the origins of conscience in Freud's case studies and metapsychological texts. The metapsychological texts locate the origins of the superego in the father-son tension of the Oedipus complex, especially in the father's castrative threats toward the son. But, Sagan contends, the case studies reveal a different theoretical formulation: conscience emerges out of the relationship with the mother in a sense of human relationality and reciprocity. Insights Freud developed could not be integrated into his Oedipal theoretical framework and were thus suppressed.

See also Madelon Sprengnether, *The Spectral Mother: Freud, Feminisim, and Psychoanalysis* (Ithaca: Cornell University Press, 1990). Sprengnether's major focus is on the displacement and denial of the figure of the mother in Freud's life and thought. She inquires as well into the notion of matriarchy and its role in the evolution of culture and religion in Freud's writings. She shows that "[m]atriarchy, as representative of a developmental stage (in the individual as well as in culture) in which the mother-infant relationship supersedes the Oedipus complex, remains unintegrated into Freud's evolutionary scheme, threatening to disrupt it from within" (86).

She exposes the contradictions between Freud's assumptions about the developmental inferiority of the pre-Oedipal and his attempts in *Totem and Taboo* and *Moses and Monotheism* to project the Oedipal scenario into the origins of culture, religion, and morality. "His struggles to incorporate matriarchy and mother goddesses in his system of cultural and religious progress attest to the fascination she holds for him as well as the threat she embodies to his construction of patriarchal authority and the Oedipal masculinity on which it rests." Sprengnether reveals "subversive" contents within Freud's texts. Freud is led again and again to an analysis of the pre-Oedipal mother and to an analysis of cultural periods of matriarchy but his Oedipal theoretical framework cannot accommodate this material. She argues that this subversive material unsettles "the smooth system of hierarchies which maintains the superiority of patriarchy to matriarchy, and Oedipal to pre-Oedipal development, as reflected in the ascendance of civilization over nature" (118).

35. Eilberg-Schwartz, "Homoeroticism," 130.

36. Ibid., 138.

37. Ibid., 135. See also Eilberg-Schwartz's feminist psychoanalytic biblical interpretation in *God's Phallus*. Other biblical scholars who have found feminist and psychoanalytic interpretive perspectives useful in textual hermeneutics are Ilona N. Rashkow (*The Phallacy of Genesis: A Feminist-Psychoanalytic Approach* [Literary Currents in Biblical Interpretation] [Louisville: Westminster/Knox, 1993) and Mieke Bal (*Death and Dissymmetry* [Chicago: University of Chicago Press, 1988]). See Gananath Obeysekere, *Medusa's Hair: An Essay on Personal Symbols and Religious Experience* (Chicago: University of Chicago Press, 1981) for the work of a psychoanalytic anthropologist attentive to gender.

38. See for example David Bakan, *Sigmund Freud and the Jewish Mystical Tradition* (Boston: Beacon Press, 1958); Susan Handelman, *The Slayers of Moses: The Emergence of Rabbinical Interpretation in Modern Literary Theory* (Albany: State University of New York Press, 1982); Yosef Hayim Yerushalmi, *Freud's Moses: Judaism Terminable and Interminable* (New Haven: Yale University Press, 1991), Dennis Klein, *Jewish Origins of the Psychoanalytic Movement* (Chicago: University of Chicago Press, 1985), and Peter Homans, *The Ability to Mourn: Disillusionment and the Social Origins of Psychoanalysis* (Chicago: University of Chicago Press, 1989).

39. Geller, "(G)nos(e)ology" and "A Paleontological View."

40. Diane Jonte-Pace, "Analysts, Critics, and Inclusivists: Feminist Voices in the Psychology of Religion," 132.

41. Estelle Roith, *The Riddle of Freud: Jewish Influences on His Theory of Female Sexuality* (London: Tavistock, 1987), 3.

42. Ibid., 136.

43. Gilman, *Freud, Race, and Gender,* 7

44. Ibid., 206, note 11. See also Daniel Boyarin, *Unheroic Conduct: The Rise of Heterosexuality and the Invention of the Jewish Man* (Berkeley: University of California Press, 1997).

45. Ibid., 10

46. See, for example, hooks, *Talking Back* and *Yearning;* Cherrie Moraga and Gloria Anzaldua, eds., *This Bridge Called My Back: Writings by Radical Women of Color* (New York: Kitchen Table: Women of Color Press, 1981); National Council for Research on Women, *Mainstreaming Minority Women's Studies Programs* (1991).

47. See Lisa Appignanesi and John Forrester, *Freud's Women* (New York: HarperCollins, 1992). Sabina Spielrein, Lou Andreas-Salomé, Helene Deutsch, Marie Bonaparte, Melanie Klein, Karen Horney, Hilda Doolittle (H.D.), and of course the psychoanalyst's own daughter Anna Freud are the best known of these figures.

48. See, for example, Jeffrey Masson, *The Complete Letters of Sigmund Freud to Wilhelm Fliess: 1887–1904,* ed. and trans. Jeffrey Moussaieff Masson (Cambridge: Harvard University Press, 1985), 271–272; Roith, *The Riddle of Freud;* Paul Vitz, *Sigmund Freud's Christian Unconscious* (New York: Guilford, 1988); Samuel Slipp, *The Freudian Mystique: Freud, Women, and Feminism* (New York: New York University Press, 1993).

49. Homans, *The Ability to Mourn,* 99–100.

50. See Jonte-Pace, "At Home in the Uncanny," and *Speaking the Unspeakable.*

51. See Jonte-Pace "Analysts, Critics, and Inclusivists" for a different formulation of this material.

52. Christianity is Jung's major focus, although he directs attention to Judaism, ancient religions, tribal religions, and Eastern religions, as well. In his approach to Christianity he was as interested in the heretical, repressed traditions (gnosticism and alchemy, for example) as in traditional doctrines.

53. Carl G. Jung, *The Collected Works (CW) of C. G Jung,* ed. H. Read et al., trans. R. F. C. Hull (Princeton: Princeton University Press, 1953–1980), 9.1, 3–41. Hereafter cited as *CW* followed by volume number and page number.

54. See Jung, *Archetypes of the Collective Consciousness, CW* 9.1.

55. Jung, *Psychology and Religion, CW* 11.

56. Jung, *Answer to Job, CW* 11, 464.

57. Jung's writings are ambiguous regarding the incorporation of matter, evil, and the feminine into the new understanding of Trinity. Philp asks Jung in an interview if this formulation wouldn't constitute a five- or six-figured figure, rather than a quaternity. See Howard Littleton Philp, *Jung and the Problem of Evil* (London: Rockliff, 1958).

58. Erich Neumann, *The Great Mother: An Analysis of the Archetype* (Princeton: Princeton University Press, 1972).

59. Joan Chamberlain Engelsman, *The Feminine Dimension of the Divine* (Philadelphia: Westminster Press, 1979), 41.

60. These include Mary Esther Harding, *Women's Mysteries, Ancient and Modern* (New York: Pantheon, 1935), Neumann, *The Great Mother;* Christine Downing, *Women's Mysteries: Toward a Poetics of Gender* (New York: Crossroad, 1992); Nor Hall, *The Moon and the Virgin: Reflections on the Archetypal Feminine* (New York: Harper, 1980); Jean Shinoda Bolen, *Goddesses in Everywoman: A New Psychology of Women* (San Francisco: Harper, 1984); Ann Bedford Ulanov, *The Feminine in Jungian Psychology and in Christian Theology* (Evanston: Northwestern University Press, 1971) and *Receiving Woman: Studies in the Psychology and Theology of the Feminine* (Philadelphia: Westminster Press, 1981); and others.

61. Engelsman, *The Feminine Dimension of the Divine,* 132–133.

62. Ibid., 156.

63. Naomi Goldenberg, "Jung after Feminism," in *Beyond Androcentrism: New Essays on Women and Religion*, ed. Rita Gross (Missoula, Mont.: Scholars Press, 1977), 57–58.

64. Ibid., 66. See Erich Neumann, *The Origins and History of Consciousness* (Princeton: Princeton University Press, 1954) for an example of the Jungian association of masculinity, development, civilization, and consciousness.

65. Goldenberg, *Returning Words to Flesh*, 17.

66. Ibid., 75.

67. Ibid., 99–100. On Jung and antisemitism, see also Aryeh Maidenbaum and Stephen A. Martin, eds., *Lingering Shadows: Jungians, Freudians, and Anti-Semitism* (Boston: Shambala Press, 1991); and Gilman, *Freud, Race, and Gender.*

68. Demaris S. Wehr, *Jung and Feminism: Liberating Archetypes* (Boston: Beacon Press, 1987), 120.

69. Ibid., 25.

70. Jung and some of his disciples, however, were interested in the dark and destructive manifestations of the "terrible mother" archetype. This focus in Jungian work might prove a useful starting point for further analysis.

71. See Peter Homans, *Jung in Context* (Chicago: University of Chicago Press, 1979), which does bring Jung into the cultural and historical discourse of the "psychology and religion movement."

72. For a discussion of this relationship see, for example, Ferne Jensen, ed., *C. G. Jung, Emma Jung, and Toni Wolff: A Collection of Remembrances* (San Francisco: Analytical Psychology Club of San Francisco, 1982); Barbara Hannah, *Jung: His Life and Work: A Biograghical Memoir* (New York: Putnam, 1976); Paul Stern, *C. G. Jung: The Haunted Prophet* (New York: George Braziller, 1976); and Vincent Brome, *Jung: Man and Myth* (New York: Atheneum, 1981).

73. Antonia Wolff, "Einfuhrung in die Grundlagen der komplexen Psychologie," in *Studien zu C. G. Jungs Psychologie* (Zurich, 1959). Wolff's work has been significant for Nor Hall, Mary Esther Harding, and many other Jungian theorists.

74. See John Kerr, *A Most Dangerous Method: The Story of Jung, Freud, and Sabina Spielrein* (New York: Knopf, 1993). Between 1907 and 1913 Jung and Freud enjoyed an intimate friendship and collaboration, which has been examined in numerous books and essays. Kerr has revealed the role of Sabrina Spielrein in this relationship.

75. Freud, *SE* 21, 226.

76. See for example Harry Guntrip, *Personality and Human Interaction* (London: Hogarth, 1961); W. D. R. Fairbairn, "Observations in Defense of the Object Relations Theory of the Personality," *British Journal of Medical*

Psychology 28 (1955): 144–156; Melanie Klein, *The Psychoanalysis of Children* (New York: Delacorte Press, 1975); Ana-Maria Rizzuto, *the Birth of the Living God: A Psychoanalytic Study* (Chicago: University of Chicago Press, 1979); D. W. Winnicott, "Transitional Objects and Transitional Phenomena," *International Journal of Psycho-analysis* 34 (1953): 89–97 and *Playing and Reality* (New York: International Universities Press, 1971); and Heinz Kohut, *The Analysis of the Self* (New York: International Universities Press, 1971). Kohut is a "self psychologist" or theorist of narcissism, rather than an "object relations theorist." However, his ideas are closely related to those of the object relations theorists.

77. See John McDargh, *Psychoanalytic Object Relations Theory and the Study of Religion: On Faith and the Imaging of God* (Lanham, Md.: University Press of America, 1983) and "God, Mother, and Me: An Object Relational Perspective on Religious Material," *Pastoral Psychology* 34 (1986): 251–263; James Jones, *Contemporary Psychoanalysis and Religion: Transference and Transcendence* (New Haven: Yale University Press, 1991), *Religion and Theology in Transition: Psychoanalysis, Feminism, and Theology* (New Haven: Yale University Press, 1996) and "Psychoanalysis, Feminism, and Religion," *Pastoral Psychology* 40 (1992): 355–368; Naomi Goldenberg, "Psychoanalysis and Religion: The Influence of Theology on Theory and Therapy," *Pastoral Psychology* 40 (1992): 343–354; Harriet Lutzky, "Reparation and Tikkun: A Comparison of the Kleinian and Kabbalistic Concepts," *International Review of Psychoanalysis* 16 (1989): 449–458, and "The Sacred and the Maternal Object: An Application of Fairbairn's Theory to Religion," in *Psychoanalytic Reflections on Current Issues,* ed. H. Siegal et al. (New York: New York University Press, 1991); Mary Ellen Ross and Cheryl Lynn Ross, "Mothers, Infants, and the Psychoanalytic Study of Ritual," *Signs* 9 (1983): 27–39; Diane Jonte-Pace, "Object Relations Theory, Mothering, and Religion: Toward a Feminist Psychology of Religion," *Horizons* 14 (1987): 310–327 and "New Directions in Feminist Psychology of Religion," *Journal of Feminist Studies in Religion* 13 (1997): 63–74; Kelley Raab, "Nancy Jay and a Feminist Psychology of Sacrifice," *Journal of Feminist Studies in Religion* 13 (1997): 75–89.

78. See Juliet Mitchell, "Introduction 1," in *Jacques Lacan and the école freudienne,* ed. Juliet Mitchell and Jacqueline Rose (New York: Norton, 1982) for a discussion of feminist debates in early object relations theory.

79. See Jonte-Pace, "Object Relations Theory," 327. See also William Beers, *Women and Sacrifice: Male Narcissism and the Psychology of Religion* (Detroit: Wayne State University Press, 1992); and Raab, "Nancy Jay."

80. Judith Butler, *Gender Trouble: Feminism and the Subversion of Identity* (New York: Routledge, 1990), 66.

81. Jane Flax, *Thinking Fragments: Psychoanalysis, Feminism, and Postmodernism in the Contemporary West* (Berkeley: University of California Press, 1990). See also Patricia Elliot, *From Mastery of Analysis: Theories of Gender in Psychoanalytic Feminism* (Ithaca: Cornell University Press, 1991), and Diane Jonte-Pace, "Psychoanalysis after Feminism," *Religious Studies Review* 19 (1993): 110–115.

82. This term is D. W. Winnicott's. See *Playing and Reality.*

83 Freud, *SE* 11, 123.

84. Rizzuto, *Birth of the Living God;* McDargh, "God, Mother, and Me"; Jones, *Contemporary Psychoanalysis* and "Psychoanalysis, Feminism, and Religion."

85. Freud *SE* 21, 72. Freud admitted that the oceanic feeling might involve "the restoration of limitless narcissism" but he felt that this sense of boundless unity was a defense against a sense of helplessness, an attempt at religious consolation: "I can imagine that the oceanic feeling became connected with religion later on. The 'oneness with the universe' which constitutes its ideational content sounds like a first attempt at religious consolation, as though it were another way of disclaiming the danger which the ego recognizes as threatening it from the external world" (*SE* 21, 72). For Freud, in other words, the primary human experience is one of helplessness and separation (not one of unity and merger), a sense of merger is a later development, a defense against the sense of helplessness, and the source of religion lies in the sense of helplessness, not in the later, secondary, compensatory illusion of unity and connectedness.

86. Guntrip, *Personality and Human Interaction,* 383. Heinz Kohut's notion of cosmic narcissism is similar. Well known for his theory of narcissism and "self psychology," Kohut argues that narcissism is not necessarily pathological, nor is it something healthy people outgrow. Rather, transformations of narcissism may contribute to the healthful adaptation of the mature personality and may be the source of wisdom, humor, creativity, empathy, and a "cosmic narcissism" that transcends individual boundaries and participates in a supraindividual and timeless existence. See Heinz Kohut, "Forms and Transformations of Narcissism," *Journal of the American Psychiatric Association* 14 (1966): 243–272.

87. Lutzky, "The Sacred and the Maternal Object," 41.

88. Lutzky, "Reparation and Tikkun," 455.

89. See for example Shirley Nelson Garner, Claire Kahane, and Madelon Sprengnether, eds., *The (M)other Tongue: Essays in Feminist Psychoanalytic Interpretation* (Ithaca: Cornell University Press, 1985); Flax, *Thinking Fragments; Jessica Benjamin, The Bonds of Love: Psychoanalysis, Feminism, and Problem of Domination* (New York: Pantheon, 1988).

90. Melanie Klein, *The Psychoanalysis of Children,* 242, cited in Wulff, *Psychology of Religion,* 326.

91. Goldenberg, *Returning Words to Flesh,* 161.

92. Ibid., 166.

93. Ibid., 164.

94. Winnicott believes that the infant creates "transitional objects" and "transitional spaces" in order to accomplish the necessary separation from the mother. Examples of the transitional object are the teddy bear, the security blanket, or even the thumb. Objects selected by the child from the environment, these are often highly charged with meaning. The transitional object, Winnicott says, originates in the transitional space, the potential space between the baby and the mother. It functions as a symbol of the mother's comforting and reassuring presence when she is absent See Winnicott, "Transitional Objects."

95. Ross and Ross, "Mother, Infants," 27.

96. Ibid., 39.

97. Nancy Jay, *Throughout Your Generations Forever: Sacrifice, Religion, and Paternity* (Chicago: University of Chicago Press, 1992).

98. Beers, *Women and Sacrifice,* 144.

99. Raab, "Nancy Jay," 79.

100. Ibid., 82.

101. Ibid., 87.

102. In Beers's view the Roman Catholic exclusion of women from the priesthood is the significant paradigm, while the recent Anglican decision to ordain women to the priesthood is something of an exception. I support Beers's thesis, arguing that sacrificial rituals (including the Eucharist) are, in the words of Nancy Jay, "remedies for being born of woman." My view is that in our complex and contradictory cultural systems, these "remedies" are occasionally enacted by women who, as priests, temporarily take on the "matriphobic" role of men. But these remedies are paradigmatically enacted by men. See Jonte-Pace, "New Directions."

103. Object relations theory, like psychoanalysis, has had an influence on feminist theory more broadly. See, for example, Dorothy Dinnerstein, *The Mermaid and the Minotaur: Sexual Arrangements and Human Malaise* (New York: Harper, 1976); Flax, *Thinking Fragments;* Nancy Chodorow, *The Reproduction of Mothering* (Berkeley: University of California Press, 1978); and Benjamin, *The Bonds of Love.*

104. Homans's *The Ability to Mourn* is perhaps the single most important work utilizing "revisionist psychoanalysis" (or self psychology) to examine religion, modernization, secularization, and the rise of psychoanalysis.

105. See Jean-Francois Lyotard, *The Postmodern Condition: A Report on Knowledge,* trans. Geoff Bennington and Brian Massum (Minneapolis: University of Minnesota Press, 1984).

106. Hazard Adams, "Introduction," in *Critical Theory Since 1965,* ed. Hazard Adams and Leroy Searle (Tallahassee: University of Florida Press, 1986), 8–9.

107. Michel Foucault, in *The Order of Things* (New York: Random House, 1970), announced the disappearance of "humanist man," which he regarded as the creation of the Renaissance episteme. See also Foucault, "What Is an Author?" in *Critical Theory Since 1965,* ed. Hazard Adams and Leroy Searle (Tallahassee: University of Florida Press, 1986) and *The History of Sexuality, An Introduction: Volume 1,* trans. Robert Hurley (New York: Pantheon, 1978).

108. Jacques Lacan, *Ecrits: A Selection,* trans. Alan Sheridan (New York: Norton, 1977).

109. Kristeva, Irigaray, and Cixous are often grouped together as the "three French feminists." See Francoise Meltzer, "Transfeminisms," in *Transfigurations: Theology and the French Feminists,* ed. C. W. Maggie Kim, Susan M. St. Ville, and Susan M. Simonaitis (Minneapolis: Fortress Press, 1993), 17–30, for some caveats about the term *French feminism* and about the problems in conflating Kristeva, Irigaray, and Cixous.

See Julia Kristeva, *Powers of Horror: An Essay on Abjection,* trans. Leon S. Roudiez (New York: Columbia University Press, 1982), "Stabat Mater," in *The Kristeva Reader,* ed. Toril Moi (New York: Columbia University Press, 1986), 160–186, *In the Beginning Was Love: Psychoanalysis and Faith,* trans. Arthur Goldhammer (New York: Columbia University Press, 1987), *Black Sun: Depression and Melancholia,* trans. Leon S. Roudiez (New York: Columbia University Press, 1989), and *Strangers to Ourselves,* trans. Leon S. Roudiez (New York: Columbia University Press, 1991). See Cixous's widely anthologized essay "The Laugh of the Medusa," trans. Keith Cohen and Paula Cohen, in *Critical Theory Since 1965,* ed. Hazard Adams and Leroy Searle (Tallahassee: University of Florida Press, 1986), 309–321. Luce Irigaray's writings on religion include "Divine Women," in *Local Consumption Occasional Papers* 8 (1986), "Women, the Sacred, and Money," *Paragraph* 8 (1986), and "Equal to Whom?" *differences* 2 (1990). See also Elizabeth Grosz, "Irigaray and the Divine," in *Transfigurations: Theology and the French Feminists,* ed. C. W. Maggie Kim, Susan M. St. Ville, and Susan M. Simonaitis (Minneapolis: Fortress Press, 1993), 199–214. Irigaray is highly critical of psychoanalysis, although she has been said to stand "on the borders of psychoanalytic theory" (Grosz, "Irigaray and the Divine," 200).

110. Many poststructuralists have written provocative, challenging, and often enigmatic texts touching on religion, on God, on mysticism, and on theology. See, for example, Lacan, *Ecrits.* The significance of this poststructuralist perspective for religious studies became apparent during the 1980s and '90s with the publication of theological texts and analyses such as Edith Wyschogrod,

David Crownfield, and Carl A. Rasche, eds., *Lacan and Theological Discourse* (Albany: State University of New York Press, 1989); Sheila Greeve Davaney, "Problems with Feminist Theory: Historicity and the Search for Sure Foundations," in *Embodied Love: Sensuality and Relationship as Feminist Values,* ed. Paul M. Cooey, Sharon A. Farmer, and Mary Ellen Ross (San Francisco: Harper and Row, 1987), 79–95; Elisabeth Schüssler-Fiorenza, *But She Said: Feminist Practices of Biblical Interpretation* (Boston: Beacon Press, 1992); Rebecca Chopp, *The Power to Speak: Feminism, Language, God* (New York: Crossroad, 1989); C. W. Maggie Kim, Susan M. St. Ville, and Susan M. Simonaitis, eds., *Transfigurations: Theology and the French Feminists* (Philadelphia: Fortress, 1993); and Sharon Welch, *A Feminist Ethic of Risk* (Minneapolis: Fortress, 1990).

Davaney, for example, argued that poststructuralism mounts a radical critique of the foundationalism of both feminist theory and feminist theology. Drawing from the work of Michel Foucault, she argues for a radical relativism that acknowledges that "truth" is determined by the play of power within particular historical contexts.

111. Kristeva, "Stabat Mater."

112. Kristeva, *Strangers to Ourselves.*

113. Kristeva, *In the Beginning.*

114. Kristeva, *Powers of Horror,* 58.

115. Ibid., 64.

116. Kristeva, *Black Sun,* 27-28.

117. For important critiques of Kristeva, see Butler, *Gender Trouble;* Gayatri Chakravorty Spivak, *In Other Worlds: Essays in Cultural Politics* (New York: Routledge, 1988), and others. For an excellent discussion of this debate, and for a defense of Kristeva's feminism as "analysis" rather than "mastery," see Elliot, *From Mastery to Analysis.*

118. In my view, most of these critiques can be answered: I see Kristeva as a *feminist analyst of both feminism and religion.* Her position as "feminist analyst" puts her in a slightly different relation to feminism and to religion. With regard to religion, she stands outside of any institutional religious tradition, seeking to understand how it functions without promoting or attacking it: her task is to analyze how religious ideas and images fulfill conscious fantasies and desires. With regard to feminism, she stands squarely within it, but her stance is self-reflexive and critical: she cautions against turning feminism into an absolutist ideology, and she shows that one cannot step entirely outside of patriarchy, arguing that within culture as currently constructed, women invariably are markers of silence, sacrifice, and otherness. Her relation to psychoanalysis is, perhaps, idealized. See Diane Jonte-Pace, "Julia Kristeva and the Psychoanalytic Study of Religion: Rethinking Freud's Cultural Texts," in

Religion, Society, and Psychoanalysis: Readings in Contemporary Theory (Boulder: Westview, 1997), 240–268.

119. Marilyn Edelstein, "Metaphor, Meta-Narraive, and Mater-Narrative in Kristeva's 'Stabat Mater,'" in *Body/Text in Julia Kristeva: Religion, Women, Psychoanalysis,* ed. David Crownfield (Albany: State University of New York Press, 1992), 27–52. See also Edelstein, "Toward a Feminist Postmodern Polethique: Kristeva on Ethics and Politics," in *Ethics, Politics, and Difference in Julia Kristeva's Writing,* ed. Kelly Oliver (New York: Routledge, 1993), 196–214.

120. David Crownfield, "The Sublimation of Narcissism in Christian Love and Faith," in *Body/Text in Julia Kristeva: Religion, Women, Psychoanalysis,* ed. David Crownfield (Albany: State University of New York Press, 1992), 57–64.

121. Martha Reineke, "The Mother in Mimesis: Kristeva and Girard on Violence and the Sacred," in *Body/Text in Julia Kristeva: Religion, Women, Psychoanalysis,* ed. David Crownfield (Albany: State University of New York Press, 1992), 67–86. See also Reineke, "Life Sentences: Kristeva and the Limits of Modernity," *Soundings* 71 (1988): 439–461 and "This Is My Body: Reflections on Abjection, Anorexia, and Medieval Women Mystics," *Journal of the American Academy of Religion* 58 (1990): 245–266; and *Sacrificed Lives: Kristeva on Women and Violence* (Bloomington: Indiana University Press, 1997).

122. David Fisher, "Kristeva's *Chora* and the Subject of Postmodern Ethics," in *Body/Text in Julia Kristeva: Religion, Women, Psychoanalysis,* ed. David Crownfield (Albany: State University of New York Press, 1992), 91–104.

123. Cleo McNelly Kearnes, "Art and Religious Discourse in Aquinas and Kristeva," in *Body/Text in Julia Kristeva: Religion, Women, Psychoanalysis,* ed. David Crownfield (Albany: State University of New York Press, 1992), 111–124. See also Kearnes, "Kristeva and Feminist Theology," in *Transfigurations: Theology and the French Feminists,* ed. C. W. Maggie Kim, Susan M. St. Ville, and Susan M. Simonaitis (Minneapolis: Fortress Press, 1993), 49–80.

124. Jean Graybeal, "Joying in the Truth of Self-Division," in *Body/Text in Julia Kristeva: Religion, Women, Psychoanalysis,* ed. David Crownfield (Albany State University Press of New York, 1992), 129–138. See also Graybeal, "Kristeva's Delphic Proposal: Practice Encompasses the Ethical," in *Ethics, Politics, and Difference in Julia Kristeva's Writing,* ed. Kelly Oliver (New York: Routledge, 1993), 32–40.

125. Jonte-Pace, "Situating Kristeva."

126. See Tomoko Masuzuma, *In Search of Dreamtime: The Quest for the Origin of Religion* (Chicago: University of Chicago Press, 1994).

127. See, for example, Kristeva, "Women's Time."

128. See, for example, Benjamin, *The Bonds of Love;* Butler, *Gender Trouble;* and Flax, *Thinking Fragments*

129. Katherine Ewing, "Can Psychoanalytic Theories Explain the Pakistani Woman? Intrapsychic Autonomy and Interpersonal Engagement in the Extended Family," *Ethos* 19 (1991): 131–160; Fatna A. Sabbah, *Woman in the Muslim Unconscious* (New York: Pergamon Press, 1984). See also Carol Delaney, *The Seed and the Soil* (Berkeley: University of California Press, 1991); and Obeysekere, *Medusa's Hair.* Jung's work is, in some ways, less Eurocentric than the work of other psychological theorists of religion, although it cannot be said that his approach avoids orientalism.

130. It should be noted that the efforts of Foucault, in *The History of Sexuality,* to trace shifts from religious discourse to psychological discourse resonates with efforts of scholars in the psychology and religion movement. Foucault has, of course, been the subject of feminist critique: he is notorious for ignoring gender, even while he analyzes sex and sexuality.

131. See for example, Sudhir Kakar, *Shamans, Mystics, and Doctors: A Psychological Inquiry into India and Its Healing Traditions* (New York: Knopf, 1982) and Jeffrey Kripal, *Kali's Child: The Mystical and Erotic in the Life and Teachings of Ramakrishna* (Chicago: University of Chicago Press, 1998) for psychoanalytic investigations of Indian culture.

132. Homans, *Jung in Context* and *The Ability to Mourn;* Henking, "Placing the Social Sciences."

6

Feminist Philosophy of Religion

MARY ANN STENGER

R eferences to feminist theology or to feminist philosophy receive positive recognition of the disciplines from educated colleagues. But mention of "feminist philosophy of religion" often draws a furrowed brow or a questioning look, followed by, "Exactly what is that?" While there are many well-known feminist theologians and feminist theorists, the same is not true of feminist philosophers of religion. In the introduction to a special edition of *Hypatia* devoted to feminist philosophy of religion, Nancy Frankenberry asks the question: "Where are all the feminist philosophers of religion?"[1] Unlike feminist theology, no names dominate the literature nor specific approaches set the agenda for feminist philosophy of religion. In many cases, people engaging in feminist philosophy of religion are trained in theology as well as philosophy, with the philosophical tasks often included in their theological works. Our central task will be to analyze the implications of feminist work for methodology in philosophy of religion, discussing both work which has been done as well as future areas of research for feminist philosophers of religion.

The Development of Feminist Philosophy of Religion

Our first task is to look at how scholarship in Women's Studies has impacted philosophy of religion. There are three broad approaches that have been part of feminist scholarship in philosophy of religion: (1) a major part of this scholarship has been the critique of patriarchy, uncovering political implications of philosophical claims of universality and objectivity; (2) feminist scholarship also builds upon and reconstructs traditional[2] philosophy in order to be more inclusive of diverse communities; (3) new philosophical options that focus on nontraditional issues, such as body and community, are being developed.

147

All of these will be explored by focusing on traditional topics in philosophy of religion and demonstrating the impact feminist work has had or should have on methodology and content.

A survey of recent books on philosophy of religion (published in the 1990s) shows a near-absence of women thinkers and of feminist approaches to philosophical issues in religion. This suggests that the impact of women's studies and feminist issues is yet to be felt as broadly as it has been in other areas of the study of religion. Nancy Frankenberry suggests four reasons why this is so: "the historical antecedents of the discipline; contemporary academic gerrymandering; feminist suspicion of religion; and mainstream resistance to feminism."[3] All of these factors are true, which makes the task for feminist philosophers of religion quite daunting. Because most feminist philosophers choose not to deal with religion and most feminist theologians have not been trained philosophically, part of the effort of feminist philosophers of religion must be to combine creatively and critically the insights of feminist philosophy and feminist theology. To this point, there has been little dialogue between traditional (mostly white male) philosophy of religion (especially of the analytic mode) and feminist thinkers.[4] Such a dialogue must begin, both to increase the impact of feminist thought as well as to strengthen and broaden the often-too-narrow approaches of traditional philosophy of religion.

Feminist analysis shares assumptions, approaches, and issues often identified as "postmodern," for example, recognition of context, relativization of universal claims, interest in subjectivity, analysis of metaphor, and interest in otherness. Even when these topics are explored by male postmodern philosophers of religion, generally the application to the context, subjectivity, and otherness of gender (or race, class, etc.) is ignored. Feminist analysis also discusses issues of power, views of the human body, and implications of sexuality. In what follows we will look at the impact of feminist analysis on the following topics: epistemology, language and hermeneutics, ultimacy, and persons (self, subjectivity, and others), with a focus on religious ideas and theories.

Epistemology of Religion

A study of feminist critiques of traditional epistemology shows that feminists question the objectivity and universality claimed by many philosophers because they fail to recognize their hidden assumptions and androcentric bias.[5] "Everyone" really means male (and usually educated, white males). Philosophers traditionally see themselves rising above concrete contexts of gender, class, race, the body, issues of power, etc. Such abstraction is what enables them to make universal rational claims. But postmodern critiques in general and more recognition of the plurality of religions have led to greater recognition of the relativity of philosophical analysis. More political awareness is necessary to broaden the recognition to include issues of gender, race, and class. The focus here will be gender although many points are equally applicable to race and class.

The major issues explored here are (*a*) the role of experience in religious knowledge and (*b*) criteria of religious truth.

The Role of Experience in Religious Knowledge. The primary focus here will be on the understanding of experience through historicist and relativist approaches and the inner subjective experience of transcendental reflection. Feminist critique of both of these broad approaches will be presented along with a summary of key issues feminists include in their discussion of the role of experience in religious knowledge.

Relativist approaches. Issues related to historicism and subjectivism focus on the historical-cultural conditioning affecting people's thought and actions (historicism) and the influence of a person's subjective state (subjectivism). Both historicist and subjectivist approaches arose as critiques of claims of absolute values, standpoints, criteria, or truths. Using the term *relativism* to include both the historicist and subjectivist approaches, we can see that relativism precludes claims of universal experience or universally valid knowledge but might include claims of universal, formal structures of experience. The very critique of absolutism given by relativism assumes such structures even while doubting universal claims of content.

Earlier relativist critiques of religious knowledge range from those based in historical biblical criticism to philosophical analyses of how humans know. Such efforts were strong in the late nineteenth century and early twentieth century, a time period that also included feminist critiques of society and political action for women's suffrage. It is interesting to note that parallel to current philosophy of religion, most relativist critiques do not include any discussion of gender conditioning even though women were writing about and reacting to their socialization as females.[6]

While relativist critiques pointed out the social conditioning of both knowledge and texts and did engage in their own period-based evaluation of those social understandings, most did not offer any assessment of the implied social roles for women (or any other nondominant group) nor analyze the implications of such social conditioning. That work has been left for the most part to feminist critiques. Feminists push the relativist analysis one step farther, to focus on the assumptions underlying the social-cultural conditioning. For example, a relativist approach to Augustine could argue that Augustine's theology reflects the decreasing political power of the Roman Empire as well as the influence of Greek philosophy. But a feminist critique would further analyze the implications for women of Augustine's use of Greek dualism, which split reason from body and more closely identified males with reason and females with body.

With relativism and, more recently, postmodernism, feminists share an emphasis on the centrality of historical-cultural context in human knowledge. Feminists as well as patriarchal scholars cannot escape the social construction of reality. Thus, the claim is not that feminist analysis is the only right way to understand the world but rather that feminist analysis is another way to understand the world that often challenges the assumed universality of earlier patriarchal approaches.

To privilege experience, especially embodied cultural experience, presumes diversity. William James's *The Varieties of Religious Experience*[7] or John Hick's *An Interpretation of Religion: Human Responses to the Transcendent,*[8] as well as Judith Plaskow and Carol Christ's *Weaving the Visions: New Patterns in Feminist Spirituality*[9] and Susan Brooks Thistlethwaite and Mary Potter Engel's *Lift Every Voice: Constructing Christian Theologies from the Underside,*[10] are clear testimonies to the diversity of religious and cultural experiences. But as we shall see in our discussion of criteria of truth, diversity does not have to mean foregoing claims of truth or criteria of truth. Yet such claims and criteria are necessarily conditioned by and limited by the context.

Underlying most feminist philosophy of religion is an assumption that men's experiences and women's experiences are not necessarily the same. But that assumption does *not* include the additional assumption that all women share experiences or that all men share experiences. Rather, the claim is that rooted in our diverse historical and cultural contexts are gender-based differentiations. These differentiations, to which we are socialized from birth, are not the same across cultures, religions, or historical periods. But the important issue is that "male" and "female" are used as categories in social-cultural norms of behavior. Given that base assumption (supported by much feminist anthropological and sociological work), what are its implications for the role experience plays in religious knowledge?

For women, the liberating dimension of these discussions of relativism and contextualism is that the definitions of female roles as subordinate or of women as weak, submissive, irrational, etc. should not be taken as universal or absolute. This is not just a matter of extending the relativist claim to be specific about gender. Rather, the key issue for women is liberating both women and men from their social conditioning as part of a political effort to produce more just societies. The relativist and postmodern critiques of knowledge are not just intriguing theoretically for women but are compelling socially and politically.

These critiques have special significance when dealing with religious knowledge and truth because religious truth is presumed to have a more absolute root and ultimate authority than other areas of knowledge. And that ultimate grounding has been used to back up social structures that enforce the domination of men over women. Feminist critiques have been seen as more

political than other relativist critiques because they press the social implications of contextual approaches and challenge the understanding of ultimacy
that is used to ground injustice. Thus, feminist religious theories focus on
experience in religious knowledge, not just to provide a legitimate basis for
women's spiritual experiences but also to connect theory to the lived experiences of women (in all of their diversity) and to bring more justice for women
to the social world.

The relativist and post-modern critiques of knowledge provide a point of
contact between feminist philosophy of religion and philosophical approaches
to religious pluralism.[11] Both feminist and pluralist critiques challenge claims
of universal religious truth by pointing out the religious and cultural relativity
of any specific claims and by rejecting patriarchal forms or imperialist expressions of religion that justified the domination of one group of people over
another. While sharing critical approaches, feminist and pluralist constructive
efforts in theology have developed in quite different directions, a point that
will be addressed later in this essay.

Transcendental Subjectivity versus Embodiment. Another approach to the
role of experience in religious knowledge is to focus on transcendental subjectivity in an attempt to find truth that is less limited by the historical-cultural
context in which the thinker lives. Such efforts pay verbal respect to the fact
that human subjectivity is embodied subjectivity, but most of the analyses
focus on the inner and deeper levels of subjectivity as a structure that all humans
can experience. For example, in *The Reason of Following*, Robert Scharlemann argues that the ecstatic experience of following another, where the
other is experienced subjectively as one's authentic self, is a form of reason, an
essential possibility for any human self. Scharlemann recognizes the self's
embodiment and the particularity of each person's life (both embodied and
psychical experiences),[12] but the focus of his self-reflexive theology is on the
inner subjectivity much more than on the particular embodiment or the
social-cultural context. Similarly, Steven Laycock acknowledges the truth of
phenomenology as transcendental subjectivity[13] and argues that "phenomenology is primarily a theory of *experiencing*, not of 'experience.'"[14] In experiencing God, Laycock argues that God is not separate from the intersubjective world.[15] But the intersubjective world is reflective subjectivity, not the
social-political community, which shares concerns and actions in its historical-cultural context. Embodiment in relation to transcendental subjectivity is
acknowledged but not analyzed for its political implications.

Feminist criticism of transcendental reflection can value the importance
of subjectivity, including reflexive analysis and intersubjectivity, but it will
connect these with analysis of the implications of female embodiment versus
male embodiment. Given Western society's focus on the body, especially female

bodies, and the social roles and definitions assigned on the basis of bodily differences (gender, race), feminists reject both explicit and implicit patriarchal understandings of the body and envision new, more positive meanings of body which can be used to work toward reducing the violence applied to all bodies.

The issue of embodiment in feminist philosophy of religion must include critique of the traditional Christian and Western philosophical attitudes toward body, especially female bodies. In looking at most philosophy of religion, one might think that only women had bodies! And in a certain sense, because of traditional views of female bodies, that has been true. Perhaps male philosophers of religion have seen little reason to deal with embodiment in anything except a general way because they have been influenced by the centuries-old view that men are associated with reason and women with bodies and by a view of philosophy that focuses on reason and leaves study of bodies to biology, medicine, anthropology, or sociology. For the most part, it is women who have addressed the issue of body because it is women who have been the victims of patriarchal identification of females as primarily bodies.

Whether one looks at Augustine or Descartes, mind and reason are seen as a higher dimension of being human than is the body, male or female. Ironically, we know much of Augustine's life in his body even while we learn of his assumption that becoming a Christian means that he must give up his concubine. We know less of Descartes's personal life, but his philosophy does make material reality secondary to subjectivity and rationality. Some feminist approaches prefer to continue the traditional abstraction from body because they see such neutrality as treating all humans, male or female, as autonomous beings.[16] Other feminist theories have rejected the dualism underlying these approaches and have argued for a more integrated approach to mind and body.[17]

Because women are often seen as bodies with minds instead of minds with bodies, the liberal approach of ignoring bodies is tempting and initially liberating. But women also know that negative views of bodies have been intertwined with degradation of women through rape, incest, and abuse. And whether she is directly a victim of these forms of violence or not, a woman knows her own vulnerability and shares in the suffering of her sisters. Feminist philosophers of religion have a special role in analyzing this topic because some religions have been so influential in perpetuating negative views of the body and directly or indirectly of female bodies. Feminist philosophy of religion needs to analyze the implications of ignoring body in traditional philosophy of religion as well as the constructive possibilities of including body in philosophical analysis of religion.

Abstracting minds from bodies is not only a philosophical method but often a method for religious experience found cross-culturally. While some religious approaches have a more positive view of the body (arguably, biblical Judaism or some tantric approaches), many religious traditions encourage an enhanced spirituality through repression of or transcendence of one's body (physical and psychical desires). Yet traditionally, only an elite few have had the opportunity and freedom from worldly cares to develop their spirituality while reducing their focus on their bodies. Most people in the world find it difficult to meet their bodily needs of food and shelter, and most women in the world find their efforts to meet those bodily needs complicated by their own bodies (menstruation, pregnancy, menopause) and by the effects of others' bodies (husband, boyfriend, children, strangers). Thus, feminist philosophers of religion need to analyze the significance of the religious attitudes toward body and of spiritual ideals abstracted from bodies in relation to most women's lives.

Some of the constructive possibilities stemming from a feminist analysis of body in religious thought include the challenge that traditional analyses of religion have not been body-free and the recognition that more positive views of body conform to recent cultural concerns about ecology and health. Ecological concerns have helped us realize our interdependence with the natural world, and health issues have made people more focused on their personal fitness. But our theoretical discussions need to emphasize the interconnection between attitudes toward bodies and attitudes toward nature as well as the interdependence of physical and earthly health. Moreover, for women, more positive views of body can be part of a process of increased self-esteem and empowerment, which are necessary deterrents to abuse and violence against women. Because religions often establish root understandings of the relationship between the ultimate/God, humans, and nature/material world, philosophy of religion needs to address the way the issues of body and nature are treated religiously and to show the practical and political implications of the religious approaches. Inclusion of both Western and Eastern religious perspectives can be helpful here.

Feminist philosophical analysis of religious experience, then, should address not only the theoretical issues of context, relativity, diversity, and transcendental reflection but also the practical implications of looking at the religious treatment of women's experiences, including their bodies. Such analysis has ethical goals of better treatment for women and by extension better treatment for the world around them.

Critique of Focusing on Women's Experience. Before leaving the topic of experience, it should be pointed out that some feminists are critical of the reliance on women's experience as the basis for feminist epistemology. They fear that such reliance reinforces rather than transforms a biological "essentialism" that splits the world into male and female.[18] The emphasis on women's experience spoken of here relies primarily on social differences that may have biological roots. Women's social experience of the world does differ from men's social experience of the world, but a key issue is whether such differences should be seen as essential or a necessary characteristic.

While there are some theorists who want to celebrate the biological and social differences of females as an antidote to patriarchal subordination of those differences, other theorists want to use the analyses of women's experiences as the basis for moving beyond essentialism. In other words, the emphasis on women's experience can be seen as a political strategy to challenge the explicit and implicit patriarchal assumptions.[19] Women's experiences not only can serve as a balance to men's experiences but can challenge implicit assumptions of universality or hierarchy.

But the critical warning about essentialism should not be taken lightly. As social theorist Marnia Lazreg argues, "[T]he establishment of a subjectivist epistemology based on the body may only end where it began: in the body."[20] But Lazreg also suggests that women's experience can be used to help understand the social conditions through which human activity becomes identified as female or male.[21] In other words, she suggests using an analysis of women's experiences to move to more universal claims about gendered experience in relationship to knowledge.

Philosophers of religion often question how much can be claimed on the basis of some people's experiences. The fact that William James can report many people's claims of religious experiences neither leads skeptics to become believers nor proves the truth of the religious claims in any universal way. But philosophers of religion can analyze believers' experiences for how religious knowledge works for them. Similarly, feminist philosophers of religion do not need to claim a universality for women's religious experiences or for their experiences of patriarchy within religion. Rather, they can use women's experiences of patriarchal religion or of their own spirituality to analyze the social construction of such experiences and to show how such social construction can affect both the form of the experience and the content. In other words, feminist philosophers of religion can abstract from concrete experiences of religious women to develop "more universal" claims about the social construction of religious experience. As shown above, such claims point to issues of power, cultural relativity, subjectivity, embodiment, and the importance of one's community. These claims are not universalizing women's religious experiences but using those experiences in comparison with traditional discussions of experience to argue some general effects of social conditions on religious experience.

Criteria of Religious Truth. Even without raising the issue of gender, discussions of truth and knowledge in religion exhibit varying and conflicting theories, with the conflicts often centering on the extent to which religious truth should follow the same criteria of truth and rules of meaning that other systems of discourse follow. Because the ultimate ground and object of religious truth is *ultimate*, meaning beyond ordinary reality and to a great extent unattainable in its full reality, religious knowledge becomes suspect when compared to knowledge in the natural sciences. Much contemporary epistemology of religion, then, works on describing the distinctive criteria and rules of meaning in religious knowledge. Such deliberations generally ignore issues of gender, but the issues raised could receive further illumination from feminist analysis. The following discussion will offer application of feminist critique to some of the issues addressed in traditional epistemology of religion.

In an article on religious truth, Louis Dupré correlates traditional criteria of truth (correspondence, coherence, and disclosure) with approaches to religious truth.[22] A correspondence theory of truth expects claims of truth to conform to reality. In religion this has been taken to mean conforming to ultimate reality, thereby involving moral and ontological claims that would not be there (at least not overtly) for truths in the natural sciences. Dupré argues: "For truth in religion always presents itself as a *relatedness* to what ultimately *is:* a conversion, both moral and ontological, toward Being as it is in its very roots and origins, contrary to appearance and deception. . . . Moreover, the 'truth' thus attained is presented as *revealed*—that is, *given* to the mind from a principle or level of being that surpasses the mind's own reality."[23] "Being as it is" would seem to be beyond gender, and so also truth corresponding to it would be expected to have a neutral impact on issues of gender.

Women's experiences and feminist analysis suggest that in addition to correspondence between truth claims and Being as it is, there is often a correspondence between such religious truth claims and male experience of the world or male ideals for religious truth. This is not to say that a desire for correspondence between religious truth and ultimate reality is wrong. Rather, the correspondence theory needs to be broadened to take into account the critiques of gender, race, and class. One must ask whether the conformity to ultimate reality that is demanded as a moral and ontological experience is as nongendered as the discussion of it. The subjective dimension of religious correspondence allows for the influence of the knower's specific human experience, including gender, race, and class, as well as the knower's specific religious experience within a particular religious tradition and cultural history. The abstract reference to being or ultimate reality often hides such influences and assumptions.

The criterion of coherence relates to consistency within a particular system of discourse, but Dupré points out the importance of dialogue between various systems of discourse.[24] Relating to religion, coherence applies first within a particular religious community's system of discourse, using its own rules of consistency, and secondarily in relation to other systems of discourse, which may have different rules for coherence. Religious discourse gains some legitimacy under this understanding, but it also needs to be in dialogue with other systems of discourse and approaches to truth.

Because there is recognition of the role a community plays in setting the rules of discourse, the criterion of coherence could take account of the role of gender, race, and class in that community. But in spite of that recognition (or illustrating its truth) is the fact that the assumptions about gender, race, and class generally are not discussed as part of the rules of discourse. Feminist philosophers should address these assumptions, especially in the area of religion, where people often believe the community is inclusive. But analysts must look at the politics of the community: Who sets the norms of discourse or whose discourse is termed normative within the community? Sojourner Truth's call to be recognized as a woman ("Ain't I a Woman?") even though she did not fit the religious leaders' structures of meaning when they spoke about women illustrates the political dimensions of speech.

Dupré points out that structuralist theories of meaning see thought determined by linguistic structures, thereby restricting truth to a "social, linguistic problem."[25] From a feminist point of view, the truth in that perspective is the impact of language on thought. To the extent that language masks the politics that ignores or devalues women, nonwhites, and the poor, then language supports the status quo, reinforcing the hidden assumptions of their inferiority or irrelevance. Ignoring the politics does not make the language or the truth formed coherently within the community's structure of meaning nonpolitical or universal or objective; it simply misleads the knowers in that community to think they are objective when they are not.

Theories of truth that allow for disclosure of truth have been attractive to theologians and to philosophers attempting to justify religious modes of knowing. Whether using Plato, Hegel, Heidegger, or Gadamer, disclosure theories leave room for revelation or truth gained through religious experience or mystical insight. Although these philosophers affirm *ontological* disclosure of Being, theologians and mystics may correlate that with religious ultimacy or God. And to the extent that Being is disclosed only partially, the theories fit well with the religious view that God or the ultimate cannot be attained fully.

In discussing these theories of disclosure, Dupré points out that the religious claims of truth require "an involved participation that philosophy cannot, and should not, reproduce."[26] In other words, these religious claims are not justified on a universal basis but only within the community of those who have experienced or who at least acknowledge the disclosure. Dupré also notes that aesthetic experiences share the same restriction of *experience* of the artistic qualities and truth, setting religious and aesthetic truth apart from scientific or historical truth in that respect (even though they all may share some rules of knowledge).[27]

Feminist philosophical analysis of these issues suggests that the assumption of scientific and historical truth as more obviously universal than aesthetic or religious truth may not hold. Feminist and other political critiques of historical and scientific knowledge suggest that hidden political and subjective factors raise questions about how universal those forms of knowledge are.[28] The insights of these political critiques of universality can help those philosophers who want to justify religious disclosure or religious knowledge generally because they suggest another similarity among major types of knowledge. These critiques do not undermine all claims of universality, but they do put knowledge within the limits of perspectives, whether it be the perspective of the scientific observer or that of a religious person.[29]

It must be acknowledged that scientific experiments and historical evidence have a more public dimension to them than individual religious or aesthetic experiences. But these various areas of knowledge reflect broad cultural assumptions, which include structures of power. With respect to nondominant groups, including women, these cultural assumptions have influenced histories, anthropologies, and scientific studies that "prove" or at least legitimate inferior status to those groups. Claims of universal truth, whether scientific or historical or religious, may have seemed universally true within a given culture and historical period and for an educated elite. Feminist recovery of the history of women, along with feminist critiques of science, social sciences, theology, and philosophy, argue that these "truths" cannot be claimed as universal but are rooted in the cultural experiences of their knowers as well as in their own systems of evidence and coherence.

Applying these political insights to the criterion of disclosure suggests that disclosure of truth is not free from these political dimensions either. Disclosures of truth, if they are to have any meaning beyond the individual, are usually expressed linguistically and therefore draw upon the personal, cultural, and historical perspectives of the individual. Although not addressing feminist or other political dimensions of truth, Dupré points out that "religious disclosure occurs *within* a highly personal or intensely communal experience and, even when raised to the level of full and universal truth, retains this personal or communal quality in being a *truth-for-me* or a *truth-for* us."[30] The question for feminists is who is the "me" and who is the "us"? (In spite of the extensive work of feminist philosophers and theologians in the last two decades, it is revealing to note that most male philosophers of religion ignore that work, even when its insights have direct bearing on their own arguments.)

But the political critiques of claimed universality should not mean a pure relativism or a rejection of efforts for universality. Feminist philosopher Sandra Harding argues that "feminist inquiry can aim to produce less partial and perverse representations without having to assert the absolute, complete, universal, or eternal adequacy of these representations."[31] Harding wants to place feminist inquiry between objectivism and "interpretationism" because she sees the claimed "disinterested, value-free" objectivism as incompatible with feminist approaches and interpretationism as unwilling to judge between differing interpretations of phenomena.[32] The effort for a middle position that takes account of context yet aims for intersubjective truth is necessary if feminists want their theories taken seriously by other thinkers and expect their ideas to have ethical effects in the broad community.

For example, efforts to offer either "value-free" descriptions of religious practices and ideas or relativist analyses that argue that each religious faith is entitled to its own approach leave a moral void. Consideration of the practice of clitoridectomy in some religious traditions will show the pitfalls of the two approaches for developing religious truth. One can offer descriptions of the procedure, the rituals connected with the procedure, the people involved, the religious legitimations offered for the event, etc. Such information can be helpful to understanding the practice, but it does little for addressing the morality or truth of the practice. On the other hand, one can present different interpretations of clitoridectomy, ranging from seeing it as mutilation to defending it as the method for a woman to achieve the highest experience of God in her own tradition. If one leaves these as differing but equally valid approaches, one has no basis for dealing with the moral and very human issues involved. Some kind of middle ground, which claims some values and truths beyond mere opinion, is needed.

One way that this effort to transcend the particular shows up in feminist work is the emphasis on community as a criterion of truth. Community here does not just mean a group of people who are brought together by their physical location. Rather, community refers to an ideal relationship of persons through which they accept each other, feel each other's pain, and work together to transform the world to be less oppressive. Although actual communities seldom live up to this ideal, feminist thinkers use it as a counterposition to the emphases on individual knowledge or on abstract truths that often ignore the pain of the other.

Another element of religious truth that transcends particularity is what Edward Farley has called a "wisdom of enduring."[33] Farley argues that "the truth of religion is historical and universal at once."[34] The issues of religious faith can be described in categories and symbols that transcend the particular experiences, but their meaning for people relates to their ongoing but changing experiences of life. And the meaning for specific experiences often is found when people turn to religion to connect with a wisdom, with truth that transcends their own particularity. Feminist philosophers of religion need to analyze not only the devaluation of women in traditional philosophies and religions but also to articulate the extent to which religions have provided a wisdom and a liberating perspective for women by transcending the particular.

"Wisdom" as a name for religious truth combines the personal, historical, and social dimensions of truth. Interestingly enough, wisdom has been a much more liberating category for women than truth. In the Hebrew Bible, there are roles for wise women, and the divine quality of wisdom is characterized as feminine. Several feminist and womanist[35] scholars have used the term *wisdom* both in recovering female leadership and ethnic roots and in developing new religious imagery.[36] The enduring quality of wisdom lends a universality that is directed toward ultimacy but does not name its own expression of it as ultimate. Wisdom transcends the individual thinker and yet connects with individuals through their social-cultural past and present.

Feminist criteria of religious truth can include correspondence, coherence, and disclosure, but they will qualify these with additional criteria of just relationships of power and recognition of the importance of community. The criteria of religious truth should include the recognition that truth is contextual but also directed toward universality and ultimacy, as expressed in the concept of wisdom. Feminist philosophy of religion, then, should take account of perspective but also aim for truths that can apply across perspectives even if they are not "value free" or fully universal.

Language and Hermeneutics

Connected to our discussion of epistemology is the issue of the power of language, a shared concern of postmodernism and feminism.[37] Feminists have been especially interested in analyzing the power of language in constructing people's self-identity. For feminist philosophers of religion, the key issue is the relationship between religious language and women's identities and roles. The discussion here will focus first on the critique of patriarchal language (both philosophical and religious) and on the implications of using metaphors versus concepts in religious discourse. Then we will turn briefly to a discussion of feminist hermeneutics in philosophy of religion.

Critique of Patriarchal Language. Traditional philosophical and religious discourse often leaves females invisible or else relegated to matters relating to female bodies. It is not surprising that many women begin philosophical or theological studies with a sense of inclusiveness, that the theorists are talking about humans when they describe "man's rational nature." But in time, they learn through specific references to women that many male philosophers were describing male modes of being, identifying rationality as a male or masculine characteristic. Thus, one issue of language is who is the subject of the discourse, males and/or females? And secondly, when females are discussed, how are they defined? Language reflects the construction of meanings in a social-cultural context that is most often patriarchal.

Feminists have been interested in the extent to which females have been defined as other than males. As mentioned earlier, such differentiation has been connected with other dichotomies, such as reason versus body and strong versus weak. One theory of meaning suggests that meaning is constructed through creating such dichotomies. Michele Barrett argues: "Meaning is constructed through the counterposition of differing elements, whose definition lies precisely in their difference from each other."[38] If one accepts such a theory of language, then differentiation will continue, but one could work to eliminate the priority given to the male side of the dichotomy. Emphasis should be given to the social construction of such differentiation in order to avoid the essentialism discussed earlier.

Feminist philosophers of religion explore the dimensions of power and domination in religious language as they relate to gender, race, class, and other religious traditions. These analyses show the lack of inclusivity that was masked under the assumption of patriarchal universality or female invisibility. Attention to dichotomies also will reveal the hierarchical differentiation between God and human that can justify the powerlessness of nondominant groups. Discourse about God within patriarchal traditions can be linked to the construction of female identity (or identity of other nondominant groups).

In *Beyond God the Father,* Mary Daly addresses the interconnection between the naming of God and female identity. "Exclusively masculine symbolism for God, for the notion of divine 'incarnation' in human nature, and for the human relationship to God reinforce sexual hierarchy. . . . The entire conceptual systems of theology and ethics, developed under the conditions of patriarchy, have been the products of males and tend to serve the interests of sexist society."[39] She calls for a new naming of God in order to castrate the patriarchy from traditional religious language and to liberate women to name themselves, their world, and God.

Rebecca Chopp articulates the underlying patriarchal implications of Christian emphasis on the Word as God's primary revelation, noting that traditionally only men could present or represent God's Word.[40] But she also argues for a transforming, liberating understanding of God's Word.

> There is, however, pushing against the Word which has dominated our ordering, and ordered the domination, another reality of Word, known to women on the margins of the order. This is a reality of Word as creative, interrupting, and transforming process.[41]

By transforming the traditional understanding of God's Word, Chopp wants to transform women's lives by empowering them to speak their own word. Her reconfiguration develops a more intimate relationship between God and women, connecting with their embodied lives and enabling them to transform themselves and their world. By connecting Word to materiality, Chopp rejects the traditional patriarchal dichotomy between spirit/reason and nature and affirms the goodness of creation.

Both Daly and Chopp recognize that language has power and that religious language has generally supported patriarchal domination. But both also acknowledge that religious language can have liberating, transforming power if women are allowed to speak their own religious words. Women speaking their own words raises the issue of what type of words can best express women's religious experiences, an issue that focuses on the value of concepts versus the value of metaphors.

Concepts vs. Metaphors. A striking characteristic of much contemporary philosophy of religion is its reliance on concepts rather than symbols or metaphors. Broad, abstract concepts such as Being, the Real, the ultimate, and the transcendent are used to convey either the divine reality itself or else the common structure of an ultimate referent in most religious traditions. As abstract and broad, such concepts can be applied to diverse religious traditions.[42] But feminists have pointed out that such abstractions can hide patriarchy or other forms of domination.[43] They also provoke a more distant projection of ultimacy, less tied to the cares of the everyday human world. And such concepts may imply a sameness to the diverse religious expressions when in fact great differences in the conception and expression of ultimacy exist across diverse religions and cultures. Yet the abstraction and distance implied in such concepts also gives them a certain protective or guardian quality, preserving difference between ultimacy and ordinary, finite reality and keeping ultimacy as ultimate.

On the other hand, metaphors and symbols often play the role of creating a more intimate connection between ultimate power and ordinary persons. Using Paul Tillich's understanding that symbols participate in the reality to which they point, one can see symbols as concrete images that are both ordinary (not ultimate) and yet present ultimacy through themselves. While some may want to distinguish metaphors from symbols, seeing metaphors as more playful and less identified with the reality to which they point, for our purposes here I will treat metaphors and symbols as serving the same function.

A real advantage of a metaphor or symbol is that generally it is drawn from the real life experiences of persons rather than abstracted from those experiences. Much feminist theological work has developed metaphors for expressing ultimacy because metaphors can make explicit implications about gender, body, and sexuality that abstract concepts do not avoid but hide. Sallie McFague's use of Mother, Lover, and Friend or frequent feminist references to Goddess are examples of metaphors/symbols that together convey gender, bodily and sexual imagery, and intimacy.

While the work of the theologian may be to develop such metaphors and traditional philosophers of religion may see their work as developing abstract concepts that can apply more universally than metaphors, feminist philosophers of religion need to analyze these uses of concepts and metaphors, showing the implications of each, including both advantages and disadvantages in their uses. Both the use of abstract concepts and the use of metaphors have political implications, with each addressing a specific political agenda. Cross-cultural philosophers of religion use abstract concepts to redress the previously "imperialistic" use of only Western-identified terms in discussing religion. Feminist religious theorists use metaphors to prevent the deception of abstractions and to create religious imagery that reflects female experiences, balancing the long history of mostly patriarchal religious language.

While some feminists may substitute female religious metaphors for patriarchal expressions, Caroline Walker Bynum expresses a word of caution regarding female symbolism:

> Those who wish to effect the sort of changes that will let women's experiences speak may need to work, not to substitute female-referring symbols for male-referring symbols, but to open new symbolic modes. If we take as women's rituals and women's symbols the rituals and symbols women actually use, and ask how these symbols mean, we may discover that women have all along had certain modes of symbolic discourse different from those of men. Even where men and women have used the same symbols and rituals, they may have invested them with different meanings and different ways of meaning. To hear women's voices more clearly will be to see more fully the complexity of symbols.[44]

Bynum's point about the complexity of symbols is well taken, especially her suggestion that women may have found meanings in male-referring symbols. Also, she points out that the recognition of the complexity of symbols has happened in part through the creation of female-rooted symbols. Working with female-referring symbols for ultimacy makes the gendered quality of traditional religious symbols more apparent. And while most women do participate in the same symbols and rituals as men, it is also significant that many women have felt compelled to develop female-referring symbols in order to have their voices heard. Today, to look at the actual uses women make of symbols, one would have to include the increased use of female-referring symbols. Bynum is right that we should not ignore female use of traditional symbols and should investigate how they experience them and understand them in their own lives, but we should also analyze female use of female-referring symbols and what such use has taught us about the gendered quality and political dimension of all symbols.

Once again, a middle position may be most helpful in dealing with the differing qualities of concepts and symbols. Although not dealing with the feminist dimensions of this issue, Paul Tillich analyzed the tension between the more abstract concepts of god developed by the philosophers and the more personal and intimate expressions of biblical affirmations of God.[45] While arguing for the interdependence of these two approaches and rooting that interdependence in the existential experience of the religious person, Tillich concludes that the tensions between these two approaches will not be resolved but must be lived in courageously.[46] Similarly, I would argue that both concepts and metaphors are necessary in religious discourse and that the tension between the two approaches shows the underlying paradox in the understanding of ultimacy/God as both transcendent and immanent. Concepts are necessary to express the ultimacy of the reality that empowers religious lives, and metaphors are necessary to express the more intimate, personal relationship with ultimate power.[47]

Hermeneutics. Recognizing that language entails patterns of domination and reinforces social-cultural definitions of women versus men has led feminist interpretation of discourses and texts to be a hermeneutics of suspicion.[48] As Sandra Lee Bartky stated, "[F]eminists are not aware of different things than other people; they are aware of the same things differently."[49] Feminists interpret texts and speech with an intensified awareness of the finite character of human thought and its practical implications for the domination of women, and with a suspicion that philosophical and religious discourse hides the patriarchal assumptions. Although the following description of the hermeneutics of suspicion by Merold Westphal makes no reference to feminist hermeneutics, it does capture the element of self-deception that makes such a hermeneutics necessary.

> Whether the disputes are between believers and unbelievers, between adherents of different religious faiths, or between members of different traditions/denominations within one religious faith we are reminded that the disputants are not just finite but liable to self-deception, not just situated but situated sinners whose (perceived) self-interests enter (quite unperceived, to themselves at least) into their judgments about what is reasonable.[50]

In relation to religion and women, hidden but underlying patriarchal meanings support male dominance in the symbols for the divine as well as in the social structures of religious institutions. Feminist hermeneutics, then, not only captures the manifest patriarchal symbols and assumptions but also extracts the latent patriarchy. An example would be the feminist critique of theological abstractions as neutral on the surface but able to serve the patriarchal status quo.

Such a critical hermeneutics reinforces the connection between theory and practice, between knowing and doing. Feminist philosophy of religion assumes such a connection in its focus on the political implications of language and theory and in its concern to analyze issues in philosophy of religion that will have transformative effects.

God/Ultimacy

In addition to the issue of religious language, traditional philosophy of religion has analyzed theological claims about God, with common topics including attributes of God, such as omnipotence, omniscience, and eternity, with special problems including the fact of evil in the world, the existence of God, and human free will. In relation to human experience of God/ultimacy, discussions have covered faith, mystical experience, miracles, religious emotions, and the process of belief. Although much philosophy of religion has focused on Christian theology, recently more attention has been given to the plurality of religions and the effect of that on claims about God, religious experience, mysticism, and belief.

Critique of Patriarchy. These traditional topics about God in philosophy of religion are not absent from feminist discussions, but they are deemphasized or reconstructed to focus on topics that address women's issues of underlying patriarchy or affirming relationality, both of which are issues of power. A major part of these discussions is how one talks about God—with concepts or with metaphors, as discussed earlier. But topics such as the existence of God and the attributes of God also figure in feminist philosophical discussions.

Rather than approaching the issue of God's existence through analysis of traditional arguments, feminist philosophers have been more interested in deconstructing the concept of God to show the political use of the male-identified God in perpetuating patriarchy. As discussed earlier, the legitimation of patriarchal domination through traditional theological constructs has been argued strongly by Mary Daly in *Beyond God the Father.* Her arguments do not deny the reality of ultimate power, but they do deny the existence of the patriarchal God. Parallel with Feuerbach's reduction of theology to anthropology, Daly's arguments reduce traditional theology to patriarchy. But Daly's reconceptualization of God as Verb or her later female-rooted metaphors for divine activity retain more transcendence and ultimate power than Feuerbach's approach.

Some feminist philosophers of religion have used the work of Luce Irigaray, who criticizes the traditional concept of God as a projection of male ego and develops a feminine divine as a counterbalance. For Irigaray, such change is necessary to effect transformation in women's self-identity. Penelope

Deutscher argues that Irigaray's "feminine divine" "does serve the function of a horizon of perfection in terms of which women can identify themselves. But, for Irigaray, it is crucial that one 'participates' in the divine, in this sense. The divine is not an ideal from which a woman is severed,"[51] in contrast to the male divine with which men identify and yet feel separated from it. Connection with the divine rather than alienation from it and correlation of theological constructs with actual social structures are themes that reverberate in most feminist theology.

Relationality. Rooted in their political awareness of patriarchy, several feminist thinkers have been interested in relationality as a central attribute of God/dess. Feminist interest in reconfiguring relationships of power socially, economically, and politically along with ecological concerns have strongly influenced contemporary feminist religious thought. Feminist philosophy of religion explores the reconstruction of religious concepts and imagery that can affirm the equality and dignity of all persons, support and more importantly empower the suffering and the abused, affirm interconnections with nature, and celebrate the global interdependence of people from all cultures and religions. All of these issues focus on God/dess in relationship either to humans or to nonhuman beings. These are not new issues, but they are reconfigured by the concern with positions of power and the effort to avoid dominance and hierarchy. They attempt not only to redress the traditional assumptions of female inferiority in theology but also to identify with other people and nonhuman lives that have been dominated.

One example of a feminist theologian who integrates issues of patriarchal domination of women with human domination of the earth is Sallie McFague. In *Models of God* and *The Body of God*,[52] she argues that the models of God that we use affect our self-understanding, our relationships with other persons, and our treatment of the earth. Using the metaphors of Mother, Lover, and Friend for God and the image of the earth as God's body, McFague moves beyond the imperialist, patriarchal qualities of traditional Christian theology to relational images, which she hopes will encourage justice for all persons and better treatment of our earth. The importance of McFague's theology is not only that she develops models that meet contemporary concerns but that her analyses draw out implications of patriarchy, injustice, and dominance of the earth that have been ignored.

Feminist philosophers of religion need to analyze the arguments of McFague and other feminist theologians to show the implications for traditional philosophical issues of the nature of ultimacy, criteria of truth, and religious experience. Similar to traditional philosophy of religion, feminist critics of traditional theology question whether the traditional attributes of God are appropriate. But the contexts in which those questions arise differ greatly for traditional philosophers of religion and for feminist religious thinkers. While most traditional philosophers of religion raise their questions against the conventional Christian construct of God as a transcendent supreme being who is omniscient, omnipotent, eternal, etc., most feminist thinkers reject that construct as oppressive, imperialistic, and destructive for human lives and for our earth. Traditional philosophers of religion focus on the rationality of Christian claims while feminist thinkers see the practical implications of thought as most significant. This does not mean that feminist theorists reject arguments about rationality, but if the images themselves are rejected as inadequate to life, then their rationality or nonrationality is irrelevant. Feminist theories, like other theories, can be judged on criteria of coherence, correspondence, etc., but even these criteria have been broadened under feminist analysis (see above).

Resources in Diverse Religious Traditions. For traditional philosophers of religion, awareness of non-Christian traditions raised new questions about the truth of Christian claims and demanded a relativization of Christian absolutism. As indicated earlier, feminist work also demands a relativization of Christian absolutism. But feminist approaches to diverse religious traditions assume the possibility of truth outside Christian theology, rather than that being the major issue, and search the traditions for insights and images that can be part of the feminist reconstruction of religious thought and transformation of our world.

For example, a number of feminists have incorporated insights from early European goddess traditions, Greek and Egyptian mythologies, ancient Near Eastern traditions, Native American divine imagery, and Hindu goddesses.[53] Once the critique of extensive patriarchy in traditional Western theology had been demonstrated, then the question arose of alternatives to patriarchy. A natural place to turn was to existing traditions of female-identified divinity, in part because many of those female divinities predate and were replaced by the patriarchal images. Just as John Hick's effort to incorporate diverse approaches to the Real exposes traditional Western concepts to critique and relativizes them, so also feminist efforts to incorporate goddess traditions devalue the patriarchal constructs and make apparent elements that are missing in conventional formulations. For example, feminist analysis of goddess traditions reveals divine qualities of holistic interconnection of humans and nature and celebration of physical birth and other natural processes as well as female identification. These elements correlate well with feminist reconstruction of traditional theology and with feminist concerns for transformation of individuals and society. Many of the goddess traditions stem from earlier, less complex cultures that seem to have allowed more balanced complementary roles. Many feminists have developed a spirituality rooted in those traditions as part of their efforts to develop more just structures in our own society.

Feminist philosophers of religion also should note that not all cultures with goddess traditions can be seen as affirming of women and other oppressed peoples. Many cultures with goddesses express the interconnection of humans with nature as a divine relationship,[54] but this does not always lead to justice for women or to better treatment of the earth. Examples here could include the Shinto goddess Amaterasu versus the traditional position of women in Japanese culture and the Hindu mother-goddess Durgā versus the traditional position of women in Indian culture. And historical studies will show that patriarchy and hierarchy predate Western influences. Female divine imagery alone does not lead to a holistic world view or justice for all.

Multivalent Symbolism and Ultimate Power. Several facts raise questions about the feminist critique of patriarchal power in religion: (1) There is not an automatic or direct connection between concepts and imagery for the divine and social-cultural structures. (2) Many women are very active in patriarchal traditions and do find meaning in them. (3) Many feminists have chosen to reconstruct traditional theological constructs rather than abandon them. These three points suggest that we cannot make a simplistic connection between conceptual or symbolic constructs and social reality. Rather, I would argue that the human ability to construct meaning and the fact that humans do that in relationship to their personal and cultural contexts suggest that reality is multivalent and not restricted to one set of meanings. So also our social and political construction of reality is not monolithically driven but the result of numerous social, political, cultural, and personal forces. So where does that leave the feminist critique of patriarchal constructs? Why do patriarchal structures still develop in the midst of complementary or multivalent symbolism for the divine?

In a recent study of meanings given to the Cross of Jesus, I have argued that the same symbol has been used to legitimate violence and evil and yet has been found to be a liberating image, often by the very victims of that violence and evil.[55] Similarly, one could argue that while the image of God as a patriarchal, dominating figure legitimating the oppression and abuse of women is there in Christian tradition, Christian imagery of God also suggests God as an ultimate power that supports the oppressed and empowers them to challenge the oppression and to work to eradicate evil.

This paradox of meanings can be seen in Mary Daly's use and later rejection of Paul Tillich's theology. In *Beyond God the Father,* she reconstructed Paul Tillich's nongendered language for God because she obviously found it more empowering of women than traditional language. Yet Daly later rejects Tillich's formulations and criticizes Tillich's abuse of women as recorded in his wife Hannah Tillich's book.[56] With respect to Tillich's language, one could certainly pull in the feminist critique of abstractions supporting although hiding the underlying patriarchy. Yet females have responded to some of Tillich's ideas as liberating[57] in spite of his personal life.

For feminist philosophy of religion, these points raise key questions about the relationship between religious meanings and the social-cultural-political world. Paul Ricoeur's discussion of intentionality and hidden desires as part of the hermeneutic of suspicion may be relevant here, and deserves further investigation. But even that discussion rests on the differences between spoken intentions and meanings and hidden intentions and meanings. While those discrepancies play a role in this issue and deserve more attention, so also we need to analyze the multivalent quality of religious symbolism and the power of the divine/God in legitimating social structures.

Ultimacy however named, conceptualized, or symbolized has power. It does not even matter whether the ultimacy named is an accurate name or if it really exists. What is important about ultimacy is its ultimate power, which people accept as real and draw on for their own purposes. Those who hold dominating roles in a society can envision ultimate power as backing them in their domination. For example, religious texts that show God(s) as vengeful, destructive of enemies, supportive of hierarchical power such as kingship, etc. reflect such responses to ultimate power. Religious legitimations of Nazi power, expressing that Hitler was the new Holy Ghost or the carrier of a new revelation, are an extreme case, but they show the effort people make to draw on ultimate power in support of their own actions. On the other side, the victims of such oppression also turn to ultimate power to sustain them in the midst of their suffering and to empower them to have the courage to challenge, resist, or transform the current oppressive situation.

What this suggests is that ultimate power or ultimacy is open to multiple symbolism and that one's personal, social, cultural position influences greatly what aspects of that symbolism a person or a community unveils. Power can always be abused, and certainly ultimate power becomes especially dangerous because the qualities of ultimacy (eternal, unchanging, absolute, unlimited, unquestionable) are attached to the finite structure of power.

Paul Tillich's critique of idolatry combined with a hermeneutic of suspicion can be helpful here. While Tillich's critique of idolatry is rooted in the Christian symbol of the Cross, it is also tied to the basic religious paradox of all symbols, that they are at the same time ultimate and finite.[58] The critique of idolatry warns against absolutization of the finite, against drawing the qualities of ultimacy onto the finite meanings and structures of our finite world. Sallie McFague develops a similar critique in her discussion of metaphors as showing and not showing divinity, both is/is not.[59]

Tillich recognized the connection between idolatry and injustice, and that connection needs to be part of our hermeneutic of suspicion.[60] When ultimate power is drawn on and tied to *any* personal, social, political, or cultural construct, then we should be on guard for injustice. In general, the absolutization of finite structures entails the domination of one group of people over another and is generally enacted in unjust and often violent treatment of others.

This suggests that it is as important for feminists to apply the critique of idolatry and hermeneutic of suspicion to their own work as well as to past patriarchal work. It also suggests that new namings or symbolisms for God/dess will not automatically prevent oppressive personal interactions or social structures. What people *do* with the namings and symbols of God becomes more important than the new theological constructs. New namings of ultimacy may be strategic politically and comforting personally to many feminists, but the new names alone will not bring justice or prevent new injustices.

Using the critique of idolatry as part of a hermeneutic of suspicion, feminist philosophy of religion needs to analyze the use of God not only in traditional and feminist theological texts but also in popular culture (novels, movies, television) and in politics.[61] To the extent that feminist philosophy of religion deconstructs the understanding of God/dess in these various uses and makes clear the injustice that results from absolutizing the finite, it can contribute to the transformation of our social world toward greater justice. The challenge is for feminist philosophy of religion to remain self-critical in its own analyses.

Personhood: Self-identity and Others

The final topic of philosophy of religion to be discussed here focuses on personhood, especially the relationship between self-identity and interaction with others. Some attention was given to the feminist critique of the universality claimed for transcendental subjectivity and to the issue of embodiment under the epistemological discussion of experience. The focus here will be on the extent to which individual self-identity is affected by others and the relationship of that to religious experience.

For many feminist theories, one's self-identity is formed in relationship with other persons. This involves both the negative recognition that others have often given women their identity and the positive understanding that support from others and empathy with others can form a strong community. In spite of analyses that show women as named and defined by others (as discussed above under epistemology and language), many feminists support a relational understanding of self and argue for the centrality of community to any ethic.

In response to patriarchal false naming of women, Daly and others have encouraged women to participate in their own naming. This is part of "raising one's consciousness" and daring to be one's own self. But that process is not seen as private but rather as an individual experience occurring within a community of supportive women. It is not that now a different community does the naming but that the community supports the individual in developing her own self-identity. And that self-identity only comes into being through relation with others.[62] In contrast to earlier views of the self that saw the pure self identified by removing the individual from all social-cultural factors, this view of the self sees relationships not just as part of the context but rather as in some part constituting an individual's self-identity.[63] Self-identity does not come through detaching from others primarily but through one's interconnection with others. The individual person is both affected by others and also affects their understandings, feelings, and needs.

For many religious feminists, to exist and to come into being in community is supported by a religious ethic of caring for others and giving of oneself to others. In an ideal community, the giving of oneself would be matched by others giving of themselves. But Rita Nakashima Brock has analyzed the actual experiences of the self that involve experiences of damaging relationships and "broken-heartedness."[64] Yet she argues that the healing process will come through the power of "primal interrelatedness," which she names erotic power.[65] Just as ultimate power has multivalent meanings, so also the element of power in relationships can have many meanings and diverse effects. Interpersonal relationships can be empowering, liberating, and healing, but they can also distort, dominate, and oppress. The liberation of one's self from patriarchal relationships and the participation in supportive feminist communities are seen as religious experiences by Daly, Brock, and other feminist thinkers.

Feminist theories have analyzed extensively the destructive power of patriarchal relationships. Their alternative vision demands transformation of interpersonal relationships to become more balanced, just, compassionate, and empowering. The religious dimension of that vision often entails relational understandings of ultimacy and inclusion of relationships to the natural world, as discussed earlier. Religious self-identity, then, builds on ultimacy experienced in relationships rather than on a privatized, inner spiritual experience.

Carol Christ describes women's experiences of self-hatred and self-negation induced by ordinary patriarchal reality as experiences of nothingness.[66] But she also argues that such experiences of nothingness make women reject ordinary meanings and open themselves "to the revelation of deeper sources of power and value."[67] Such experiences of revelations are described by Christ as mystical experiences that occur through relationships with nature or with other women. Christ acknowledges similarities with other descriptions of mystical experiences of nothingness and awakening but argues that the experience for women is more strongly one of gain rather than loss. "Women often describe their awakening as a coming to self, rather than a giving up of self, as a grounding of selfhood in the powers of being, rather than a surrender of self to the powers of being."[68] Unlike most traditional mystical experiences, interconnections with others (persons and nature) are very much a part of the awakening.

Anne Klein uses Buddhist theories of subjectivity to develop an understanding of self that integrates body and mind.[69] She criticizes postmodern theories of subjectivity as too focused on language and as needing to include bodily experience as well. In contrast to postmodern views that deny the possibility of full presence of a subject, Klein argues that Buddhist mindfulness allows for full self-centering in the present where self includes mind and body but is not dependent on essentialist definitions of male and female bodies. She sees the Buddhist experience of emptiness and mindfulness as developing personal strength and agency that are compatible with the contemporary complexity of a woman's identity.[70]

Underlying Brock's, Christ's, and Klein's proposals is the desire to develop a religious understanding that empowers women's self-identity and encourages transforming the social world without sacrificing that identity. All of these efforts show the liberating possibilities for self that can be drawn from various understandings of ultimacy. But it must also be recognized that others have based patriarchal structures on similar understandings of ultimacy. For example, Klein's feminist reading of Buddhist subjectivity has not been the common experience of Buddhist women in other cultures and historical periods. The challenge, then, is to broaden the impact of these new proposals of self-identity through practical efforts to transform women's lives.

Conclusion

In conclusion, the impact of feminist work on philosophy of religion has been a broadening and shifting of traditional methods and issues rather than creation of a new methodology and content.[71] Critique of explicit and implicit patriarchal assumptions has been applied to traditional methods of philosophy of religion (phenomenology, transcendental reflection, analysis of experience, hermeneutics, analysis of language) and to traditional issues in the content of philosophy of religion (ultimacy, language, religious experience, self-identity, subjectivity). The effects of such critiques include questioning claims of objectivity and universality, emphasizing the significance of historical-cultural context for method and content, and drawing out the structures of power implicit in various methods and theories. Constructive proposals include more concern with embodiment, community, and liberation of women. In turn, proposed understandings of ultimacy are more relational, focusing on interconnections with persons and nature. Language to express these understandings is both conceptual and metaphorical, with strong preference given by many feminists to metaphorical expression.

Feminist philosophy of religion, like feminist theology, is interested in transformation and liberation, in connecting theory with action.[72] That agenda makes apparent the political implications of theory, with a recognition that all theory has political implications whether supporting the status quo or encouraging change. Feminist philosophy of religion, like feminist theology, participates in the liberation of women through giving voice to women's experiences, ideas, and goals. But unlike feminist theology, feminist philosophy of religion has not moved from the margins of the discipline. Throughout this chapter, we have seen shared issues and approaches between traditional philosophy of religion and feminist philosophy of religion. Even when the feminist arguments would enhance their arguments, most male philosophers of religion have ignored feminist analyses. Dialogue among these theorists must happen if they take seriously their avowed concerns for particularity, diversity and some universality. That feminists challenge traditional philosophies of religion is clear; what remains is for that challenge to impact more broadly and more deeply both male and female philosophers of religion.

The diversity of approaches in philosophy of religion points to the multivalent qualities of ultimacy, selves, and religion. And these multiple possibilities of meanings and of structures of interaction point to the contextual freedom we have in determining meanings and in creating social structures. Some use that freedom to theorize in ways that support or at least do not challenge current social structures. Others freely challenge the patriarchal status quo and propose meanings that can liberate and empower those on the margins of society. But for theory to become more effective practically, structures must be transformed as well as theories. Self-identity, understandings of ultimacy, religious language, and religious knowledge can be and are being transformed by feminist scholarship. New understandings alone do not create justice although they assist efforts toward justice. Scholarship in women's studies generally has that practical goal of transformation of society toward justice, but justice will require establishment of new, more equitable structures in religions and society as well as the transformation of ideas.

This chapter is both an analysis of various examples of feminist philosophy of religion as well as an exercise in feminist philosophy of religion. The examples used are far from exhaustive, but many are drawn from feminist theories not focused on religion and from feminist theologies. Feminist philosophy of religion as distinct from these approaches is developing but needs much more critical reflection on these approaches as well as more constructive proposals. Because feminist approaches are experienced by many women as liberating, their commitment to these approaches may make it difficult for them to be self-critical, a task that is crucial to the credibility of feminist philosophy of religion and in women's struggle for justice.

Notes

1. Nancy Frankenberry, "Introduction: Prolegomenon to Future Feminist Philosophies of Religions," *Hypatia* IX, no. 4 (Fall 1994): 1.

2. The term *traditional* is used throughout this essay to refer to approaches and topics that have dominated the discipline in recent decades.

3. Frankenberry, "Introduction," 2. Frankenberry develops these points (2–4): (1) Mostly white males have dominated the discipline of philosophy of religion, setting its focus mostly on Christianity until recently and relating to each other's work more than responding to the changing religious cultures. (2) In the last few decades, many philosophy departments grew increasingly skeptical of association with religion and did not become involved in the broadening, dynamic new fields within religious studies. Frankenberry points out that most women interested in philosophy of religion chose to do their Ph.D.s in religion or theology rather than in philosophy. (3) Many feminists have been so critical of the negative effects of religion on women that they have little interest in religious issues. (4) Mainstream philosophers of religion see their work as unaffected by gender issues, thus resisting feminist work.

4. Ibid., 5.

5. For example, see Jane Duran, *Toward a Femunist Epistemology* (Savange, Md.: Rowman and Littlefield, 1991), 3–15; Christine DiStefano, "Dilemmas of Difference: Feminism, Modernity, and Postmodernism," and Susan Bordo, "Feminism, Postmodernism, and Gender-Scepticism" in *Feminism/ Postmodernism*, ed. Linda J. Nicholson (New York and London: Routledge, 1990).

6. For example, Elizabeth Cady Stanton and the Revising Committee's *The Woman's Bible* (1895) (republished by the Coalition Task Force on Women and Religion, Seattle, 1974) focuses on the role of the Bible in setting social roles and meanings for women. Recognizing the political implications of such an effort and fearing repercussions in their academic settings, most female biblical and historical scholars would not participate.

7. William James, *The Varieties of Religious Experience* (1901–1902 Gifford Lectures) (New York: New American Library, 1958).

8. John Hick, *An Interpretation of Religion: Human Responses to the Transcendent* (New Haven and London: Yale University Press, 1989).

9. Judith Plaskow and Carol Christ, eds., *Weaving the Visions: New Patterns in Feminist Spirituality* (New York: Harper and Row, 1989).

10. Susan Brooks Thistlethwaite and Mary Potter Engel, eds., *Lift Every Voice: Constructing Christian Theologies from the Underside* (New York: Harper and Row, 1990).

11. For a longer analysis of common points between feminist and pluralist critiques of Christian theology, see Mary Ann Stenger, "Feminism and Pluralism in Contemporary Theology," *Laval Théologique et Philosophique* XLVI, no. 3 (October 1990): 291–305.

12. Robert Scharlemann, *The Reason of Following: Christology and the Ecstatic I* (Chicago and London: University of Chicago Press, 1991), 41.

13. Steven W. Laycock, "God as the Ideal: The All-of-Monads and the All-Consciousness," in *Phenomenology of the Truth Proper to Religion*, ed. Daniel Guerriere (Albany: State University of New York Press, 1990), 254.

14. Ibid., 263.

15. Ibid., 271–272.

16. For a discussion of "Enlightenment liberal feminists" who assume that women are or can be included under Enlightenment discussions of rationality, see Josephine Donovan, *Feminist Theory; The Intellectual Traditions of American Feminism* (New York: Frederick Ungar Publishing Co., 1985), chapter 1. Also, Philipa Rothfield notes: "The concept that the subject is an autonomous, self-constitutive being is articulated within the framework of liberal humanism, and therefore appears in the discourse of liberal feminism. The identity contained in the liberal paradigm would appear to be an abstract individual. However, the tradition of liberal humanism has been critically reviewed by feminist authors who tease out the implicitly male gender of such an 'abstract' individual." ("Feminism, Subjectivity, and Sexual Experience," in *Feminist Knowledge: Critique and Construct*, ed. Sneja Gunew [London and New York: Routledge, 1990], 132).

17. See Rothfield, "Feminism, Subjectivity," 136–141; Donovan, *Feminist Theory*, 27–30, 141–169; Duran, *Toward a Feminist Epistemology*, 161–181.

18. Robyn Rowland and Renate D. Klein, "Radical Feminism: Critique and Construct," *Feminist Knowledge*, 296. After pointing out the critique of biological essentialism, Rowland and Klein argue that the differences should be argued more strongly from differences in social worlds than from biology (p. 297). See also the critique of biological essentialism by Gisela T. Kaplan and Lesley J. Rogers, "The Definition of Male and Female; Biological reductionism and the sanctions of normality," *Feminist Knowledge*, 205–228.

19. See Elizabeth Grosz, "Conclusion; A note on essentialism and difference," in *Feminist Knowledge*, 340–343.

20. Marnia Lazreg, "Women's Experience and Feminist Epistemology; A critical neo-rationalist approach," in *Knowing the Difference: Feminist Perspectives in Epistemology*, ed. Kathleen Lennon and Margaret Whitfore (London and New York: Routledge, 1994), 58.

21. Ibid., 59.

22. Louis Dupré, "Truth in Religion and Truth of Religion," in *Phenomenology of the Truth Proper to Religion*, 19–42.

23. Ibid., 31.

24. Ibid., 32.

25. Ibid., 34.

26. Ibid., 37.

27. Ibid., 38.

28. See Joseph Rouse, *Knowledge and Power: Toward a Political Philosophy of Science* (Ithaca: Cornell University Press, 1987); Holmes Rolston, III, *Science and Religion: A Critical Survey* (Philadelphia: Temple University Press, 1987); Sandra Harding, *The Science Question in Feminism* (Ithaca: Cornell University Press, 1986). Also see, Philip Clayton, "Religious Truth and Scientific Truth," in *Phenomenology of the Truth Proper to Religion*, 43–59 for an analysis denoting important similarities as well as differences between scientific and religious truth.

29. In "Religious Truth and Scientific Truth," in *Phenomenology of the Truth Proper to Religion*, Philip Clayton argues: "As to *the attitudes and activities of scientific researchers*, the coherential understanding of truth already suggests science-religion parallels in practice as well as in theory or doctrine. As already indicated, the identity theorist holds that there are reasons for viewing science not as a basically theoretical endeavor but in the first place as a particular species of human activity, one reflecting the perspectives of its participants" (51).

30. Louis Dupré, "Truth in Religion and Truth of Religion," 40.

31. Sandra Harding, "Feminism, Science, and the Anti-Enlightenment Critiques," in *Feminism/Postmodernism*, 100.

32. Ibid., 87–88.

33. Edward Farley, "Truth and the Wisdom of Enduring," in *Phenomenology of the Truth Proper to Religion*, 60–74.

34. Ibid., 74.

35. The term *womanist* was first used by Alice Walker in *In Search of our Mother's Gardens: Womanist Prose* (San Diego: Harcourt, Brace Jovanovich, 1983) to affirm both African American and feminist connections.

36. For example, Elizabeth Johnson's *She Who Is* (New York: Crossroad, 1992) develops a trinitarian theology rooted in Sophia/Wisdom.

37. For a discussion of this shared interest between postmodernism and feminism, see Susan J. Hekman, *Gender and Knowledge; Elements of a Postmodern Feminism* (Boston: Northeastern University Press, 1990), 30.

38. Michele Barrett, "Words and Things: Materialism and Method in Contemporary Feminist Analysis," in *Destabilizing Theory: Contemporary Feminist Debates*, ed. Michele Barrett and Anne Phillips (Stanford: Stanford University Press, 1992), 203.

39. Mary Daly, *Beyond God the Father: Toward a Philosophy of Women's Liberation* (Boston: Beacon, 1973), 4.

40. Rebecca Chopp, *The Power to Speak: Feminism, Language, God* (New York: Crossroad, 1991), 26.

41. Ibid., 27.

42. It is noteworthy that several philosophers of religion, in dealing with religious pluralism, turned to abstract concepts like the Real (John Hick)

or transcendence (Wilfred Cantwell Smith). For more discussion of this topic, see my article, "Feminism and Pluralism in Contemporary Theology."

43. See Rosemary Ruether, *Sexism and God-Talk* (Boston: Beacon Press, 1983), 67 and Sallie McFague, *Models of God: Theology for an Exological Nuclear Age* (Philadelphia: Fortress Press, 1987), xi.

44. Caroline Walker Bynum, "The Complexity of Symbols," in *Experience of the Sacred: Readings in the Phenomenology of Religion,* ed. Sumner B. Twiss and Walter H. Conser Jr. (Hanover, N.H.: Brown University Press/University Press of New England, 1992), 272.

45. Paul Tillich, *Biblical Religion and the Search for Ultimate Reality* (Chicago: University of Chicago Press, 1955).

46. Ibid., 1, 65, 85.

47. See my fuller discussion of this issue in "Feminism and Pluralism in Contemporary Theology," 297–302.

48. The term *hermeneutics of suspicion* comes from Paul Ricoeur, who argued for a strong connection between language and consciousness, leading to interpretations that attempt to bring out both the underlying sense of language as well as the surface meanings.

49. Sandra Lee Bartky, "Toward a Phenomenology of Feminist Consciousness," in *Feminism and Philosophy,* ed. Mary Vetterling-Braggin, Frederick A. Elliston, and Jane English (Totowa, N.J.: Rowman and Littlefield, 1977/1981), 26.

50. Merold Westphal, "Phenomenologies and Religious Truth," in *Phenomenology of the Truth Proper to Religion,* 122–123.

51. Penelope Deutscher, "'The Only Diabolical Things About Women . . .': Luce Irigaray on Divinity," *Hypatia* IX, no. 4 (Fall 1994): 102.

52. Sallie McFague, *The Body of God: An Ecological Theology* (Minneapolis: Fortress Press, 1993).

53. For examples, see several articles on Native American, Old European, Greek, and Mesoamerican goddesses in *Weaving the Visions*; Kartikeya C. Patel, "Women, Earth, and the Goddess: A Shakta-Hindu Interpretation of Embodied Religion," *Hypatia* IX, no. 4 (Fall 1994): 69–87; *The Book of the Goddess Past and Present: An Introduction to Her Religion,* ed. Carl Olson (New York: Crossroad, 1986).

54. For example, one can see such a divine interconnection in Shinto or in Hindu views of all living beings as connected to ultimate reality.

55. Mary Ann Stenger, "The Ambiguity of the Symbol of the Cross: Legitimating and Overcoming Evil," in *Evil and the Response of the World Religion,* ed. William Cenkner (St. Paul, MN: Paragon House, 1997), 56–69.

56. Hannah Tillich, *From Time to Time* (New York: Stein and Day, 1973).

57. In addition to my own use of Tillich's ideas, see Anne Carr, *Transforming Grace* (San Francisco: Harper and Row, 1988); Sallie McFague, *Models of God*; and Carter Heyward, *The Redemption of God: A Theology of Mutual Relation* (Lanham, Md.; University Press of America, 1982).

58. For fuller discussion of this point, see my discussion in "Paul Tillich's Theory of Theological Norms and the Problems of Relativism and Subjectivism," *The Journal of Religion* LXII, no. 4 (October 1982): 359–375.

59. Sallie McFague, *Models of God*, 33–35.

60. See my discussion of the connection between idolatry and injustice in "Male Over Female or Female Over Male: A Critique of Idolatry," *Soundings* LXIX, no. 4 (Winter 1987): 464–478.

61. For example, one could analyze Margaret Atwood's *The Handmaid's Tale* (New York: Fawcett Crest, 1985) as an illustration of both the ambiguity in meanings that are latent in our contemporary politics, both liberal and conservative, and the injustices that result from absolutizing one group of people (elite white males). She portrays the society of Gilead as a divinely legitimated ("God is a National Resource") social order that celebrates the fertility of women (what remains of that fertility after ecological disasters) and ensures the safety of women in public. But that society also reinforces the position of women as subordinate objects to be used for procreative purposes or as household servants on the basis of religious legitimations. Parallels to contemporary political uses of religious power to support set agendas for society are easily drawn.

62. Ruth Smith, "Feminism and the Moral Subject," in *Women's Consciousness, Women's Conscience*, ed. Barbara Hilkert Andolsen, Christine E. Gudorf, and Mary D. Pellauer (San Francisco: Harper and Row, 1985), 236, 246. See also Charles Winquist, *Desiring Theology* (Chicago: University of Chicago Press, 1995): "What is at stake is that self becoming is always relational (communal), always contingent, and always unfinished" (141). In "Feminism and the Ethic of Inseparability," in *Women's Consciousness, Women's Conscience*, Catherine Keller argues that interconnection and loving another are central values which affirm community but also assume differentiated selves (262). In *Journey by Heart: A Christology of Erotic Power* (New York: Crossroad, 1991), Rita Nakashima Brock describes the self as a "relationship-seeking activity" (9).

63. Ruth L. Smith, "Feminism and the Moral Subject," 236.

64. Rita Nakashima Brock, *Journey by Heart*, 13, 16, 22, 24.

65. Ibid., 26.

66. Carol Christ, "Nothingness, Awakening, Insight, New Naming," in *Experience of the Sacred: Readings in the Phenomenology of Religion*, 121. Compare Mary Daly's discussion of women's experience of nonbeing in *Beyond God the Father*, chapters 1 and 5.

67. Christ, "Nothingness," 121.

68. Ibid., 126.

69. Anne C. Klein, "Presence with a Difference: Buddhists and Feminists on Subjectivity," *Hypatia* IX, no. 4 (Fall 1994): 112–130.

70. Ibid., 126. See also Rita M. Gross, *Buddhism After Patriarchy: A Feminist History. Analysis, and Reconstruction of Buddhism* (Albany: State University of New York Press, 1993).

71. For a parallel but somewhat different analysis of trends in feminist philosophy of religion, see Marilyn Thie, "Epilogue: Prolegomenon to Future Feminist* Philosophies of Religions," *Hypatia* IX, no. 4 (Fall 1994): 229–239.

72. In "The Idea of God in Feminist Philosophy," (*Hypatia* IX, no. 4 [Fall 1994]), Marjorie Hewitt Suchocki argues that feminist theorists "insist that the ultimate judge of any philosophical thinking is not simply coherence and consistency, but the pragmatic criterion of the philosophy's impact on communities of inclusive well-being" (67).

7

Methodologies in Women's Studies and Feminist Theology

ROSEMARY RADFORD RUETHER

Feminist theology is both a critical reflection on the effects of androcentric bias on theology, and also a reconstruction of theology so that women are fully included and affirmed as full and equal human beings in the symbolic content of theology, as well as in the teaching and pastoral ministries of the church. In this essay on methodologies in feminist theology, I will focus on Christian feminist theology, although much of what I say could also be applied to other religions where formal systems of theology exist, such as Judaism, Islam, or Buddhism.[1]

Feminist theology starts with the recognition that Christian theology has been created primarily from male elite experience. Its symbols and world view have reflected these sociological origins, and have functioned to legitimate male elite monopoly on both teaching and pastoral ministry in the churches in particular and in society in general. Feminist theology arises out of a fundamental shift in consciousness. Instead of this male monopoly on leadership in the church and society being accepted as both "natural" and "divinely ordained," it is seen as wrong, as a fundamental violation of justice to women that impedes women's full human development in society and the full vision of redemption in Christ.

Proceeding from this fundamental shift in evaluation of the "facts" of male monopoly of theology, feminist theology proceeds with a threefold process. It begins by developing a systematic critique of the effects of this male bias on the symbols and norms of Christian faith. Secondly it seeks alternative traditions within the collective historical heritage and religious experience of women and men that provide more inclusive images of women. Thirdly, feminist theology moves toward the revisioning of the basic symbols of Christian faith that will undo male bias and create a wholistic theology in which women are no longer overtly or covertly marginalized by theological discourse.

179

This process of criticism of androcentric and misogynist symbols in theology, the recovery of more inclusive alternatives and the systematic reinterpretation of Christian symbols, such as God, Christ, sin, salvation, and church, so that women are equally affirmed, necessarily involves a wide variety of methodologies. Feminist theology draws on feminist methodologies across the academic disciplines: in literary criticism, history, philosophy. psychology, sociology, and anthropology, in order to both analyze how the symbols of Christian faith have been shaped by androcentric bias, and to lay the historical, hermeneutical, and cultural symbolic basis for an inclusive restatement of theological terms.

Feminist Methodologies in the Academic Disciplines

Feminist methodology in each of the academic disciplines starts with the basic recognition that women have been excluded from the discipline, both as practitioners of it and as objects of its research. The net effect of this double exclusion is that women are generally invisible in the discipline. When they are mentioned at all, it is primarily to enforce ideologies that justify women's exclusion from public leadership and their limitation to separate roles in the private, domestic sphere, ideologies that the discipline has presented as if they were unasssailable "truths" that arise from and are confirmed by the discipline itself.

This androcentric bias in all the academic disciplines itself reflects the basic sociology of the production and control of knowledge. Women have been largely excluded from higher education in all the traditions that have shaped Christian thought: Judaism, classical Greek and Roman societies, and medieval and early modern Europe. Men, specifically an elite class of men, have had an almost total monopoly on the production of all fields of knowledge, both the learning and the teaching of it. Male dominance of education thus has created a social context in which all fields of knowledge both reflected and justified male control of knowledge and the uses of knowledge.

It is only in the late nineteenth and early twentieth centuries that women in Western Europe and North America gained access to colleges and universities, and they were not present in theological schools in more than token numbers until the early 1970s. An elite class of women did gain education through women's monastic life in the Middle Ages, but the Church's control over public intellectual life made it extremely dangerous to express dissenting ideas from the dominant orthodoxy, including gender orthodoxy. A few women were privately educated in their families in Renaissance and modern Europe, but had little access to the public forums of intellectual life, being excluded from universities.

Even when women gained access to higher education in the last one hundred years, the pervasive assumptions of women's intellectual inferiority and incapacity for rigorous thought meant that the first generation of academic women spent much of their energy simply learning the disciplines and proving that they were capable of the "same" intellectual achievements in various fields as men.[2] It was only when women as students and then as teachers in higher education had won their place in some numbers, that it became possible for the "second wave" of feminism to begin to challenge the androcentrism and misogyny within the fields themselves and to propose reconstruction of those fields to eliminate this male gender bias.

Thus "women's studies" and "feminist critique" in various disciplines is a phenomenon in U.S. universities beginning in the late 1960s to mid-1970s. Women's studies also arises in universities in Western Europe, as well as countries such as India, in the mid-1970s or later.[3] Women's studies and feminist critique of the theological disciplines begins about the same time as women gained access to ordination in increasing numbers of Protestant denominations from 1956 (Methodists and Presbyterians) to 1976 (Episcopalians) and thus became present as students and then as professors in theological schools in larger numbers.[4]

Women (and some men) with a feminist perspective could then begin to incorporate feminist critique and revisioning of the theological disciplines into the teaching of theology itself in theological education and so begin to change what was transmitted to the next generation of teachers and pastors as the interpretation of the "tradition." Since theological schools were training pastors for the church, as well as future teachers, both men and women, this revisioning of the content of theological education has broad effects on the church and society as well.

Feminist theology does not just begin in the late 1960s. It is possible to discover women in earlier centuries, such as Christine de Pizan in the mid-fifteenth century and Margaret Fell in the 1660s, who wrote tracts that criticized Christian symbols from a feminist perspective,[5] but these writings had virtually no effect on the public discourse of Christian thought because their criticism was not incorporated into the ongoing teaching and preaching of Christianity. Indeed, such earlier feminist writings remained largely unknown in the dominant academic world, often surviving accidently in libraries and archives. It is contemporary feminist studies that have searched out, reclaimed, and republished these earlier feminist foremothers.

Thus, one can say that feminist studies in theology, or in any discipline, make little impact on public culture until women are present in sufficiently significant numbers as teachers in a particular field of education, and feminist critique is sufficiently accepted, that they are able to incorporate this critique into academic discourse with colleagues and the way the discipline is taught to the next generation of students; in short, until women and women's critical perspective gains some ability to control and shape the educational processes themselves.

This has only begun to happen in universities and theological schools. But it is still very much a contested presence of feminist critique that is not fully incorporated into the "foundational" teaching of the discipline. In other words, women's studies and feminist critique tends to remain marginalized in separate enclaves in the universities and theological schools, either in specialized programs or in special elective courses, taken only by feminists (mostly women and a few men). The majority of the "normal" courses still mostly ignore feminist revisionism in the field and thus proceed as if androcentric bias were normative for the field; that is, they are not labeled as "men's studies."

It is often still risky for women who wish to survive in academe to take a feminist line in their field, since this is considered "soft" (and also aggressive and dissident) thinking. Consequently, many women accept the message that to ignore women's issues in their fields is the way to "make it" in academic life. Consequently, although feminist thought now has some twenty to thirty years of development in many fields and has produced an enormous amount of comprehensive and highly credible scholarship in every field, it has largely not achieved its ultimate goal, which is to transform the foundational content and methods of the disciplines so that they are no longer androcentric, but genuinely gender inclusive.

In theological schools feminist revision of theological disciplines is further embattled by backlash in the churches (reflecting backlash in the society in general). Conservatives in many Christian denominations have denounced feminism as heresy, claiming that male language for God is unchangeable truth and female imagery for God is "paganism."[6] Since feminism in theological schools aims not simply at transforming theological education itself, but also the practice of teaching, preaching, and worship in the churches, this backlash that seeks to rule out feminist questions a priori as contrary to orthodoxy puts all feminists at risk in the Christian churches.

With these provisos on the limited and still embattled nature of feminism and women's studies in academic disciplines in general and theology in particular, let me survey briefly some basic elements of feminist methodologies in the fields of history, anthropology, sociology, psychology, and philosophy. I will then discuss their use in theology.

Feminist revision of history writing starts with the obvious point that what has been regarded as "historical" has been public political, military, and cultural events from which women have been mostly excluded in patriarchal societies. Thus, "history" has been not only almost entirely men's history, but the history of a certain class of elite men in power and mostly these men only in the public, political aspects of their lives. The relations of such "great men" to men and women friends, parents, wives, lovers, children is invisible or of concern only to those interested in psychoanalytic history. The pervasive assumption has been that women are not historical actors, and appear, if at all, only in their relations to "great men".

Women's studies in history begins by trying to find the women in history. It may do so by playing by the same rules of what history is, by trying to find the occasional "great woman" who was a ruler, thinker, or creator of cultural artifacts of note. Or it can seek to widen the field of what is called history by including areas where women are more fully present, in family history or in the history of "lower levels" of the society where women are present as workers, artisans, and social actors. Since the sources for history have privileged documents of the sort that record the public lives of powerful men, women's studies in history is faced with the problem of finding the source material for this enlarged history, either by close reading of well-known sources to discover traces of women's lives that have been ignored by male scholars or by discovering new primary sources, such as diaries, letters, documents, and newspapers, that may reflect the lives of broader classes of people.[7]

Feminist historians have been interested in not only finding women as historical subjects, but also in discovering those women who began, through writing, artistic creation or social activities, to challenge the imposed limitations put on women's lives, women who opposed and protested these limits, by transgressing them in their own lives and/or by criticizing these limits as unjust. In other words, they have been interested in finding the history of feminist foremothers. If patriarchy is (and has always been) an unjust social pattern that violates women's fuller capacities, it is important to document that there were women in past generations who also recognized this, as well as to understand why so few were able (or can be known) to have challenged this and why feminism as a movement only became possible under certain circumstances in modern times.

The patterns of society that marginalized women, and the cultural constructs that reenforced this marginalization, become themselves a part of feminist historical analysis. Feminists have been concerned to show the organization of power that rendered women invisible and also where and how women transgressed these strictures. This also means that feminist historiography, and all feminist revisionist work in academic disciplines, transgresses and rejects the claims that "good science" is "disinterested" and "value free."

Feminist revisionist methods are "interested" methods, interested in changing social systems that restrict women in the name of justice for women and a more just society as a whole. This means they also challenge the claims of objectivity and disinterestedness in the dominant social sciences and show how these claims enforce a male bias that renders women invisible, a bias often overtly revealed by assertions about women's inferiority and natural place. In short, androcentric science is neither objective nor value free, but is a hegemonic knowledge that confirms male control of it, as well as in society as a whole.

Key to feminist methodologies is the rejection of notions that this marginalized place of women reflects "natural" and "inevitable" realities about
female and male biologies. Feminists analyze these social systems, and their
claims about male and female nature, as social constructions for the purpose
of giving men power and privilege over women. Feminist revisionist science
thus seeks knowledge for the sake of change, for the sake of a particular kind
of change; namely, the change of social structures that marginalize women
and the change of ideologies that reenforce that marginalization of women, in
order to create more just and inclusive social relations of men and women.

Feminist methodologies in other social sciences follow much of the same
lines as feminist historiography. Feminist anthropologists have begun by asking
about the absence of women, both as researchers and as subjects of anthropological studies. They have questioned the pervasive tendencies of male anthropologists both to take the accounts of males in the societies studied as normative
for the whole society and to impose judgments on the society drawn from the
male-dominant societies of the researchers.

Feminist anthropologists have also recognized that, in societies where
women are highly segregated from men, it is impossible for the male anthropologist to question the women or observe them in their daily functioning.
Female anthropologists also have to struggle to shed their own cultural biases,
to try to understand the other society, and women in that society, in their own
terms. Yet they can use their femaleness to be able to gain entreé to the women's
side of the society and to seek to discover thereby the female point of view.

Female anthropologists have often found that this female point of view
provides a very different set of assumptions about economic and cultural realities than that found only by seeing male activities and the male viewpoint.
For example, the male may describe the house where his wife and children
live as "his house," while the woman may understand it as her house. Actual
observation from within the house may make it evident that the man enters it
only on her sufferance. Or male hunting may be regarded by the men as the
primary source of food for the society, but observation of women's work
makes it clear that female gathering and gardening provides the actual bulk of
the food consumed. The actual functioning of a society thus cannot be
described only from the male perspective.[8]

A subject of great interest to feminist anthropologists has been the origins
of male domination in family and social structures and how the higher status
and power of men over women is justified and enforced. Many nineteenth-
and early-twentieth-century anthropologists assumed that patriarchal patterns
were universal and reflected the "natural" social arrangements that followed
from female child bearing, child care, and lesser bodily strength. Some nineteenth-century anthropologists, however, believed that the original patterns
of human society were matriarchal, and that patriarchy was a later stage of

development, although usually these writers also assumed that this development was a higher or better stage.[9]

In the twentieth century grand theories of human development, which see all societies as passing from one type of society to another, fell out of favor with anthropology, in favor of "scientific" observation of particular societies. But feminists have revived the question of whether male domination is universal and whether either more egalitarian or female-dominant patterns may have existed more commonly at earlier times in human development. Even those who have concluded that some greater power and status of men over women exists in all societies, although with much variation, reject the assumption that this is natural and inevitable. Rather, they seek to analyze the social and cultural ways these patterns are constructed and perpetuated.[10]

Since more female-dominant or gender egalitarian social patterns seem to correlate with societies that have either female-centered or gender-paired understandings of the divine and the ordering of the cosmos, while strongly male-dominant societies seem to have either an exclusively male divinity and/or myths that emphasize male dominance in the ordering of the cosmos, these questions about the social origins of male domination have been of great interest to feminist theologians and religionists as well.[11]

If the male monotheistic view of God and God's actions found in the Bible are not universal in human religion, but are a fairly recent development in the Ancient Near East that arose through the repression of more egalitarian societies and female divinities, then this has major implications for how the Biblical view of God is evaluated. Was the advent of male monotheism the vindication of the authentic God against idols and demons, as the tradition has supposed, or a problemmatic ideological expression of the rise of patriarchy?

Feminist sociology is distinquished from anthropology in that it studies contemporary "developed" societies. It too faces a pervasive pattern in classical sociology that both ignored women as subjects and, when it noticed them, justified their subordination and limitation to the domestic sphere. It seeks to widen the sociological subject matter to include the relation of family to other social structures and to show how the total pattern of social structures reenforces women's marginalization. Like other feminist methods, it rejects this marginalization as natural and "good." Feminist sociologists also study how the inclusion of women in public roles changes the way social structures function.[12]

Feminist sociologists have been divided between liberals and Marxists. Liberal feminists have primarily sought to argue for the equal inclusion of women in public economic, political, and cultural roles in the existing Western capitalist society. Marxists have argued that women's subordination, both in unpaid labor in the family and in the low-paid labor in the paid work force, is an integral part of a patriarchal capitalist socioeconomic system that allows a male capitalist ruling class to accumulate the lion's share of economic profit and political power by exploiting dependent classes of workers.[13]

For Marxists, the emancipation of women can only happen through a major overhaul in the system of ownership of the means of production. For women, this would mean, not only equal inclusion in paid labor, but also a transformation of the system of unpaid domestic labor done almost entirely by women that prevents them from entering the public world on equal terms with men. It is not enough for men to share domestic labor equally with women on a private, voluntary basis, because the public system of work and power is still predicated on the assumption that men are freed from such work by women. Men who share such work would be both handicapped in terms of time for economic opportunities and culturally derided by men who follow the traditional patterns.

Emancipation of women demands a reconstruction of the total system of home and work relations in order to make it possible for men and women to participate as equals in all areas of the social system, rather than dividing society into male and female spheres that are ordered in a hierarchical interdependence. Feminist sociologists may study democratic socialist societies, such as Sweden, where there have been more intentional efforts to achieve this equality in both domestic and public relations than has been the case in the United States.

Feminist psychology also faces a dominant tradition in its field, in the major schools of psychological thought, both psychoanalytical and empirical, which have reinforced traditional gender dimorphism. This dimorphism of men as "masculine" (rational, aggressive, independent) and female as "feminine" (intuitive, emotional, passive, and dependent) has been assumed to be both biologically based and hence necessary and, at the same time, a pattern that is to be enforced by psychocultural socialization. Masculinity and femininity are both what men and women are by nature, and what they must become in order to achieve "normal" and "healthy" psychosocial development.

This means that men who prefer what are seen as more "feminine" styles of behavior (intuitive, sensitive, gentle, interdependent) and women who prefer more "masculine" styles (intellectual, aggressive, and independent) are evaluated as deviant, unhealthy, even pathological. Older psychology labeled such "deviant" gender patterns as both cause and evidence of homosexuality, seen as the pathological failure of "normal" psychological health and development par excellence. Thus, psychology has functioned overwhelmingly to provide a new set of sanctions for traditional gender stereotypes, as these stereotypes were losing their religious justifications and were being challenged by feminism in modern societies.[14]

Feminist revisionism in psychology has sought to revise these psychological dogmas, both by suggesting much more positive views of feminine characteristics as the basis of creativity and relationality,[15] and also to challenge the binary assignment of one set of characteristics to men and another to women. Feminist psychologists have redefined the healthy personality, not as one that is exclusively masculine or feminine, but rather as one that is "androgynous"; that is, that develops toward a creative synthesis of independence and interdependence, activity and receptivity, rationality and intuitiveness, instrumental and expressive capacities.[16]

Far from bimorphic development providing optimal male-female relationships, considerable research has shown that the pairing of highly masculine men and feminine women is often unhappy and even abusive, with little capacity to communicate between such opposites, while more androgynous men and women have happier and more satisfied relationships.[17] Also, the assumption that masculinity and femininity are each a package of characteristics that normally go together has been questioned. Many psychologists today would opt for a more complex understanding of human psychological traits, present in all humans, and which each person develops in individual syntheses.

Contemporary psychologists, informed by both feminist and gay and lesbian protests, have revised the concept of feminine men and masculine women as the source and expression of homosexuality. Many have also rejected the assumption that homosexuality is a pathological condition. The aetiology of homosexual preference is seen as much more uncertain. Some claim that homosexuality is a naturally occurring variant of human sexual wiring, while others see it as a preference that develops socially from an initial capacity of all humans for bisexuality. In this context it is as much a question of how most people "become" heterosexual, as it is a question of why some people resist the dominant socialization into heterosexuality to claim a homosexual or bisexual preference.[18]

Feminist revisionist thought in philosophy also faces a pervasive tradition in Western philosophy, from Plato and Aristotle to Kant, Hegel, and Nietzsche, that both asserted the normativity of the male and disparaged women as having a lesser capacity for thought and human agency. This is of major concern for feminist theology because the incorporation of Greek philosophy, particularly that of Plato and Aristotle, as the base for Christian theology, had a major effect in reinforcing andocentric and misogynist views in theology.[19]

Plato's ontological and moral dualism of soul and body, mind and matter—with body and matter as both ontologically inferior and the cause of moral fault—which saw men as more spiritual and women as more material, had a major impact on Christian theology. Platonic dualism gave philosophical justification to the denial that women as female body (women are seen as having the image of God as gender-neutral soul, but not *qua femina*) possessed the image of God, and to doctrines of sin that condemned women as more sin-prone than men and the primary cause of the Fall. Aristotle's definition of women as lacking full humanity, being defective in the very process of biological production, underlay Thomas Aquinas's definition of women as "misbegotten males" who cannot represent Christ in the ordained priesthood because only the male possesses full normative humanity necessary for Christ's incarnation.[20]

Feminist philosophers have not only critiqued the androcentrism and misogyny in classical and modern Western philosophy, but they have also sought philosophical methods more supportive of feminist theory. Some contemporary feminist theorists have explored postmodern and poststructualist thought as particularly useful for feminist theory, while other feminists question the helpfulness of these methods for feminism.[21]

Postmodernism has particularly attacked the Cartesian concept of the individual as universal self, which has been the basis for personal identity and civil rights in modern liberal societies. Far from being a concept of the self that really includes women, liberal revolutions in the United States, France, and elsewhere initially excluded women from citizenship, based on the assumption that this sort of self was possessed only by males of property. Only with great difficulty have women, as well as various groups of propertyless and dependent men (servants, slaves), succeeded in winning recognition that they are included in this definition of the "all men" who are "created equal" and "endowed by their creator with certain inalienable rights."

Postmodernists would argue that this concept of the self as a transcendental, autonomous consciousness is both false, ignoring the actual reality of selves as the product of a network of social and cultural relationships, and also one that cannot include female difference, as well as any other kind of difference from the hegemonic norm of those ruling men who have identified their selfhood with this concept of the human person. Women, white and nonwhite, and nonwhite men may attempt to include themselves in this concept of the human person, but this will always be contradictory. The very nature of this concept of the self defines women of all races and nonwhite men as other and lesser, not full members of this universal humanity, or approximating it only to the extent that they can think and act as much as possible like white Western males.

Recently, postmodern feminists have argued, not only that feminism has pursued the wrong direction in seeking to affirm women's equality through inclusion in this modern concept of the person, they have also reduplicated the same mistake by assuming a universal normative concept of woman as the generic excluded other of patriarchical systems of society and culture. Feminism, they argue, must abandon this concept of univocal womanness and, with it, the concept of woman's experience, in favor of the recognition of an endless diversity of selves, constituted by diverse networks of culture and social relations.

Many feminists are willing to let go of any ideas of essential femaleness and maleness based on biological nature, as well as a univocal model of female experience. The increasing protests of African-American, Hispanic, Asian, lesbian, and other groups of women against a white middle-class heterosexual feminism, which assumed that its concerns were those of women, has led most feminists to seek a more plural understanding of women's concerns, based on an expanding dialogue between women of different classes, races, and cultures.

But many feminists are less convinced that they should give up any concept of a substantive basis for human personhood apart from a network of relations. Moreover, the insistence on endless differences finally dissolves any way of talking about an ongoing identity of cultural groups, or even of individuals, rooted in the interaction of self and experience. In its own way postmodernism seems to have reproduced radical Western individualism, substituting the Cartesian "view from nowhere" with a theoretical claim to embrace all diversity in a "view from everywhere."[22] We will discuss the problems of postmodernism and poststructualism in feminist methodology further in its application to feminist theology and hermeneutics.

Feminist Methodologies in Feminist Theology

Feminist theology makes use of the whole range of feminist methodologies developed in women's studies in the academy, although some feminist theologians may focus more on literary, hermeneutical, or philosophical methods, and others more on historical and sociological methods. Revisionist history of the Christian community and theology plays a key role in both the critical and the constructive work of feminist theology.

Feminist critique of Christian theology typically began with a history of misogyny in Christian theology. Mary Daly's early book, *The Church and the Second Sex*,[23] was this type of feminist revisionist history of theological thought, showing how hostility to women, and justifications of women's exclusion from church leadership, pervades the writings of the major Christian theologians, from Tertullian in the second century, with his denunciation of women as the "devil's gateway," to modern theologians, such as Karl Barth, with his insistence that men and women occupy a places of super and sub-ordination in the divinely ordained "order of creation."[24]

Feminist criticism of theology has demonstrated that such misogynist statements were not simply an idiosyncratic expression of certain personalities, who had "personal problems" with women, but were an integral part of the theological system itself. More careful study of theological history introduced a more subtle analysis of these patterns. It became apparent that the dominant thought of Christian theology was an androcentrism that rendered women invisible. The male was assumed to be the normative subject and representative of Christian faith.

Misogynist statements tended to occur in the writings of theologians or in church documents when these exclusions were violated, and movements occurred that supported women as teachers, preachers, and ministers in the church. The New Testament itself enshrines the first example of this conflict. Early Christianity had trends in it that encouraged the breakdown of gender roles and the participation of women in church leadership, but, as the church became institutionalized, it incorporated a patriarchal social order that excluded women's leadership. Thus, the secondary strata of the New Testament are rife with statements that attempt to give theological justification to the exclusion of women leaders, repressing the theologies that had included them.[25]

These theological justifications of women's exclusion from leadership draw on two arguments: the patriarchal ordering of the family and society as order of creation and the silencing of women as punishment for the sin, particularly for their primacy in causing the Fall of Man. These arguments occur classically in I Timothy 2:10–14: "I do not permit a woman to teach or to rule over man, she should keep silence. For Adam was created first, and then Eve. And it was not Adam who was deceived. It was woman who, yielding to deception, fell into sin. "

Christian theological misogyny through the centuries has been mainly an elaboration on these two assertions: that woman is intrinsically subordinate in the order of creation, and hence in the family and society, by God's intention, and that she was the cause of sin entering the world by rejecting this ordained place. Women are then to be doubly put down, both to put her back in her place, and to punish her for the transgression of getting out of her place. Variations of these arguments have been endlessly fetched up at those moments in Christian history when women have begun to gain some access to public forums in the church or Christian society.

This reading of overt misogyny in Christian theology, not as a general consensus, but as a reaction to conflictive theological views and social movements in Christian society, also opens up another avenue of historical research. It becomes evident that from the beginnings of Christian history, there were also alternative theological perspectives and practices that tended toward a more egalitarian reading of the gospel. It becomes possible to trace, on the margins and between the lines of the hegemonic male church and its theology, an alternative line of faith and practice.

From women apostles, prophets, and teachers in the New Testament, to women mystics and leaders in monastic communities of the Middle Ages, to women preachers and leaders of congregations on the left wing of the Reformation, to founders of new churches, reformers, and missionaries in the nineteenth century, leading into the gaining of women's ordained ministry in the twentieth century, there is a history of women in the Christian church that is not simply one of silence and passive reception of male dictates. Moreover, many of these women wrote tracts defending their active work, drawing on inclusive readings of Scripture and theology. A feminist revision of Christian theology draws on this alternative tradition to reshape Christian symbols in ways inclusive of women.[26]

Feminist sociology, and economic and legal history, is also important to feminist theology. Feminist work in the social sciences allow the woman theologian to define more concretely what patriarchy means as a socioeconomic and legal system in different historical periods. In first century Roman society patriarchy meant the rule of the *paterfamilias* over those defined as dependents: women, children, slaves, animals, and land. This collectivity of those ruled over by the patriarch defined what Roman law called the *familia*.[27]

Why the Bible and Christian theology not only define God in terms drawn from the patriarchal class, but also refer to the church metaphorically as the wife (bride), sons, and servants of God, comes into focus when we understand more fully this social system, which provided the base for the theological metaphors of divine and creaturely relationships. Concepts such as male headship, Christ as head of the body, the church, and the image of God as a collective sovereignty possessed by males, not only over their own bodies, but over women as well, are thereby explicated to a modern Christian audience that no longer lives in this older form of the patriarchal system.

Anthropology, or the comparative study of non-Western societies, helps Jews and Christians to better understand the societies and cultures that lay behind Hebrew society and religious thought in the ancient Near East. How to understand the prominence of goddesses in these societies, whether they represent a more egalitarian society that the Hebrews rejected for a more patriarchal one, or whether they are remnants of a more egalitarian society of a much earlier period, before the rise of "civilization," is a major area of controversy between Jews and Christians and those radical feminists who seek a Goddess-centered religious world view reclaimed from this assumed earlier stage of human religious and social history.[28]

Anthropology is also important to uncovering the silences about women's role in Hebrew religion on the margins of the dominant male practices. Phyllis Bird has argued that feminist methodology for uncovering women's roles in Hebrew religion must proceed on a different basis than that of feminist New Testament scholars, such as Elisabeth Schüssler Fiorenza. Fiorenza has argued that the New Testament's androcentric language conceals the actual participation of women in early Christian communities. When we read androcentric terms, such as *brethren*, and *deacon*, we should assume that women were included.

Bird has argued that Hebrew religion, by contrast, is highly sex-segregated. When only men are described as doing religious functions, we should assume that only men were allowed to do them. One finds the women in

Hebrew religion, not by reading them into male roles, but by looking to the excluded other spheres where women were located. There, one can often find alternative religious practices by women in the family or among other women. The comparison with anthropological studies of religious roles of Jewish and Muslim women in traditional Middle Eastern societies today can provide data for such separate female religious practices within the female sphere of activity.[29]

Feminist psychology is also a vital tool for feminist theology. This revisionist work uncovers the psychological dynamics of the binary splits of male and female as masculine and feminine that have been sanctified in Christian anthropology. The analysis of object relations and the development of the male personality by emancipation from the mother and identification with the father in family systems of female early child raising also reveals the deep fears and resistences of males (and some females) to female images of God and the emotional-laden defense of the exclusive naming of God as "Father."[30]

Concepts of God as Mother and Father reduplicate, on a more absolute level, the shaping of gender development through relationship and differentiation from the nurturing mother, and the transfer of authority to the distant father. What it means for a woman to seek a mother-God, and how that might have a different meaning for men than for women is also explored through these insights into gender psychological development.

More androgynous or wholistic accounts of the "healthy" human personality for both men and women also have important implications for Christian theology. What it means to think of both men and women as images of God, whether this points us to an anthropology of complementary opposites who together make one whole, or rather to a complex androgynous whole of each person in mutuality with others, will deeply affect one's interpretation of such theological ideas. The extent to which conversion, salvation, or sanctification point toward a process of transformative growth that is essentially the same (but with deeper theological warrants) as the psychological path toward healthy human development also has important implications for the interface between pastoral theology and psychology.[31]

Feminist revisionist work in philosophy, particularly classical philosophy, also is of great relevance to feminist Christian theology, since this philosophical tradition has underlaid the whole structure of classical Christian theology. The understanding of God as absolute Being, versus creaturely finitude; an anthropology built on mind-body dualism which also presupposed the classical disputes over Christology; the platonic view of the soul as a substantive entity separable from the body; evil as finitude and succumbing to the corruption of bodily passions; all these patterns were appropriated, with some revisions, into the systematization of Christian theology in the patristic and medieval periods.

What philosophical tradition might provide a more wholistic alternative that would not split God and matter, soul and body, as male and female, is a question that is unsettled for feminist theologians, many of whom are stronger on the critique of theological androcentrism and misogyny, than in finding a philosophical basis for an alternative. Some feminists have looked to Process Theology as conducive to a more wholistic account of God, humanity, and the cosmos, since in Process Theology God is not "unmoved mover," but both underlies and is produced through the cosmic historical process of interrelation and response.[32]

Postmodern and poststructuralist philosophies have critiqued the Cartesian concept of the universal subject, including concepts of universal woman who can be the basis for a univocal woman's experience to ground feminist theology. But they have been less convincing in providing a positive opening for theological affirmations of the "good" and hope for a transformative "newness of life" for men and women in social relations. Their strengths seem to be more in deconstruction than in reconstruction.[33]

The first wave of Christian feminist reconstruction of theology often proceeded in a somewhat intuitive and eclectic way. They identified the theological patterns that have marginalized women. These are the reading of the male as the normative human person, created first, the normative image of God; women as created to be auxiliary to man, second in creation, but first in sin; the assumption that God, although beyond gender, is normatively to be described as like a patriarchal male; that Christ, as perfect God and perfect man, must be male in order to both incarnate God and to possess full and normative humanness; and finally, only men can be ordained because only men can represent Christ.

They then searched the Biblical and historical tradition to locate more inclusive ideas; feminine images of God, such as Sophia; the image of God as both male and female in Genesis 1; the new humanity in Christ as "neither male nor female" in Galatians 3:28; early Christian understandings of ministry as inclusive of women as well as men, such as Acts 2:17, "I will pour out my Spirit upon all flesh and your sons and your daughters shall prophesy"; the descriptions of women apostles in the Gospels: Mary Magdalene, Mary and Martha of Bethany, and the "other Marys"; and women ministers in the letters of Paul, such as Phoebe, Prisca, Mary, and Junia.

Feminist theologians then set about an increasingly systematic critique of the negative patterns, but also the reconstruction of the basic symbols of Christian faith. What would this mean? For most Christian feminists this would mean an egalitarian, gender-inclusive reading of anthropology, sin and redemption, God, Christology, and ecclesiology.[34]

In anthropology this would mean the affirmation that both women and men possess the fullness of human nature. They do not relate to each other either as superior to inferior or as complementary parts of a human nature in which each has the half that the other lacks. Rather, woman as woman and man as man each have the fullness of human capacities and potential. Their relationship should be one of mutuality that enables the full and equivalent human development of one another in community.

The understanding of sin names sexism as sin and patriarchy as a sinful social system. Sexism and patriarchy express sin as a distortion of human relationality into domination and subordination, corrupting the humanity of both men and women. Grace is the critical consciousness to recognize such distortions as sinful, to be converted from them, and to struggle against them to overcome patriarchy in personal relationships and in social systems. Redemption means building new relationships, personally and socially, based on mutual co-humanity.

Christ as the redeeming presence of God reveals the nature of God as the power of co-humanity and mutual relationality. Christ is our revealed paradigm of the Word and Wisdom of God (Logos-Sophia). God's Word and Wisdom is beyond both male and female and is personified in both men and women. The maleness of the human historical person of Jesus of Nazareth in no way limits God's representation to one gender. Rather, it is one element of his historical particularity as an individual person, in the same sense as his Jewishness or the fact that he was born at a particular time and place.[35]

Jesus as an individual person nevertheless represents the fullness of redeemed personhood of all people in all times and places, and thus his representation in the Christian community must be inclusive of all people. We as the Church, who know Christ, not after the flesh, but after the Spirit; no longer limited by particularities of place, time, race, or gender, are called to encounter Christ in one another in all the diversities of class, race, gender, and culture.

God-language must also reflect this inclusive understanding of Christ's redemptive work and the Christian community. If all persons, male and female, are mutually interrelated, then God cannot be imaged only in terms of the male gender or in terms of ruling class roles of males. God is both beyond gender and is the ground of mutual personhood of both men and women. All language for God is metaphorical, not literal. If women are images of God, then God must also be imaged in metaphors drawn from female being and activity, as much as from that of males. Male and female imagery for God should not reinforce unjust gender stereotypes, but point us to the redeemed fullness of personhood of men and women.[36]

Finally, the understanding of ministry should be based on a vision of the church as both nurturing and prophetic community of liberation from personal and social evil. As church we are called to enter into loving and liberating co-humanity. Ministry is the enabling of the community of faith to develop its life together as the birthing of new humanity and as witness to the world of the exodus from oppressive social systems, such as patriarchy, and entrance into co-humanity in Christ.[37]

This thumbnail sketch of what an inclusive reading of Christian symbols would look like might be generally endorsed by many feminist theologians, but it remains much too simplistic. Critical questions about ontology and epistemology, the presumed universality of the human subject as sinner and saved; Christology as "the way" for all humans in every culture, unawareness of ethnocentrism, heterosexism, and anthropocentrism needed to be questioned.

New voices from African-Americans, Hispanics, and Asians in America, lesbians, as well as Third World feminists from Latin America, Asia, and Africa have also entered the discussion, revealing the parochial assumptions of this first wave of feminist theology. Feminist theology in the 1980s had begun to enter its second wave, in which these more critical questions about philosophical presuppositions and cultural diversity are explored.

A Comparison of Two Methodologies for Feminist Theology

In this concluding section of the chapter I wish to detail and compare two methodologies for feminist theology, my own method as a Euro-American of Catholic-ecumenical tradition and classical education and a feminist hermeneutic developed by a collective of feminist theologians in the Philippines, to provide a partial example of the particularity of feminist theological methods in different contexts.

My method made use of the concept of women's experience as a source and critical norm for feminist theology. This idea of women's experience was something of a given in the first wave of feminist theology in the '70s. However, in using this idea, I made clear that the concept of experience was not a new concept as source and norm of theology. It has always implicitly underlaid Christian theology. What had been excluded in androcentric ordering of theology was women's experience. [38]

I also increasingly refined what should be meant by women's experience. This did *not* refer to psychobiological essentialism of a separate women's nature. I assumed that gender identity, both maleness and femaleness, was a social construction. Even women's specific body differences, of womb, breasts, and vagina, the experiences of being sexually penetrated, pregnancy, and birth, menstruation and menopause, are not experienced by all women in the same way, not only because not all women are hetereosexual or become mothers, but also because these bodily experiences are not simply "natural," but are always mediated and experienced through lenses of cultural interpretation.

To experience menstruation as "polluting," one's breasts and pubic area as provocative and provoking male assault on the female body, birth as tying women to social dependency, sexual penetration as violation; all these are to experience the female body through the lens of particular cultural discourses.

There is no purely natural and universal experience of the female (or male) body, but our bodily experiences are products of these cultural discourses.

By "women's experience" I basically meant women's critical experience of patriarchy as limiting and denying a woman's creative potential. The critical perspective for feminist theology arises from this "first act" of disaffiliation with the patriarchal discourses and their attendant social relations, which women experience as oppressive, and the quest for a liberating alternative. These critical experiences are by no means univocal. The meaning and effects of patriarchal discourses and relations are highly diverse, depending on class, race, ethnic location, and particularities of personal biography.

Thus, one cannot speak of the woman's experience, but a great diversity of critical experiences that must arise from many communities of women in different contexts finding their critical and liberating voices. My own experiences, based on a great deal of intercultural dialogue between American feminist theologians, in Euro-American Protestant and Catholic contexts, African-Americans, Hispanics, and Asians, lesbians and heterosexuals, Jews, Muslims, and Buddhists, and internationally in Korea, India, Japan, the Philippines, South Africa, Zimbabwe, Mexico, Nicaragua, Costa Rica, Chile, Brazil, and Argentina, is that there are very large areas of commonalities between women in these many locations as they find their critical voices.

Patriarchal treatment of women in these many contexts has enough similarities that one finds much the same problems dealt with by woman in various cultures and contexts, although with many different nuances of detail, both in the urgency of the problems that need to be confronted and the cultural resources that can be appropriated for alternative visions. Commonalities do not mean identity, but also difference does not mean a dissimilarity that lacks large areas where shared experiences can be recognized. With these qualifications I believe it is still useful to speak of women's experience, or experiences, as a critical base and resource for feminist theology.

Perhaps even more important to discuss is the assumption about the human subject that grounds critical dissent and aspiration for liberation. If humans are simply the product of social discourses created by systems of social relations without remainder, then there would seem to be no basis by which anyone could dissent from these social discourses and systems that have shaped us. How could we experience these discourses as oppressive and aspire to liberating alternatives, if these are all there is and all "we" are?

Thus, my anthropology and cosmology, or theology of redemption, assumes an element of "transcendent" potential, which I would also identify with grace or divine power in our lives, that opens up experiences of dissatisfaction, dissent, and resistance to oppressive systems of relations and their discourses, and leads us to imagine liberating alternatives. These liberating alternatives do not exist in some transcendent place or consciousness, but rather they are themselves constructed in the process of resistance, and in the shaping of and interaction with communities of alternative discourses and relationships.

However, what is liberating and what is oppressive is not simply an arbitrary set of opinions, although it also cannot be infallibly known or definitively and fully realized in finite human relations. But there are some partial but reliable guidelines to differences between what is "good" and what is "evil", what is redemptive and what is not. This has to do with "fruits" of relationship, whether they deliver well-being or not, and whether this well-being is expansive, extending well-being to expanding communities of neighbors, or whether our well-being is predicated on some other's group's oppression. These are the concrete tests for whether a path of transformation is redemptive or not.

Four critical principles have guided my methodology. First, there is a rejection of any concept of inerrancy or infallibility in use of authoritative sources of Scripture and theological history. We base our theological reflection as Christians on dialogue with Scripture and Christian tradition, not because these are inerrant, but simply because they are *our* collective story as a community, no better and no worse than other collective stories that Muslims or Buddhists refer to in their reflection. It is a finite, particular tradition, filled with distortions and unjust violence, but also rich and insightful of transformative visions.

The second criterion is the norm of experience, specifically the critical experience of dissent from oppression and shaping of alternative hope. Here there must always be a preferential option for the excluded voices, for those who have been left out of the dominant discourses, including the discourses of feminist theology, and who seek to open these discourses to those who still remain on the margins even of "liberation movements."

Thirdly, there is the ethical norm, which I have just discussed. Here proposed communities and practices of liberating alternatives need to be judged by the fruits of expanding well-being, without victimizing "undersides" to their projects and practices and willingness to be open to further critique and transformation, when such victimizing "undertexts" are shown to exist. Finally there is the eschatological norm; that Christian redemptive hope lies, not in a fixed and realized past, but in an expanding future of gracious disclosure of power to imagine and aspire to new possibilities in the future of God's "realm."

As feminist theology enters into dialogue with the coded experience of the Christian community, beginning with the Bible, women face profound ambiguity. Since the Bible is an androcentric book, written throughout from the perspective of males, reflecting and mostly justifying patriarchal social relations, how can women use this book as Scripture, or liberating Word of God, for them?

One opening point in this dialogue is the recognition that, although Scripture is androcentric, it is not uniformly on the side of the dominant class or political system in society. The very shaping of the Bible, both Hebrew

Scripture and New Testament, is generated in and through a continual tension and conflict between discourses and practices that justify and sacralize the dominant social system and those that critique it and call for repentance and transformation. This tension shapes two fundamentally different views of the function of religion and relationship to God. I call these two views the "sacred canopy" and "prophetic critique."[39]

Sacred canopy religion is not only found throughout the Bible, but it is probably the dominant form of religiosity in all religions. Biblical religion functions to sacralize the status quo in various ways; by seeing the law codes of patriarchal society as handed down by God; by portraying the conquest of other people and their land, even the extermination of other people, as mandated by God's will; and describing the hierarchies of male over female, master over slave, as the cosmic order, mirroring the relation of God to Christ, Christ to the cosmic "body."

Prophetic critique cuts across these patterns of sacralized social power and calls elements of it into question. God is positioned, not as the author of this system, but as the destabilizer of it, mandating prophets and prophetesses to denounce it as contrary to God's mandates of justice, and calling the powerful to repent or else proclaiming that God will enter history to overthrow such social patterns, and bring about a new society where peace and justice on earth will reign. Not only unjust social systems, but also their religious justifications are denounced and rejected as contrary to true faith and obedience to God.

We find such language of denunciation in the prophets, such as Amos 5:21, 23–24: "I hate, I despise your festivals and I take no delight in your solemn assemblies . . . . Take away from me the noise of your songs; I will not listen to the melody of your harps, But let justice roll down like waters and righteousness like an everflowing stream." Prophetic denunciation and annunciation are also central to Jesus' preaching. Using the text of Isaiah for his sermon in his hometown synagogue, Jesus defined his mission "to bring good news to the poor, to proclaim release to the captives, the recovery of sight to the blind, to let the oppressed go free and to proclaim the Year of the Lord's favor" (Luke 4:18).

These two tendencies do not make for two different Biblical canons in which we can separate out the "good stuff" from the "bad stuff." Rather, these tendencies intersect, often with elements of both in the same passages. Discerning the liberating tendencies from those that justify oppression is a matter of transformative insight in constantly changing contexts. As we discern anew what is liberating in new contexts, and free ourselves from what is oppressive, we generate new discourses that will also have their insights and their blindnesses. This is the very process by which the Biblical texts were generated over the centuries, and by which Christians (and Jews, in a different line of memory) generate new insights again today in our theological dialogue with past and present texts and contexts.

Liberating insights always have their limits. Their recognition of what is making for injustice and what would make for well-being are limited by the particular interests and standpoints of the prophetic spokesperson and community. This is as true of the Bible as of ourselves today. We recognize what oppresses us, but are often blind to how we oppress others, until they bring it to our attention. Then we may or may not be able to respond graciously.

Moreover, discourse that has a liberating meaning in one context may be routinized by a new established religious leadership and used to oppress others in a different context. Thus, Jesus' denunciations of the blind and limiting clericalism of the religious leadership of his community was taken out of context and used to justify anti-Judaism, as Christians moved outside the Jewish community as an antagonistic schismatic sect. Language about Jesus as Lord, which liberated a weak and vulnerable Christian community from the great imperial power of Rome, was later used to sacralize the Lordship of the Christian Caesar as representative of the Lordship of the Cosmic Christ, when Christianity became the established religion of the Roman Empire.

Thus, prophetic truth is never a matter of simply repeating texts, but of discovering the critical and transformative shift that needs to happen in one's own inherited discourses and social systems now. We read the Bible as Word of God to the extent that we read it as a dialogue partner engaged in its own version of that same process of discernment, and spin out our own liberating discourse through this dialogue between its struggle and our own.

Christian preaching and teaching is never a matter of exegesis, in the sense of simply finding what the Bible said in the past, and then applying "unchanging truth" to our own time. Rather, prophetic preaching is midrash or new story telling. Exegesis is helpful to the extent that it helps us to discern the struggle between blindness and insight in the Biblical context, but the Word of God for us is the new liberating story we spin out from the underside of our own texts of oppression, including the way the Biblical text has been used to encode oppression. Feminist theology is a version of this same midrashic process in the context of our struggle for liberation from encoded gender oppressions.[40]

Theological hermeneutics is not simply a matter of dialogue between Biblical texts (themselves enshrining more than two thousand years of quite different contexts and genres, for the Christian Bible is not a "book," but two libraries of successive religious communities) and our context. It also draws on a configuration of resources from our cultural memory by which to discern what is liberating from what is oppressive. This constellation will be quite distinct in different cultural communities, and for particular individuals, even within the broad parameters of those who claim to work in the Christian tradition.

In my discussion of historical sources for feminist theology, I drew together a constellation of such resources that worked for me as a Euro-American ecumenical Catholic with a broad training in Western civilization from its roots in the Ancient Near East, the Hebrews, Greeks, Romans, and Latin Europe to modern Western Europe and the United States.

Thus, I spoke of five constellations of tradition from which I drew my dialogue: (1) Hebrew Scripture and the New Testament, read through the eyes of prophetic critique; (2) the countercultural Christian tradition that has its roots in the discipleship of equals of the early Christian community and was continually regenerated, from Montanists and women mystics to Waldensians and Quakers, to nineteenth-century utopians and reformers to modern feminist spirituality; (3) the prophetic, inclusive rereading of mainline discourse on the symbols of Christian faith; (4) pre-Biblical religions and extra-Biblical religious movements that are a countercultural background to the formulations of Hebrew religion and the New Testament; and (5) post-Christendom liberation theory, in its three major lines of revolutionary liberalism, romanticism, and socialism.[41]

This broad network of discourses formed my own cultural context and those of the educational community in which I was shaped. But, broad and representative as it may be for a certain network of communities of discourse, it is also very particular and limited. African-American womanist theologians may draw on some of the elements of the Biblical tradition in a similar but also distinct way from mine, but their dialogue with cultural history will privilege a quite different set of memories, from African roots, the African American history of slavery and struggle for emancipation and the distinct literature of African-American women.[42]

This is a discourse in which I am called to be, not only in dialogue, but also judged and called to account by, for the history of African-Americans is to a large extent that of oppression by European Americans of the kind that were my ancestors. But to be accountable to their discourse and critique does not mean that it is appropriate for me simply to appropriate their discourse and the distinct literature upon which they draw. I need to find the authentic way to be responsive to their discourse without trying to colonize it.

As each new community of women in new cultural contexts finds its critical and liberating voice, it will also put together the constellation of memories that shape the context for their reflection on their struggle. I will use the position statement on hermeneutical principles by a group of Filipina feminist theologians to illustrate an alternative method and constellation of memories arising from women of the Philippines.[43]

These women theologians arise from the process of developing "Third World" Liberation Theologies by theologians of Asia, Africa, and Latin American (EATWOT: Ecumenical Association of Third World Theologians), and from the particular version of Asian liberation theology (Theology of Struggle) developed by Filipino theologians. These women use the methodology of theological reflection developed by Third World liberation theology in general, and the Filipino Theology of Struggle in particular. But they also arise from the recognition that Third World male liberation theologians were not able to take the feminist questions of their sisters seriously. And so it was necessary for Third World women theologians, each in their distinct national communities, to develop their own Third World feminist theology in dialogue with each other, through the Women's Commission of EATWOT.[44]

This methodology starts by gathering in small circles and each person telling their story. After the stories are generated, there is reflection on the stories to understand how each of them and in their relation to each other reveal the social system that encompasses and oppresses the community. The reflection then moves to the discernment of Biblical insights, and also resources from one's historical culture, for liberating discourses, moving toward a more systematic reading of theological themes. These reflections should lead back to renewed praxis. Hermeneutical method moves in a dynamic interaction of praxis, reflection, and praxis.

Following this method, but from the Filipina context, the study begins with five stories that encapsulate a variety of women's experiences in the Philippines. There is the story of Lucy, a factory worker struggling to form a union to improve working conditions for women, against the intransigence of the owners and the insensitivity of male union leaders to women's issues. There is Norma, a college student from a middle-class family, who is sexually abused by her father (who also batters her mother) and forced to drop out of school in order to hide from him.

There is Elisa, a political activist who was imprisoned and tortured by the military, who feels strengthened by the support of her family and friends and her own ability to resist and survive. There is Lolita, a waitress in an American-owned bar, who struggles with low wages, demands of prostitution, the need to care for her infant son, and the fear of contracting AIDs from the American military customers. She hopes the American father of her baby or some other American will marry her. Finally, there is Jannie, a religious sister from one of the hill tribes of the Cordillera who struggles against the repressive training and ethnic prejudice of her order to define her authentic vocation for her people.

These stories then lead to the second step, the analysis of the stories to reveal women's historical and social situation in the Philippines; how each of these women's stories reveals a facet of the interrelation of class hierarchy, ethnicities, sexism, the unjust economic and political system, and the ambivalent role of the Catholic church in this reality.

The paper then moves to an analysis of the construction of the Filipino cultural and social system in terms of its basic periods of history: (1) the pre-colonial Filipino culture; (2) the reshaping of Filipino culture and society, including gender relations, by four hundred years of Spanish colonization, and then (3) the further reshaping of Filipino culture and society by fifty years of American colonial occupation, followed by a neocolonial relation to the United States.

Filipino women thus have to struggle for a liberating identity in the context of triple layers of culture: indigenous cultures, which often had stronger roles for women in society and in religion, such the Babaylans or priestesses; Spanish Catholicism; and Americanization. As Filipinas, joking, summarize this history: "Four hundred years in the convent, fifty years in Hollywood." Their historical heritage is also one of resistence to Spanish and American colonization, a heritage of women leaders, such as Gabriela Silang, who led a rebellion against the Spanish in the eighteenth century, women union leaders of the nineteenth and twentieth centuries and feminist reformers and liberationists.

Filipina hermeneutical principles call for both a critical analysis of the forces that have shaped women's oppression, in the context of the oppression of the Filipino people, but also claim the liberating aspects of this dual heritage, as Filipinas and as Christians. This leads to a claiming of religious myths and symbols from indigenous tradition, such as Philippine creation stories in which a female deity creates the world or where a male and female deity create the world together. It also allows the claiming of those liberating stories from the Bible and the Christian tradition. Filipinas do not need to choose between these heritages, but claim both of them.

The paper then moves to the enunciation of four key principles by which this dual heritage is to be evaluated theologically. "From the perspective of Filipino women committed to authentic womanhood and societal transformation, we interpret and judge texts, events and realities as in accordance with God's design when they: 1) promote the authentic personhood of women; 2) foster inclusive communities based on just relationships; 3) contribute to genuine national sovereignty and autonomy; and 4) develop caring and respectful attitudes, not only among human beings, but toward the rest of Creation as well. We interpret and judge as sinful and contrary to God's intentions whatever goes counter to the development of authentic womanhood, imposes domination of any kind, deviates from the vision of the peacefilled community and prevents the coming of God's reign in our world."

The paper ends with a number of further tasks for theological evaluation: questions concerning cosmology, religious anthropology, Christology, Mariology, moral theology, spirituality, and worship. For these women of the Philippines, hermeneutics is a series of tentative guides in the process of making a new way into the future. They have no assurance of victory, but they are committed to the struggle for justice as the expression of their faith in God. This, finally, is what any theological method should be about.

Notes

1. Judith Plaskow, *Standing Again at Sinai: Judaism from a Feminist Perspective* (San Francisco: Harper and Row, 1990); Rita Gross, *Buddhism after Patriarchy: A Feminist History. Analysis and Reconstruction* (Albany: State University of New York Press, 1993; Riffat Hassan, "Woman-Man Equality in Islamic Tradition," *Harvard Divinity School Bulletin* 17, no. 2 (Jan.-May 1987): 2–4.

2. Edward Clarke, who introduced Freudian thought in America, wrote *Sex in Education* in 1873, arguing that women had limited energy and needed this energy for reproduction. If women used their energy for higher education, they would become sterile and invalids. For the struggle of women to enter American colleges after the Civil War, see Eleanor Flexner, *Century of Struggle: The Women's Rights Movement in the United States* (New York: Atheneum, 1972), 113–130.

3. See Maithreyi Krishna Raj, ed., *Women's Studies in India: Some Perspectives* (Bombay: Popular Prakashan, 1986).

4. See Rosemary R. Ruether, "Christianity and Women in the Modern World," in *Today's Woman in World Religions,* ed. Arvind Sharma (Albany: State University of New York Press, 1991), 276, 279–284, 289–293.

5. Christine de Pizan (1363–1431), *The Book of the Ladies* (New York; Persea Books, 1982); Margaret Fell, *Women's Speaking Justified and Other Seventeenth Century Quaker Writings about Women* (London: Quaker Home Service, 1989).

6. See "Re-imagining" from the Steering Committee of the Ecumenical Decade: Churches in Solidarity with Women, Greater Minneapolis Council of Churches, 122 W. Franklin Avenue, suite 218, Minneapolis, MN 55404.

7. See essays by Gerda Lerner, Hilda Smith, Juliet Mitchell, and Sheila Ryan Johansson, in *Liberating Women's History: Theoretical and Critical Essays,* ed. Berenice A. Carroll (Chicago: University of Illinois Press, 1976), 345–430; also Joan Kelly, *Women, History, and Theory* (Chicago: University of Chicago Press, 1989).

8. See Rayna R. Reiter, *Toward an Anthropology of Women* (New York: Monthly Review Press, 1975). For an anthropological study showing the difference of male and female perspectives in a society, see Yolanda Murphy and Robert Murphy, *Women of the Forest* (New York: Columbia University Press, 1974).

9. The matriarchal thesis was founded in nineteenth century anthropology by writers such as J. J. Bachofen, *Das Mutterrecht* (Stuttgart: Krais and Hoffmann, 1861) and Lewis H. Morgan, *Ancient Society: Research into the Lines of Human Progress from Savagery through Barbarianism to Civilization* (New York: H. Holt, 1877). A major nineteenth century feminist reinterpretation of this thesis is found in Matilda Joslyn Gage, *Woman, Church, and State* (Chicago: C.H. Kerr,1893). For a critique of this thesis, see Joan Bamberger, "The Myth of Matriarchy: Why Men Rule in Primitive Society," in *Women, Culture, and Society,* ed. Michelle Zimbalist Rosaldo and Louise Lamphere (Stanford: Stanford University Press, 1974), 263–280.

10. See Sherry R. Ortner, "Is Female to Male as Nature is to Culture," in Rosaldo and Lamphere, 67–88.

11. Peggy Reeves Sanday, *Female Power and Male Dominance: On the Origins of Sexual Inequality* (New York: Cambridge University Press, 1981).

12. See Cynthia Fuchs Epstein, "Women in Sociological Analysis: New Scholarship Versus Old Paradigms," in *A Feminist Perspective in the Academy,* ed. Elizabeth Langland and Walter Fove (Chicago: University of Chicago Press, 1981), 149–162.

13. See Zillah R. Eisenstein, ed., *Capitalist Patriarchy and the Case for Socialist Feminism* (New York: Monthly Review Press, 1979); for a critique of women's status under Eastern European communism, see Hilda Scott, *Does Socialism Liberate Women* (Boston: Beacon, 1974).

14. See Jean Baker Miller, *Psychoanalysis and Women* (Baltimore: Penguin, 1973); also Janet T. Spence, "Changing Conceptions of Men and Women: A Psychologist's Perspective," in Langland and Gove, 130–148.

15. Carol Gilligan, *In a Different Voice: Psychological Theory and Women's Development* (Cambridge: Harvard University Press, 1982); also Mary F. Belensky, Blythe M. Clinchy, Nancy R. Goldberger, and Jill M. Tarule, *Women's Ways of Knowing: The Development of Self, Voice, and Mind* (New York: Basic Books, 1986).

16. See Carolyn G. Heilbrun, *Toward a Recognition of Androgyny* (New York: W.W. Norton and Co., 1982.

17. Spence, *op. cit.,* 138–140.

18. See Rosemary R. Ruether, "Homophobia, Heterosexism, and Pastoral Practice," in *Homosexuality in the Priesthood and the Religious Life,* ed. Jeannine Gramick (New York: Crossroad, 1989), 21–35.

19. See Hilde Hein, "Liberating Philosophy: an End to the Dichotomy of Spirit and Matter," in *Beyond Domination: New Perspectives on Women and Philosophy,* ed. Carol C. Gould (Totowa, N.J.: Rowman and Allenheld, 1983), 123–141.

20. See Aristotle, *Generation of Animals,* 729, 737–738, 775. Thomas Aquinas, *Summa Theologica,* pt. 1, q. 92, art. 1.

21. See Linda Nicholson, *Feminism/Post-Modernism* (New York: Routledge, 1990); also Tania Modleski, *Feminism without Women: Culture and Feminism in a Post-Feminist Age* (New York: Routledge, 1991); Judith Butler, *Gender Trouble: Feminism and the Subversion of Identity* (New York: Routledge, 1990).

22. See Susan Bordo, "Feminism, Post-Modernism, and Gender Scepticism," in Nicholson, *Feminism/Post-Modernism*, 133–156; also Allison M. Jagger and Susan R. Bordo, eds. *Gender/Body/Knowledge: Feminist Reconstructions of Being and Knowing* (New Brunswick: Rutgers University Press, 1989).

23. Mary Daly, *The Church and the Second Sex* (New York: Harper and Row, 1968).

24. Rosemary R Ruether, ed. *Religion and Sexism: Images of Women in the Jewish and Christian Traditions* (New York: Simon and Schuster, 1974).

25. See Elisabeth Schüssler Fiorenza, *In Memory of Her: A Feminist Theological Reconstruction of Christian Origins* (New York: Crossroad, 1983), 243–334.

26. Rosemary R. Ruether and Eleanor McLaughlin, *Women of Spirit: Female Leadership in the Jewish and Christian Traditions* (New York: Simon and Schuster, 1979).

27. See "The Household in Late Antiquity" in David Herlihy, *Medieval Households* (Cambridge: Harvard University Press, 1985), 1–28.

28. See Marija Gimbutas, *Goddess and Gods of Old Europe: 6500–3500 B.C.* (Berkeley: University of California Press, 1982). For a popularization of this thesis, see Riane Eisler, *The Chalice and the Blade* (San Francisco; Harper and Row, 1987). For a Jewish feminist critique and alternative construction of the relation of Babylonia and Syrian Goddesses and Hebrew religion, see Tikva Frymer-Kensky, *In the Wake of the Goddesses: Women, Culture, and the Biblical Transformation of Pagan Myth* (New York: Macmillan, 1992).

29. Phyllis Bird, "The Place of Women in Israelite Cultus," in *Ancient Israelite Religion*, ed. Paul Hanson, et al. (Minneapolis: Fortress Press, 1987), 397–419; for an example of the anthropological method in contemporary Jewish religious studies, see Susan Starr Sered, *Women as Ritual Experts: The Religious Lives of Elderly Jewish Women in Jerusalem* (New York: Oxford University Press, 1992).

30. Nancy Chodorow, *The Reproduction of Mothering* (Berkeley: University of California Press, 1978).

31. For example, see Ana-Maria Rizzuto, *The Birth of the Living God: A Psychoanalytic Study* (Chicago: University of Chicago Press, 1979)

32. Sheila G. Davaney, *Feminism and Process Thought* (New York: Mellen Press, 1981).

33. Mary McClintock Fulkerson, *Changing the Subject: Women's Discourse and Feminist Theology* (Minneapolis: Fortress, 1994).

34. Rosemary R. Ruether, *Sexism and God-talk: Toward a Feminist Theology* (Boston: Beacon, 1983), 12–20; also Rosemary R. Ruether, "The Task of Feminist Theology", in *Doing Theology in Today's World,* ed. John D. Woodbridge and Thomas E. McComisky (Grand Rapids: Zondervan Publishing House, 1991), 359–376.

35. Rosemary R. Ruether, "Can Christology be Liberated from Patriarchy," in *Reconstructing the Christ Symbol: Essays in Feminist Christology* (New York: Paulist Press, 1993), 7–29.

36. Elizabeth A. Johnson, *She Who Is: The Mystery of God in Feminist Theological Discourse* (New York: Crossroad, 1993).

37. Rosemary R. Ruether, *Woman-church: Theology and Practice of Feminist Liturgical Communities* (San Francisco: Harpers, 1986); also Letty Russell, *The Church in the Round: Feminist Interpretation of the Church* (Louisville: Westminister/John Knox, 1993).

38. Rosemary R. Ruether, *Sexism and God-talk,* 19.

39. Rosemary R. Ruether, "Feminist Interpretation: A Method of Correlation," in *Feminist Interpretation of the Bible,* ed. Letty Russell (Philadelphia: Westminister, 1985), 111–124.

40. See Rosemary R. Ruether, *Women-Guides: Texts for Feminist Theology* (Boston: Beacon, 1985), xii, and 247–254.

41. Ruether, *Sexism and God-talk,* 20–45.

42. Delores S. Williams, *Sisters in the Wilderness: The Challenge of Womanist Godtalk* (Maryknoll: Orbis Press, 1993).

43. *Toward an Asian Principle of Interpretation: A Filipino Women's Experience* (Manila: Institute of Women's Studies, St. Scholastica College, 1992).

44. For the history of EATWOT and the rise of the Women's Commission within it, see Virginia Fabella, *Beyond Bonding: A Third World Women's Theological Journey* (Manila: Institute of Women's Studies, St. Scholastica College, 1993). The term *Third World* has been criticized as both demeaning to Asian, African, and Latin American people and also obsolete, now that the Eastern European communist world has disintegrated. I use the term here because it is the term that is still used by this network of theologians of Asia, Africa, and Latin America. Moreover, as Fabella notes in her book (3) this term did not connote to this group, either that these areas of the world were a "third" in some hierarchical scale of value, nor only a third of the world in size and population, but rather the term was used analogously to the *Third estate* in the French Revolution, meaning the emergence of a new revolutionary class that would revolutionize and displace the old class structure of aristocracy and clergy.

8

Method in Women's Studies in Religion

A Critical Feminist Hermeneutics

ELISABETH SCHÜSSLER FIORENZA

This volume seeks to explore the methodological contributions that women's, or feminist, studies in religion are making to religious studies. Its aim is to investigate the affinities, interactions, and differences between the still new discipline of women's/feminist studies and the study of religion. It wants to do so especially with respect to malestream[1] methods, among them hermeneutics, which both areas of study engage.

To approach the topic of "Women's Studies: Hermeneutics,"[2] I must first explicate my own perspective and location since feminist theory, together with malestream hermeneutics, has insisted that scholarship is not done from a disembodied, value-neutral position or a "god's eye view," but that it is always perspectival and sociopolitically situated. My own work therefore has sought to articulate feminist theology and studies in religion not just as hermeneutical but rather as rhetorical-critical studies.

As I have elaborated in *Bread Not Stone*[3] and theorized in both *But She Said*[4] and *Sharing Her Word*,[5] feminist biblical interpretation is best understood as a practice of rhetorical inquiry that engages in the formation of a critical historical and religious consciousness. Whereas hermeneutical theory seeks to understand and appreciate the meaning of texts, rhetorical interpretation and its theo-ethical interrogation of both texts and symbolic worlds pays close attention to the kinds of effects religious discourses produce and how they produce them.

While wo/men always have participated in religion and interpreted scriptures[6] and traditions, hermeneutics, understood as the theoretical exploration of the cultural and political presuppositions of inquiry and the meaning of texts, that is feminist in the interest of wo/men is of very recent vintage. Only in the context of the wo/men's movement of the last century, and especially in the past twenty-five years or so, have feminists in religion begun to explore the possibilities and implications of scholarship that takes the silencing of wo/men by institutionalized religions as its point of departure. In the last decade numerous books and articles on women's/feminist studies in religion have appeared. They have not only won a wide general readership but have also made inroads, albeit very slowly, into the academy. This growing body of feminist research and publications seeks to address and redress the centuries of wo/men's silencing and exclusion from religious leadership and theological studies.

Feminist studies in religion are therefore best understood as critical research that explores the history of wo/men's subordination and exclusion. Hence, the starting point and interests of feminist hermeneutics are different from those of malestream hermeneutics, which is concerned with the understanding, appreciation, and validation of cultural and religious traditions. Feminist studies are therefore closer to critical theory, rhetorics, and ideology critique than to a universalizing ontological hermeneutics. Nevertheless, a critical hermeneutics is important for feminist inquiry. Hence, it is necessary to critically explore and assess the contributions that a critical hermeneutics, understood as a rhetorics of emancipation, can make to feminist studies in religion. Yet before I can engage this question it is necessary to address the hermeneutical impediment that the word *feminism/feminist* constitutes for popular and scholarly audiences.

A Critical Theoretical Perspective and Methodological Framework

Since, for many, feminism is still or again associated with ideological prejudice and unscientific bias, it is necessary to explain why and how I use the term for delineating my theoretical perspective. I begin with the insight that being a woman is not sufficient for generating feminist knowledge. Rather, feminist inquiry is a critical theory[7] and intellectual practice that requires both a process of conscientization[8] and of engagement in struggles for transformation. The title *women's studies* is ambiguous and can be understood either in an objectifying scientific sense as the study *about* wo/men[9] or in feminist terms as the study *by* wo/men. In contrast, feminist studies explicitly adopt a critical theoretical framework that stresses the agency and authority of wo/men as intellectual religious subjects. They seek not just to understand but to change and transform wo/men's situation of religious-theological silencing, marginalization, and oppression. Strictly speaking feminist studies move beyond hermeneutics. Therefore, it is necessary to braid together the theoretical approaches of hermeneutics, rhetorics, and ideology critique for fashioning a method of critical inquiry that is oriented toward justice, emancipation, and liberation.

Although there are many divergent forms and even contradictory articulations of feminism today so that it is appropriate to speak of feminisms in the plural,[10] most feminists agree nevertheless that contemporary feminism is not only a political movement akin to other emancipatory movements, it also is an intellectual process for theorizing the situation of wo/men in kyriarchal[11] societies and religions.

> Feminist Thought gives women new knowledge of social life, the power to think about our circumstances, and the power to act upon them. Feminism then has a claim to exist as scientific knowledge. In common-sense terms it is a pursuit of truth.[12]

The diverse theoretical articulations of feminism come together in their critique of elite male supremacy and hold that gender is socially constructed rather than innate or ordained by G*d.[13]

Feminist "conscientization" makes one realize that cultural common sense, dominant perspectives, scientific theories, and historical knowledge are not only androcentric but that they are kyriocentric, that is, elite male or master-centered. Malestream language and science do not give an objective, value-neutral account of reality. Rather, by making marginalization and stereotypes appear as "natural" or "commonsense," they interpret, construct, and legitimize reality from the perspective of elite Western men and in the interest of relations of exclusion and domination.

My preferred definition of feminism is expressed by a well-known bumper sticker, which, with tongue in cheek, asserts, "Feminism is the radical notion that women are people." This definition accentuates that feminism is a radical concept and at the same time ironically underscores that at the end of the twentieth century feminism is a commonsense notion. Wo/men are not ladies, wives, handmaids, seductresses, or beasts of burden but full citizens. It alludes to the democratic motto "We, the people" and positions feminism within radical democratic discourses that argue for the rights of all the people. It evokes memories of struggles for equal citizenship and decision-making powers in society and religion.

Theologically, feminism understands wo/men as the people of G*d and indicts the death-dealing powers of oppression as structural sin and life-destroying evil. Feminist theologies, therefore, have the goal not only to alter the nature of malestream knowledge about G*d and the world fundamentally but also to change religious institutions that have excluded wo/men from leadership positions for centuries. Feminism thus, in my view, is best understood as a theoretical perspective and historical movement for changing sociocultural and religious structures of domination and exploitation.

The "root-experience" of feminism realizes that cultural "common sense," dominant perspectives, scientific theories, and historical knowledge are androcentric , male biased, and therefore not objective accounts of reality but ideological mystifications of domination and subordination. Generally, feminists have used *patriarchy* as a key-concept for analyzing such relations of oppression. Whereas prior to feminism patriarchy was understood in the fields of anthropology and social studies as the power of the father over his kinship group, in the 1970s feminists developed theories of patriarchy as a social system that maintains "men's social, ideological, sexual, and political dominance"[14] over wo/men.

Since such a universalizing, dualistic analytic of patriarchy has been consistently criticized by black and "Third World" feminists, since the late 1970s I have redefined patriarchy in the classical Aristotelian sense as subordination and exploitation of wo/men who are differently located on the patriarchal pyramid of intermeshed structural oppressions. Then, in the early 90s, I introduced the neologism *kyriarchy /kyriocentrism* (from Grk. *kyrios* = lord, slave master, father, husband, elite propertied man) as a substitute for the commonly used term patriarchy for three reasons: first, to avoid the misunderstanding of patriarchy in the dualistic, generalized sense as power of men over wo/men; second, to underscore the complex interstructuring of domination; and third, to situate sexism and misogyny in a broader range of oppressions. In short, this neologism seeks to expose the embeddedness of the oppression of wo/men in the entire domain of Western society, culture, and religion and thereby to reveal that the subordination and exploitation of wo/men is crucial to its maintenance. Hence, no adequate theory or praxis of emancipation and liberation is possible that does not take explicitly into account the multiplicative interlocking structures—sexism, racism, colonialism, class exploitation and ageism—of wo/men's oppression.

Feminism as I understand it is not just concerned with gender inequities and marginalization. Kyriarchy not only perpetrates dehumanizing sexism and gender stereotypes but also other forms of wo/men's oppression, such as racism, poverty, religious exclusion, and colonialism. Feminist studies therefore have the goal of altering fundamentally the nature of our knowledge of the world by exposing its deformations and limitations in and through androcentrism, racism, classism, and cultural imperialism, as well as by reconstructing different, more comprehensive, and more adequate accounts of the world.[15]

In the past as in the present feminist movements have emerged from the participation of wo/men in emancipatory struggles, such as the struggles for full democratic citizenship, religious freedom, abolition of slavery, civil rights, national and cultural independence as well as those of the ecological, labor, peace, and gay movements. In these struggles for religious, civil and human rights, feminists have learned that words such as "human" or "worker" or "civil society" are gender-typed and often do not mean, nor do they include the rights and interests of wo/men. Therefore, it becomes necessary to focus specifically on the struggle for wo/men's rights and self-determination in society and church.

Feminist movements are engendered and renewed by wo/men's participation in emancipatory democratic struggles, a participation that leads to a different self-understanding and systemic analysis of "commonsense" perceptions and visions of the world. Such a different understanding in turn leads to the articulation of a feminist politics and spirituality that can empower wo/men to bring about further change of society and religion. In sum, in my understanding feminism is a theory and practice of justice that does not seek simply to understand but to change relations of marginalization and domination.

As a theory and practice of justice feminist studies in religion can be appreciated only if seen in their entirety and in their particular historical-social locations. Their rhetorical aims, theoretical arguments, and theological passion must be understood as both empowered and limited in significant ways by the sociopolitical and academic-religious contexts in which they operate. Consequently, a critical feminist hermeneutics of liberation aims at the transformation of malestream theoretical and theological discourses. In order to elaborate the theoretical framework of such a critical feminist hermeneutics, it is necessary to delineate the key methodological components that are braided together in this theoretical articulation.

Since "voice," positionality, and heterogeneity are key-categories in feminist studies, feminist theory and theology have always insisted that scholarship cannot be done from a disembodied value-neutral position. Research is always perspectival and sociopolitically situated. Insofar as they share this critique of positivist science with malestream hermeneutics, feminist religious studies and theologies have found hermeneutical method and theory helpful. However, hermeneutics, with its great appreciation of tradition, does not take sufficiently into account the centuries of women's silencing and exclusion and the systematically distorted communication that has resulted from it.

Although I have introduced and shaped the field of feminist biblical hermeneutics,[16] my own work has sought to articulate feminist theology and studies in religion not simply as hermeneutical but as critical rhetorical studies. By rhetorics I mean a form of cultural practice and critical investigation that is no longer circumscribed by the scientist objectivism, liberalism and nationalism of the Enlightenment, which have relegated classical rhetoric to the dustbins of history.

> Rhetoricality, by contrast, is bound to no specific set of institutions. For this reason it allows for no explanatory metadiscourse that is not already rhetorical. Rhetoric is no longer the title of a doctrine and a practice, nor a form of cultural memory; it becomes instead something like the condition of our existence. . . . Rhetoricality

names the new conditions of discourse in the modern world and, thus, the fundamental category of every inquiry that seeks to describe the nature of discursive action and exchange.[17]

In a rhetorical research paradigm, method is understood differently. Whereas in a scientific positivist paradigm methods are understood as rules and regulations, in a critical-rhetorical paradigm they are seen as modes of inquiry, as questions to be asked and perspectives to be clarified.

Feminist theory has shown that malestream scientific methods and theoretical perspectives have been formulated and shaped in the context of kyriarchal (that is, master/ lord/husband/father dominated) academic institutions that until very recently have been exclusive of women and other "inferior status" scholars. Feminist studies in religion, therefore, cannot simply assume that academic research will produce knowledge that has the power to accurately describe and analyze kyriarchal relations of domination in order to change them. Hence, it must submit its methods to a critical process of rhetorical analysis and reconfiguration, a process of "braiding" or "blending together" various methods if they should serve liberatory goals. Such a braiding or hybridization of methods must be accomplished within a critical feminist framework. In short, by method I do not mean primarily technical procedures and rules but rather modes of critical reflection and analysis.

Even though I have consistently elaborated a critical feminist biblical hermeneutics, I have also argued nevertheless that feminist interpretation must be developed not just in terms of hermeneutics but rather in terms of the overall context of critical theory and feminist theologies of liberation.[18] As a theory and practice of justice feminist critical studies can not be limited to hermeneutical studies, which seek to understand, appreciate, and appropriate the texts and traditions of malestream culture and religion. Rather, they must draw on and braid together several methodological approaches in order to reconfigure them as a critical feminist rhetorics of liberation.

What do I mean by critical? Since "critique and critical" is often understood in a negative, deconstructive, and cynical sense, I use the term in its original sense of "crisis" which is derived from the Greek word *krinein/ krisis*, meaning judging and judgment. A critical method is interested in weighing, evaluating, and judging, in crisis situations and adjudications. A critical method thus has the opposite goals and functions from those which a positivist scientist method espouses. Moreover, in difference to hegemonic hermeneutics it focuses not only on the rhetoricality of all inquiry and the rhetoricity of texts but also on the power relations in which they are embedded.[19]

Whereas the literary formalist and the historical positivist paradigms of interpretation were still reigning in religious studies two decades ago, today epistemological and hermeneutical discussions that are critical of the positivist scientific paradigm of religious studies determine academic discourses. Their theoretical and practical force has destabilized the foundations of the field of religious studies. Feminist hermeneutics has played a great part in this transformation of academic scholarship in religion. Nevertheless, even a cursory glance at the literature can show that the hermeneutical contributions of critical feminist scholarship are rarely recognized and much less acknowledged by white malestream academic and religious institutions. Even feminist scholars still feel compelled to "prove" the legitimacy and validity of their arguments by showing how these "fit" into the hermeneutical frameworks and epistemological theories of the "great men" in the field.[20]

Hermeneutics

The notion of hermeneutics[21] derives from the Greek word *hermeneuein* and means to interpret, exegete, explain, or translate. It owes its name to Hermes, the messenger of the gods, who has the task of mediating the announcements, declarations, and messages of the gods to mere mortals. His proclamation, however, is not a mere communication and mediation but always also an explication of divine commands in such a way that he translates them into human language so that they can be comprehended and obeyed.

While hermeneutics can be understood, with Derrida, as a matter of the free play of signs[22] and with Rorty[23] as merely keeping the lines of communication open, according to Gadamer[24] hermeneutics has the task of translating meaning from one "world" into another.[25] Like Hermes, the messenger of the gods, hermeneutics does not only communicate knowledge but also instructs, directs, and enjoins. Hermeneutics thus has affinities to mantic and prophecy. It conveys revelation and interprets signs and oracles. It is a matter of practical understanding that involves the Aristotelian virtue of *phronesis* (practical judgment) and adjudication, which is not secured by an a priori method but only in the process of understanding

As a discipline, philosophical hermeneutics has its roots in biblical interpretation. It is best understood as a theory and practice of interpretation that explores the conditions and possibilities of understanding not just texts but other practices[26] as well. As such hermeneutics is not so much a disciplined scientific method and technique but rather an epistemological perspective and approach. It

> represents not so much a highly honed, well-established theory of understanding or a long-standing, well-defined tradition of philosophy as it does a family of concerns and critical perspectives . . .[27]

Since Schleiermacher, Dilthey, and Gadamer,[28] hermeneutics has maintained, over and against scientific positivism, that understanding takes place as a process of engagement in the hermeneutical circle or spiral, which is characterized by the part-whole relation. It stresses that understanding is not possible without preunderstandings or prejudices and therefore that understanding is always contextually dependent. Hermeneutics does not ground intelligibility in the "pregiven, essentially changeless human subject, but in the public sphere of evolving, linguistically mediated practice."[29] Thus, hermeneutics seeks to remain open for change and difference.

Hermeneutics insists on the linguisticality of all knowledge, on its contextuality and its immersion in tradition. It stresses that human understanding can never take place without words and outside of time. Its key concepts are *empathy, historicity, linguisticality, tradition, preunderstanding, fusion of horizons,* and *the classic* with its notion of *effective history*. However, all seven aspects and theoretical emphases of hermeneutics are problematic from a critical feminist perspective because they do not take sufficiently into account relations of domination and power.

1. *Empathy* invites one to cultivate emotional identification, sympathy, and appreciation in the process of understanding. Wilhelm Dilthey[30] has argued that "through an act of "empathy" (of *sich einfühlen*) one could achieve objective validity. In such an act of empathy the historian of religion can extricate herself from her own immersion in history and determination by contextuality and transpose herself into the minds and lives of those whom she studies.[31]

Rita Gross has emphasized the centrality of empathy in the study of religion. According to her, the hermeneutical approach of empathic understanding involves two steps: First, the bracketing of one's own world view, values, and visions as much as possible and second, the imaginative entering into the world of the text or religious practice that is being studied. She concedes, that a feminist hermeneutics cannot relinquish critical evaluation, but she nevertheless insists on empathy as a central method in the feminist study of religion.

> Although empathy involves appreciatively entering into the spirit of that which is being studied, one could not agree with all the positions that one understands emphatically because many are mutually exclusive.[32]

I would argue instead that feminists cannot adopt such an empathic hermeneutical method not because positions and theories are mutually exclusive but because kyriarchal religious texts, traditions, and practices are destructive of wo/men's well-being. The statement by her student, that Gross teaches all those religions as if they were true, a statement she quotes as a compliment, highlights the practical implications of such an empathic hermeneutics. To teach, for instance, kyriarchal religious vilifications of wo/men "as if they were true" is to intensify kyriarchal identifications and socialization rather than to interrupt and change them.[33]

2. *Historicity (Geschichtlichkeit) and Contextuality* are central to hermeneutic method. Historicity signifies our participation in and belonging to history and makes us historical beings through and through. It colors our rational capacity to know and make sense out of the world. By shaping our preunderstandings and prior assumptions it makes it impossible for scholars of religion to free ourselves from the impact of our own historical context in order to represent other religions or the past "as they actually are." Scholars can produce more or less true accounts but we can never free ourselves from the influences of our historical contexts and locations.

Moreover, historicity means that we can never be reduced to an essential ahistorical core or to a universal" human nature" that is the same in all historical circumstances. Rather, who we are must be understood as a function of the historical circumstances, languages, and communities in which we live.

> According to the hermeneutical perspective, human beings are neither given an immutable essence by God or nature, nor do we make ourselves (at least not as isolated individuals), but we are rather the particular mode of historical existence we in part find ourselves in and in part shape in co-operation with others.[34]

Yet while hermeneutics stresses that "human beings *are* their history," feminist theory would specify that wo/men are determined by the historical power relations of domination in which they live. Historicity and contextuality always also mean domination. Utilizing the hermeneutical emphasis on historicity and the liberationist critique of contextuality and social location, feminists, for instance, have critically destabilized the foundational concept of "woman." In her book *Am I That Name?*[35] Denise Riley has distinguished three overlapping and blurred levels of indeterminacy, the individual, the historical, and the political level, which are characteristic of "women."

Wo/men are not a unitary group. They are not just determined by their gender and sex but also by their race, class, able-bodiedness, and ethnicity. Taking the ambiguity of the term into account, I have begun to write the word in a broken form as wo/men, in order to indicate that I do not understand "women" in essentialist or naturalized terms. In this way I seek to lift into consciousness that "woman/women" is not a unified concept but an ambiguous one. This way of writing seeks to point out that there are many historical and structural differences *between* wo/men and *within* wo/men themselves, which cannot be reduced to gender difference. Moreover, in light of a systemic analysis the term *wo/men* can be seen as being inclusive of all non-persons, to use an expression of Gustavo Gutierrez. It is not female nature or feminine essence that defines the concept of wo/men but historical-political contextuality.[36]

3. *Linguisticality:* Hermeneutics insists further that all knowledge and understanding is determined by and mediated through language. Language

transports meaning from one context to another. The notion of linguisticality underscores that all understanding is historically and culturally mediated. By learning a language or the discourse of specialized fields of study we come to understand our world and ourselves. The recognition of the totalizing linguisticality of our being in the world is crucial for feminist work but at the same time raises difficult problems for feminist theory, knowledge, and understanding.

Feminist analyses have underscored that grammatically masculine, so-called generic language is a major cultural force in maintaining women's second-class status in culture and religion. If according to Wittgenstein the limits of our language are the limits of our world,[37] then grammatically masculine language that constructs the universe of women and men in androcentric—or better, kyriocentric—terms engenders a world in which wo/men are marginal or not present at all. Hence, it does not suffice to understand the kyriocentric religious-cultural language, tradition, and classic. What is necessary is to change them.

A critical feminist hermeneutics, therefore, insists that we must analyze language as an instrument of power and ideology rather than as simply descriptive and communicative. Language is always rhetorical. Hence, hermeneutical theory must be "braided" with rhetorics, for rhetorics not only inscribes but also makes explicit the relation of language and power in a particular moment.[38]

> If all language is rhetorical, if even objectivity is the product of a certain strategy, then discourses are no longer to be measured in terms of their adequacy to an objective standard (which Nietzsche's perspectivism exposes as a myth) but rather to be analyzed in terms of their strategic placement within a clash of competing forces themselves constituted in and through the very rhetorical dissimulations they employ.[39]

4. *Tradition* is a foundational term in hermeneutics and religious studies. Gadamer stresses that we always stand within a tradition and likens this to our standing within a river of life. Hermeneutics is the attempt to understand the stream of tradition of which we are a part. Thus, Gadamer understands tradition in affirmative ways, "as belonging," rather than in critical terms, as a place of distortion and domination. To belong to a tradition means to have a shared language and/or understanding. Accordingly, hermeneutics does not sufficiently problematize that traditions are rhetoricized, valorized, and shaped by the interests of those in power.

The emphasis of hermeneutics on tradition and its authority clearly stands in tension with feminist preunderstandings and goals because in most societies and religions wo/men have been excluded from the authoritative traditions and classic texts not just by historical accident but by law and custom. Tradition is not just distorted; rather, it consists of and continues to serve practices of exclusion and domination, because major religious traditions have both eliminated wo/men from the ranks of their leadership and have been shaped by the ideology of subordination and inferiority which is structured by gender, race, class, and colonialist relations of power.

5. *Preunderstanding:* The well-known hermeneutical circle insists that all understanding is conditioned by our preunderstanding. If we are part of a language and world that is not of our own making we can never leave it behind even if we adopt a "disinterested" theoretical attitude. No presupposition-less understanding is possible.

> The languages we speak, the practices we unconsciously appropriate, the institutions we live out our lives in, the theoretical debates we inherit, and so forth, all form a loosely packed amalgam of meaningful relations that we can never entirely objectify and that we always presuppose in our thematic understanding of anything whatever.[40]

In short, our very ability to understand becomes defined by our preunderstandings, which we cannot simply cast off as we would a coat or a hat. Furthermore, our presuppositions are not roadblocks that prohibit a true grasp of reality itself, but rather, by inheriting a set of linguistically mediated preunderstandings we gain the possibility of understanding the world. Utilizing this insight a feminist hermeneutics insists that critical scholarship requires the critical articulation of one's kyriocentric preunderstandings. Yet, understanding the kyriocentric world of the text does not suffice. Feminist studies in religion must seek to enable wo/men to recognize this world for what it is, a world of subordination and oppression. At this point it becomes evident that a critical feminist hermeneutics must move beyond hermeneutics to the critique of ideology that can lift into consciousness the distortions and rhetorical constructedness of this world.

6. *Fusion of Horizons:* Gadamer understands the hermeneutical event as a fusion of horizons *(Horizontverschmelzung)*. Interpreters have to inquire into the unspoken horizon of meaning behind the text and of their own historical preunderstandings. The well-known "hermeneutical circle" means that understanding can only take place if we situate a phenomenon in a larger context, that is, the parts of some larger reality can only be grasped in terms of the whole. What we can do in this "to and fro" of the hermeneutical spiral is to fuse our horizon with that which we seek to understand.

All interpretation involves a fusion of horizons between that of the text and that of the reader, between past and present, between the classic and its interpreters. Such a fusion of horizon presupposes that a conception of the actual course of history

> linking the past with the present situation and its horizon of the future forms the comprehensive horizon within which the interpreter's limited

horizon of the present and the historical horizon of the text fuse together. For only in that way are the past and the present preserved in their historical uniqueness and difference in contrast to one another within the comprehensive horizon.[41]

The image of the fusion of horizons seeks to articulate effective hermeneutic communication. The appropriation of a tradition through understanding can be likened to translation. The horizon of the present is not formed without the past. Such an interlacing of horizons belongs to the very conditions of hermeneutic work. No horizon is closed because we are able to place ourselves in another point of view and to comprehend another culture.

However, it has been pointed out that Gadamer does not mean to say that past and present are separate horizons, although the image suggests a melting or flowing into each other of two distinct horizons.

When we understand the past, with its many differences, we are expanding our horizon, not stepping out of our horizon into the other horizon.[42]

Yet to understand the fusion of horizons either as expanding our horizon with that of the other's horizon or as submission of one's own to that of the other, means to construe understanding in kyriarchal terms, either as appropriation or as submission. Rather than to conceive of understanding as a fusion of horizons it is necessary, as Susan Shapiro has argued,[43] to articulate hermeneutics as rhetorics. If horizon means "the field to which the perceptual object belongs," or is the "inactual, nonthematic halo that surrounds and decisively affects the structure of the thematic object,"[44] then hermeneutics must become a critical inquiry into the rhetoricity of the structures of domination and utopias of emancipation.

7. *The Classic:* Finally, the notion of classic and its history of effects underscores the authority of the great works of the tradition and pays attention to the effects of the classics and its reception history. David Tracy has argued over against the modern hermeneutical emphasis on regarding all texts, including sacred texts, in the same critical manner, that the classic text exerts a previous claim upon us. We expect such a text, especially a sacred text, to be significant, to speak to us, to be meaningful, and to have a certain authority that is based on tradition. We always read in front of the cultural or religious "influential" classic or canonical text. Cultural classics and canonical scriptures in turn always already inform our readings. Insofar as they are cultural or religious "classics," they have "performative authority" that is of continuing significance and influence in shaping people's thought and life. They function as persuasive rhetorical texts that continue to influence Western cultures and biblical religions. Because of their persuasiveness they must be critically

scrutinized as to how much they re-inscribe structures of domination and silencing.

Tracy insists that "the interpreter must risk being caught up in, even being played by, the questions and answers"[45] which the classic raises for us today. However, such advice is dangerous for those whose subordination and silencing the classics, such as scripture, have promoted and legitimated. Feminist and ideological criticism has pointed out that a culture's or religion's classics are selected and valorized by those in power.

The claim of hermeneutics that one must accept and enter the text's world of vision cannot be sustained by a critical feminist hermeneutics. Rather, this claim must be critically scrutinized as to its rhetorical structures of domination that distort communication. One must investigate the genealogy of the kyriocentric classic in order to evaluate its persuasive impact and power. Since the debates of the "culture wars" have amply documented that relations of power condition the formulation, function, and effective history of the classic, works considered as classics require especially a critical rhetorical investigation into their function as distorted communication.

Hermeneutic as Ideology Critique

With Jürgen Habermas, a representative of the Frankfurt School of critical theory, a critical feminist hermeneutics insists over and against the malestream hermeneutical program that the question of power is integral to understanding, linguisticality, tradition, and the classic. Habermas distinguishes

> three basic forms of our scientific interest in knowing about the world: the empirical-analytical, the hermeneutical-historical, and the critical-emancipatory. We seek to know in order to control social and natural realities (the empirical-analytic interest), to qualitatively understand and interpret such realities (the hermeneutical-historical interest), and to transform our individual and collective consciousness of reality in order to maximize the human potential for freedom and equality (the critical-emancipatory interest).[46]

Whereas hermeneutics is concerned with the surplus of meaning, critical theory focuses on the lack and distortion of meaning through contextualization and relations of domination. Just as feminist analysis so also critical theory stresses the distortion of language and tradition. The endurance of the classic, for instance, is not so much due to its outstanding representation of meaning but rather to the persistence of kyriarchal power constellations that legitimate it and in turn are legitimated by it. Cultural and religious linguistic practices and traditions have been constituted within unequal power relationships. A feminist critical theory thus insists on and makes possible the concrete analysis of structures of power and domination that determine the classics, such as, for example, scripture. It engages in hermeneutics for the sake of ideology critique.

With the feminist theorist Michèlle Barrett, I understand ideology as referring to a process of mystification or misrepresentation. Ideology is distorted communication rather than false consciousness.

> The retrievable core of meaning of the term ideology is precisely this: discursive and significatory mechanisms that may occlude, legitimate, naturalise or universalise in a variety of different ways but can all be said to mystify.[47]

A fundamental assumption of critical theory holds that every form of social order entails some forms of domination and that critical emancipatory interests fuel the struggles to change these relations of domination and subordination. Such power relations engender forms of distorted communication that result in self-deception on the parts of agents with respect to their interests, needs, and perceptions of social and religious reality. Theologically speaking these power relations result in structural sin.

> The notion of ideology must be situated with a theory of language that emphasizes the ways in which meaning is infused with forms of power. . . . To study ideology is not to analyze a particular type of discourse but rather to explore . . . the modes whereby meaningful expressions serve to sustain relations of domination.[48]

John B. Thompson has pointed to three major modes or strategies that are involved in how ideology operates: legitimization, dissimulation, and reification (literally: to make into a thing).[49] All three modes can be identified in the discourses of wo/men's silencing and censure. The first strategy is an appeal for legitimacy on traditional grounds, whereas the second conceals relations of domination in ways that are themselves often structurally excluded from thought. Or as Jürgen Habermas puts it, ideology serves to "impede making the foundations of society [and, I would add, of religion] the object of thought and reflection."[50]

The third form of ideological operation is reification or naturalization, which represents a transitory, culturally, historically, and socially engendered state of affairs as if it were permanent, natural, outside of time, or directly revealed by G*d. For instance, this ideological strategy comes to the fore in the questionable theological arguments for wo/men's special nature. Ideology moreover contributes to the distorted self-understanding of oppressed people who have internalized the belief in the legitimacy of their own subordination and innate status as inferior. Religious texts and traditions that represent and mystify kyriocentric texts and kyriarchal structures of domination as revealed truth call for ideology critique.

Relying on a critical theory of language and the insights of liberation movements, I have sought to develop such an ideology critique as a critical feminist rhetoric of liberation and transformation. Such a critical hermeneutical theory attempts to articulate interpretation both as a complex process of reading and reconstruction and as a cultural-religious praxis of resistance and transformation. It moves from hermeneutic to metic.

From Hermeneutic to Metic

Since feminist studies in religion are primarily interested in the critical-emancipatory interests of knowledge production, "hermeneutics" seems to be a misnomer for the method used to pursue such emancipatory interests. Thus, it is not the myth of Hermes but that of Metis and Athena that articulates the task of a critical feminist rhetoric. Athena, the patron goddess of the classic Athenian city-state, was not only the patron of the arts, and technological and scientific knowledge but also a war goddess. According to Hesiod, she came fully grown and armored from the head of her father Zeus. However, she only appears to be motherless. Her real mother is the Goddess *Metis*, the "most wise woman among Gods and humans."[51]

According to the myth, Zeus, the father of the gods, was in competition with Metis. He duped her when she was pregnant with Athena because he feared that Metis would bear a child who would surpass him in wisdom and power. Hence, he changed her into a fly. But this was not enough! Zeus swallowed the fly Metis whole in order to have her always with him and to benefit from her wise counsel. This mythical story of Metis and Zeus reveals not only the father of the gods' fear that the child of Wisdom would surpass him in knowledge, but it also lays open the conditions under which wo/men in kyriarchal cultures and religions are able to exercise wisdom and to produce knowledge.

Read with a hermeneutics of suspicion the myth of Metis and Athena shows that kyriarchal systems of knowledge and power objectify wo/men and swallow them up in order to co-opt their wisdom and knowledge for their own interests of domination. Women's studies remains therefore an ambiguous notion since it has wo/men rather than structures of domination as objects of its research. Feminist studies in contrast seeks to empower wo/men by recognizing and changing such knowledges and structures of marginalization and oppression.

Since the goal of feminist hermeneutics is not simply to interpret and communicate divine revelations and religious insights but to undo kyriarchal mystification and dehumanization, it must derive its name and inspiration from Metis and not from Hermes, the trickster god. A feminist critical hermeneutic—or better metic—critically investigates malestream religious myth, texts, traditions, and practices as to how much they marginalize, make invisible, or distort experience, tradition, language, knowledge, and wisdom in such a way that they lead to women's elimination from cultural and religious consciousness and records. Positively it seeks to produce knowledge not as divinely or naturally given which is hidden and must be unearthed, but as practical wisdom—*sophia* and not just *phronesis.*

I have proposed, therefore, a complex method for the critical process of a feminist interpretation for liberation.[52] Such, a critical feminist hermeneutic-rhetorical method of interpretation does not subscribe to one single reading strategy and method but employs a variety of theoretical insights and methods for articulating its own practices of interpretation. The following seven hermeneutical strategies of interpretation are constitutive for such a critical rhetorical model. They are a hermeneutics of *experience,* of *domination,* of *suspicion,* of *critical evaluation,* of *memory* and reconstitution, of *imagination,* and of *transformation.*

This model of a critical feminist interpretation for liberation seeks to recast interpretation not in positivist but in rhetorical terms. It does not deny but rather recognizes that religious texts are rhetorical texts, produced in and by particular historical debates and struggles. It argues positively for the integrity and indivisibility of the interpretive process as well as the primacy of the contemporary starting point of interpretation. Such a complex model of reading that engages in a hermeneutical process of deconstruction and reconstruction, of critique and retrieval, applies both to the level of text and to that of interpretation. It seeks to overcome the hermeneutical splits between sense and meaning, between explanation and understanding, between critique and consent, between distanciation and empathy, between reading the text "behind" and "in front of " the text,[53] between the present and the past, between interpretation and application,[54] between realism and imagination.

This rhetorical model for a critical process of feminist biblical interpretation for liberation requires feminist conscientization and systemic analysis. Its interpretive process or "hermeneutical dance" does not commence by beginning with malestream texts and traditions and by placing them at the center of its attention. Rather, it begins with a hermeneutics of experience.[55]

Such a critical hermeneutics of experience in a feminist rhetoric of liberation focuses in particular on the struggles of wo/men at the bottom of the kyriarchal pyramid of domination and exploitation, because their situation lays open the fulcrum of oppression and dehumanization threatening every wo/man. The victories in the struggles of multiply oppressed wo/men reveal at the same time the liberatory presence of G*d in our midst. In short, a feminist critical interpretation for liberation does not simply begin with experience. Rather, it begins with a reflection of the experience of wo/men on the bottom of society who struggle for survival and well-being.

Feminist liberation theologies of all colors take the experience and voices of the oppressed and marginalized, of those wo/men traditionally excluded from articulating theology and shaping communal life, as the starting point of their epistemological and theological reflection. Long before postmodern feminist theories, feminist liberation theologies have not only recognized the perspectival and contextual nature of knowledge and interpretation but also asserted that knowledge and theology are—knowingly or not—always engaged for or against the oppressed. Intellectual neutrality is not possible in a historical world of exploitation and oppression. Yet, as the Brazilian educator Paolo Freire pointed out a long time ago, the oppressed have also internalized oppression and are divided in and among themselves.

> The oppressed, having internalized the image of the oppressor and adopted his *[sic]* guidelines, are fearful of freedom. Freedom would require them to eject this image and replace it with autonomy and responsibility. Freedom . . . must be pursued constantly and responsibly.[56]

Since both the oppressed and their oppressors are "manifestations of dehumanization,"[57] the methodological starting point of all liberation studies cannot be simply "commonsense" experience but rather must be systemically analyzed and reflected experience. Because wo/men also have internalized and are shaped by kyriarchal "common sense" mindsets and values, the hermeneutical starting point of feminist interpretation must be the experience of wo/men that has been critically explored in the process of "conscientization" as to its location in the systems of oppression and struggles for liberation

To that end one must employ a hermeneutics of domination which insists on a systemic analysis that is able not only to disentangle the ideological (religious-theological) functions of sacred texts and traditions for inculcating and legitimating the kyriarchal order but also for explaining their potential for fostering justice and liberation.[58] Feminist readings that do not prioritize wo/men's struggles against multiplicative oppression but privilege the religious text itself and malestream doctrinal, theological, spiritual, or theoretical frameworks cannot be liberative.

Such a critical systemic analytic of kyriarchal structures of domination and dehumanization provides critical tools for a hermeneutics of suspicion. A hermeneutics of suspicion scrutinizes both the presuppositions and interests of interpreters and that of biblical commentators as well as the androcentric strategies of the biblical text itself. In my view a hermeneutics of suspicion does not employ

> a hermeneutics of discovery assuming that there is some order in the world . . . that can be discovered. . . . Truth is something discovered

by employing a hermeneutics of suspicion, wherein one is suspicious of the various disguises one can use to cover up and distort reality.[59]

Kyriocentric language not only covers up but also constructs reality in a certain way and then mystifies its own constructions by naturalizing them. Kyriocentric texts, literary classics and visual art, works of science, anthropology, sociology, or theology do not represent reality "as it is." Rather, they are ideological constructs that produce the invisibility and marginality of wo/men as a given reality. Their ideological practices must be underscored, sorted out, and assessed rather than just unmasked. A hermeneutics of suspicion must be understood as a denaturalizing and demystifing practice rather than as a working away of the layers upon layers of cultural sediment that hides or represses a "deeper truth." Hence, a critical feminist interpretation insists on a hermeneutics of suspicion in order to identify the ideological functions of kyriocentric text and commentary. It does not do so because it assumes a kyriarchal conspiracy of the classics and their contemporary interpreters but because of the ideological functions of grammatically masculine language in which women do not, in fact, know whether we are addressed or not by grammatically masculine so-called generic texts.

A hermeneutics of ethical and theological evaluation assesses the rhetorics of texts and traditions and their ideological functions and impact in light of a feminist scale of values and visions. It seeks to adjudicate the oppressive or liberatory tendencies inscribed in religious texts as well as their function in contemporary struggles for liberation. It does not, however, reify texts and traditions either as oppressive or as emancipatory. Rather, it seeks to pass judgment again and again on how they function in particular situations. Its criterion or standard of evaluation, the well-being of every wo/man, must be established and reasoned out in terms of a systemic analysis of kyriarchal domination. For theological reasons it insists that Christians must cease to preach kyriarchal texts as the "Word of G*d," since by doing so they proclaim G*d as legitimating kyriarchal oppression.

A hermeneutics of remembrance and reconstitution not only works to increase the distance between ourselves and the time of the text, but also seeks for an increase in historical imagination. It displaces the kyriocentric dynamic of the text in its literary contexts by recontextualizing the text in a sociopolitical model of reconstruction that can make the subordinated and marginalized "others" visible. It attempts to recover wo/men's religious history and the memory of their victimization, struggle, and accomplishments as wo/men's heritage. It seeks not only for historical retrieval but also for a religious reconstitution of the world. With postmodern thinkers it is fully aware of the rhetoricity of its own reconstructions but nevertheless insists that such work of historical remembrance is necessary in support of wo/men's struggles for survival and transformation. If it is a sign of the total oppression of a people not to have a written history, then feminists cannot afford to eschew such historical, reconstructive work.

A hermeneutics of creative imagination and ritualization in turn seeks to generate utopian visions and to "dream" a world of justice and well-being. It seeks to retell scriptural stories, reshape religious vision, and celebrate those who have brought about change. To that end it utilizes not only historical, literary, and ideological critical methods that focus on the rhetoric of religious texts and their historical contexts. It also employs methods of storytelling, role play, bibliodrama, pictorial arts, dance, and ritual for creating a "different" religious imagination.

Because our imagination and utopian visions are always informed and determined by our present sociopolitical location, we need to engage a hermeneutics of suspicion for scrutinizing them too. When seeking for identification and a future vision, we can only extrapolate from present experience that is always already determined by the past. Hence, we need to analyze the present and the past in order to articulate the vision and imagination for a new humanity and religious community. Only if we want to work for a different future can our imagination transcend the past and present limitations of our vision. As Toni Morrison so forcefully states in her novel *Beloved:*

> She did not tell them to clean up their lives or to go and sin no more. She did not tell them they were the blessed of the earth, it's inheriting meek or it's glory bound pure. She told them that the only grace they could have was the grace they could imagine. That if they could not see it, they would not have it.[60]

Such a hermeneutics of imagination is always also a hermeneutics of desire. Alicia Suskin Ostriker characterizes such a hermeneutics of desire as "you see what you want to see."

> I am engaged both theoretically and practically in the question of what will happen when the spiritual imagination of women, who may call themselves Jews or Christians, pagans or atheists, witches or worshippers of the great Goddess, is released into language and into history. . . . I feel desperately fractured much of the time, as anyone in a pathological culture must. But I strive for healing. And so I must confront what is toxic—but I must do more than that.[61]

The shared spiritual visions of traditional religions can evoke powerful emotions and responses and thereby create a sense of community necessary to sustain the struggles and visions for an alternative society and world. Hence, the critical feminist interpretative process or "hermeneutical dance" I have elaborated here, climaxes in a hermeneutics of transformation. Its goal is to change relations of domination that are legitimated and inspired by kyriarchal religion.

Feminist religious interpretation and inquiry must explore avenues and possibilities for changing and transforming relations of domination inscribed in texts, traditions, and everyday life. It must stand accountable to those wo/men who struggle at the bottom of the kyriarchal pyramid of discriminations and dominations. Hence, it must articulate religious studies as a site of social, political, and religious transformation.

Reconceptualizing the Authority of Scripture and Tradition

Since such a critical process of interpretation seeks not just to understand religious texts and traditions but to change kyriarchal biblical religions in the interest of the well-being of the non-person, it requires a reconception of the authority of scriptures and traditions. Understanding this authority as challenging possibility rather than as given norm redefines scripture as formative root model rather than as normative archetype. Instead of reducing the symbolic richness of scriptural and other religious expressions to abstract principles, timeless norms, decontextualized essences, or ontologically immutable types that are to be repeated and translated from generation to generation, a critical feminist hermeneutics of liberation seeks to reclaim religion and the sacred not as a mythic androcentric unchanging essence but as an open-ended paradigm that sets experience in motion and makes transformation possible.[62]

To be sure, the experiences that religious traditions and practices have generated are not always liberating. They often are oppressive not simply because of unfaithful or false interpretations and bad readings. Many religious texts and traditions do re-inscribe relations of oppression because they have been formulated in the first place for maintaining kyriarchal sociopolitical structures and religious identity formations. Therefore, a critical rhetoric of liberation must clearly identify and mark not only those religious texts and traditions that promote kyriarchal structures and religious visions that legitimate injustice and oppression but also the contexts in which they are read and their ideological functions in ever-changing situations.

Religious identity that is grounded in scripture and tradition as its formative prototypes must in ever-new readings be deconstructed and reconstructed in terms of a global praxis for the liberation not only of wo/men but of all those dehumanized by kyriarchal societies and religions. As root metaphors that are characterized by the tension between is and is not, malestream traditions and scriptures may inform but cannot provide the theological lenses for a critical feminist reading of particular biblical texts in the interest of liberation.

As I have argued above, unlike a hermeneutic-aesthetic inquiry, which strives for textual understanding, appreciation, application, and consent, a critical feminist rhetorical inquiry pays careful attention to the power structures and interests that shape language, text, and understanding. In difference to hermeneutics, a critical feminist rhetorics is not just concerned with exploring the conditions and possibilities of understanding and appreciating kyriocentric texts and traditions but also with the problem as to how, in the interest of wo/men's liberation, one can critically assess and dismantle their power of persuasion. To that end one must construct a feminist theoretical framework of interpretation that can move toward the articulation of a critical rhetoric of inquiry, an epistemological move that is often overlooked. Such a critical rhetoric of inquiry calls for a redefinition of the notion of truth in metic—emancipatory— terms of wisdom.

Examining ancient Greek legal, philosophical, and literary texts on torture, Page duBois has argued that classical Greek philosophy has developed the concept of truth as something hidden, something to be excavated or extracted by the torture of slaves.

> This logic demands a closed circle, an other, an outside, and creates such an other. And in the case of the Greek city, the democracy itself used torture to establish this boundary, to mark the line between slave and free, and to locate truth outside.[63]

In contrast, the myth of Metis makes clear that it is not the subordinated others who cover up truth but it is kyriarchal power that deforms and swallows up wisdom and truth. Truth is not located outside but within kyriarchal relations of domination. Western philosophy understands truth as something that is not known, but buried, secreted in the earth, in the body, in the woman, in the slave, in the totally "other": something that must be extricated through torture or sexual violence.

In a similar fashion, revelation has been understood in traditional theology, as an uncovering of a hidden mystery that is located in the unknown and in the beyond. It is directly known only to a select few and it can be extracted only through arduous labor. The "canon within the canon" approach, for instance, seeks to uncover, to distill or to extract a universal truth or authoritative norm from the multilayered meanings of sacred texts and the often contradictory writings collected in them.

According to Page duBois this kyriarchal understanding of "truth" is articulated in reaction to the "logic of democracy" as the notion of equal power among members of a society, which required the radical distribution of wealth as well as the elimination of social and political hierarchies. For some ancient thinkers, even slavery itself was eventually called into question. This "logic of democracy" is not represented by Zeus or Hermes but by Metis. It was Zeus, the father of the gods, who violated "this logic of equality" by dedivinizing and dehumanizing Metis and by not being able to acknowledge her power.

Such a recontextualization of religious hermeneutics in the paradigm of radical democracy produces a different notion of truth. It does not understand truth or the sacred as a metaphysical given buried in the "other" but seeks to comprehend it in and through the interactive deliberation of a multiple, polyvalent assembly of voices. Truth is a process not of discovering the hidden or lost sacred, but rather of public deliberation and creation for establishing radical democratic power relations. The truth of democratic religion is produced in struggle and debate between equals as an alternative discourse to torture and inquisition. In this radical democratic paradigm the truth or the sacred is best understood as an "absent presence," as a moment in an interpretive political process, a progressive extension of rights and equality to all residents of our expanding world community. Such a conception of "truth" comes close to the biblical notion of "doing the truth" that will set us free.

A critical feminist hermeneutics of liberation, therefore, attempts to reconstruct the traditional spiritual practice of discerning the spirits as a deliberative rhetorical practice. As religious subjects, feminists, I argue, must claim their spiritual authority to assess both the oppressive as well as the liberating function and imagination of particular religious texts and traditions in particular historical situations. They must do so because of the kyriarchal functions of authoritative religious claims that demand obedience and acceptance. By deconstructing the all-encompassing kyriarchal rhetorics and politics of subordination, critical feminist discourses are able to generate new possibilities for the communicative construction of religious identities and emancipatory practices. Reclaiming the authority of women for shaping and determining religions, feminist scholars ask new questions in order to reconceptualize the act of religious interpretation as a moment in the global praxis for liberation.

To that end they seek to interrogate religious texts, traditions, and institutional practices for religious visions that foster equality and justice and utilize the hermeneutics of desire to envision and practice the *ekklesia,* that is a radical democratic association, as a feminist public counterspace[64] to that of kyriarchal domination. Yet, only when a critical feminist rhetorics questions the kyriarchal discourses of exclusion inscribed in religious scriptures and traditions will it be able to identify such radical democratic religious roots. A critical hermeneutical integration of notions of liberty, equality, and radical democracy with radical egalitarian religious visions, I argue, can engender critical religious studies and discourses of possibility for a different understanding of human well-being. The task of feminist studies in religion is to articulate and envision a spirit-center for a radical democratic citizenry of global dimensions.

In short, the shift from a modern Western malestream to a critical liberation theological frame of reference engenders a fourfold change in hermeneutical-rhetorical inquiry: a change in interpretive goals, a change in epistemology, a change in consciousness, and a change in central theological questions.

Such a critical process of interpretation for liberation is not restricted to Christian religious and biblical texts but has been applied successfully to traditions and scriptures of other religions. It has been used in graduate education, in parish discussions, in college classes, and in work with illiterate Andean women. This critical rhetorical model of feminist hermeneutics conceives of religious studies as well as theology as a site of struggle and conscientization. It challenges other approaches in religious studies to become more comprehensive and sophisticated by problematizing their sociopolitical location and function in the global struggle for a more just and inclusive religion and world.

The Feminist Reconceptualization of Religion as a Site of Struggle

This hermeneutical paradigm shift requires a recasting of religious studies not in positivist but in rhetorical terms. As I have elaborated above, the task of feminist interpretation is not just to understand religious texts and traditions but to change Western idealist hermeneutical frameworks, individualist practices, and sociopolitical relations. For so doing, feminist liberation studies of all colors derive their lenses of interpretation not from the modern individualistic understanding of religion. Rather, they shift attention to the politics of religious studies and its sociopolitical contexts. They claim the hermeneutical privilege of the oppressed and marginalized for reading and evaluating religious texts and traditions. Whereas Schleiermacher, the "father of hermeneutics," addressed the cultured critics of religion, Gustavo Gutierrez argues that liberation theologians take up the questions of the "non-persons."[65]

Such an articulation of Religious Studies from the social position of the oppressed is not confessional and doctrinal but ecumenical and inter-religious. It seeks to enable and to defend sentient life that is threatened or destroyed by hunger, destitution, sexual violence, torture, and dehumanization. Liberationist studies seek to give dignity and value to the life of the non-person as the presence and image of G*d in our midst. Therefore, they do not restrict salvation to the soul but aim to promote the well-being and radical equality of all.

As long as kyriarchal religion is both a tool against wo/men struggling for emancipation and in support of patriarchal kyriarchy and a distortion of wo/men's self-understandings and perception of the world, feminist interpretation must pay attention not only to kyriocentric texts and traditions but also to the frameworks or "lenses" of wo/men readers. Recognizing the kyriocentric dynamics of religious texts and traditions, a critical feminist rhetorics of liberation, I have argued throughout, must abandon the quest for a liberating canonical text, unitary essence, or revealed pre-given truth, and shift its focus to a discussion of the processes and practices of interpretation in which wo/men as religious-theological subjects grapple with oppressive as well as liberating meanings of particular religious texts and traditions and their function in women's lives and struggles. Such a liberationist rhetorical understanding of religious studies stands in tension with the dominant one.[66]

The hegemonic conceptualization of religion and of religious studies is highly controverted. Three areas of debate are of special significance for feminist inquiry: First, the positivist understanding of religious studies, second, the hermeneutical definition of religion, and third, the modern definition of religion in gendered, racist, and colonialist terms.

First: Although the positivist scientific ethos of value-neutral inquiry and objective impartiality has been assiduously critiqued not only by feminist theory but also by the discipline of hermeneutics, the Enlightenment construct of positivist scientific scholarship still fuels the debate between theology and religious studies.[67] In difference to theology, religious studies allegedly seeks to produce value-detached and objective knowledge. Whereas the academic study of religion is understood as feminist-friendly because it is situated within the university, theology is generally treated with suspicion by feminists because it is understood as a confessionally typed doctrinal practice that is beholden to the hegemonic interests of organized religion. In contrast to theological studies, which are believed to be biased and parochial, the academic study of religion is deemed to be scientific, ecumenical, and global. It supposedly describes and understands the religions of the world as objectively and in as "unbiased" a fashion as possible without ranking them or identifying with any of them intellectually and spiritually. This positivist ethos of the discipline re-inscribes the modern dichotomy between religion and culture, between religious practice and the academic study of religion.

In order to avoid the positivist fallacy, I suggest, one needs to understand religion not simply as object of study but as a site of struggle. Scholars always speak from within a communal religious tradition, even when they have rejected their own religious heritage. However, by insisting that feminist studies speak from within a particular religious tradition I do not mean to claim the interpretive and descriptive authority of the insider, as does Wilfred Cantwell Smith in his often quoted methodological rule, "No statement about religion is valid unless it can be acknowledged by that religion's believers."[68]

I do not want to imply that to understand religion one must refer primarily to the testimony of believers. Rather, I want to make a hermeneutical point: As with any other subject matter if one studies religion, one always already has a preunderstanding of the subject matter that one seeks to understand. There is no value-neutral scholarship. Scholarship is always already situated—religiously, socially, culturally, and politically. Feminist or women's studies of religious practices are always already situated in religion, insofar as they are shaped by their religious intellectual traditions even if they have rejected them or claim to have surpassed them. Hence, like feminist theology so also feminist studies in religion must become conscious of speaking from within particular religious traditions or communities to which they are both insiders and outsiders[69] at one and the same time.

The Jewish feminist theologian Judith Plaskow has argued that women's studies in the United States tends to see religion within an Enlightenment frame. Speaking to a women's studies audience she points to the widespread suspicion in women's studies that anyone interested in religion must be either co-opted or reactionary and argues that their suspicion is not justified.[70] The notion that feminists must critically study and change oppressive ideologies, she argues, has not been extended to the serious work done by feminists in religion. This attitude of suspicion toward feminist studies in religion is regrettable for three major reasons.

1. Feminists need to study religion because it has played and still plays a key role in both women's oppression and liberation. Hence, a central task of feminist studies consists in understanding the implication of religion in the continuing political exploitation of wo/men as well as its active participation in social movements for change. Plaskow asserts that an explicit connection between feminist critiques and social change has been made in feminist studies in religion from its very beginnings.

2. Women's studies in religion is a variegated and vibrant field that has moved from analysis and critique of male texts toward reconstructing wo/men's heritage in and outside of hegemonic religious traditions and most recently has focused on the constructive transformation of patriarchal traditions and the creation of new ones.

3. Plaskow maintains that to a much greater extent than feminist scholars in other areas feminists in religion have sustained strong connections to wo/men's communities outside the academy. Much work of feminist studies in religion has been generated and challenged by wo/men in and outside organized religions who search for a feminist spirituality and politics of meaning for their lives. Conversely, feminist scholars also are involved either in traditional religious feminist groups or in Goddess and spirituality movements that have critically challenged and enriched biblical articulations and religious formations.[71]

Because the institutional location of feminist studies in religion is that of malestream scholarship, it is necessary to construct a different intellectual discursive space. By conceptualizing feminist studies in religion as critical rhetorical-political practices for liberation one can avoid the positivist snare. When one remains conscious of women's studies' sociopolitical location in the academy, it becomes apparent what is at stake in the theoretical construction of such a discursive position. Feminists, who have been and still are "outsiders" or "aliens" in theology and academy, engage in religious studies in order to transform the kyriarchal discourses of institutionalized religion and the academy, which have excluded wo/men for centuries. However, we can do so only if we become both qualified residents and remain foreign speakers at one and the same time.

Second: Religion as the object of religious studies is often defined in essentialist, Tillichian,[72] or phenomenological terms. Ursula King, for instance, states:

> Religion is more than an object of study. It has been described as a core concern, as expressing and addressing the sacred, or as disclosing a transcendent link to ultimate value. Religion has not only been the matrix of cultures and civilizations, but it structures reality—all reality, including that of gender—and encompasses the deepest level of what it means to be human.[73]

Most recently, this hegemonic notion of sui generis religion has been studied and critically evaluated by Russel T. McCutcheon. He argues that this concept has been used not only to constitute and institutionalize the field of religious studies but also to define its research object as an apolitical, fetishized, and sacrosanct area of study. Thereby it has created scholarly discourses that call for distinct and unique methods adequate to the interpretation of religious data and has insisted on the institutional autonomy of the scientific study of religion. Religion as sui generis is widely conceived by scholars in the field as

> autonomous, strictly personal, essential, unique, prior to, and ultimately distinct from, all other facets of human life and interaction.
> . . . In other words, the genres claim effectively brackets not only the datum but also the researcher as well from critical scrutiny.[74]

Excluding or peripheralizing social and political contents in defining what really counts as "religious" thus constitutes the "uniquely religious."

McCutcheon follows Rosalind Shaw who has criticized such a scientific sui generis notion of religion as decontextualized and depoliticized. According to her three dominant perspectives of religious studies—religion as a reality sui generis, a primarily text-based view of religion, and a positivistic self-understanding as the science of religion—account for such scholarship that renders religion as decontextualized and ungendered. The uniquely religious is understood as the distinctively apolitical, insofar as the exclusion or marginalization of social and political contents and aspects constitutes it. The distinctly religious is understandable "only on its own terms." Hence, studies of religion that engage in social-political rhetorical analysis are disqualified as "reductionist."

In short, malestream discourses on religion represent the "homo religiosus" as a collective subject, which is undifferentiated by race, gender, class, ethnicity, or age. This view from "above" is underscored not only through the sui generis nature of religion but also through the emphasis given to religious texts and privileging of scholarly elites. Wo/men who have been excluded from the articulation, proclamation, and interpretation of religious texts are thereby excluded from the higher levels of religious authority.

Since "religion" is a complex and ambiguous term, its study raises difficult methodological questions for feminist theory. If feminist studies in religion are concerned with all wo/men and not only with Western white wo/men, they must unravel the gendered colonialist hermeneutic of "othering" which permeates the study of religion, since the discourses of the history of religions have conceptualized religion in colonialist feminine terms. Hence, feminists must redefine religion in liberationist terms and refuse to engage in its further colonization. In Shaw's words:

> By re-conceptualizing power as integral to—as opposed to a detachable "dimension of"—religion, feminist Religious Studies has the potential to generate conceptual change and renewal.[75]

Third: Feminist studies have contextualized this discourse on religion historically and politically. They have shown that in modernity religion has been feminized. Religion has been conceptualized as that over and against which progress, rationality, subjectivity, and modernity have been defined. Since the industrial revolution in Europe and America institutionalized religions have been pushed out of the public realm and relegated to the private sphere of individualistic piety, charitable work, and the cultivation of home and family. Since theology was not considered to be a science and reason was defined in contradistinction to religion, religion—just as women—had no public presence in the Enlightenment university. Nevertheless, both religion and women were also crucial in maintaining public interest in the antithetical "other" and in shaping cultural self-identity.

In modernity "religion" was invented to operate within the limits of reason alone. It was feminized insofar as European Christianity was dislodged from its hegemonic role and restricted to the private sphere as well as by making it a civilizing project of colonialism. In the process of religious privatization and cultural "feminization," the clergy and theology lost their privileged intellectual status and came to be treated like "women" in polite society. This feminization of religion has led both to the emasculation of theology and clergy in society and to the reassertion of their masculine roles in theology, church, and the home.

Like the "White Lady," Christianity, the religious community from within which I speak, had the function of ameliorating the horrors of imperialism. Its task was to "civilize" the savages, who were understood as "untamed nature." The Western discourses on femininity and female nature have their sociopolitical contexts in this colonial exercise of power. Just as anthropology, so also comparative religious studies have their origin in such a colonial context. The study of religion turns religion into an object of the Western colonialist masculine gaze.

An explicit example of the power that the discourse of the history of religions exerts over the "other" can be found in the following journal entry of Mircea Eliade:

> I see the history of religions as a total discipline. I understand now that the encounters facilitated by depth psychology, with the stranger within, with that which is foreign, exotic, archaic in ourselves, on the one hand—and, on the other, the appearance of Asia and of the exotic or "primitive" groups in history—are cultural moments which find their ultimate meaning only from the perspective of the history of religions. The hermeneutic necessary for the revelation of the meanings and the message hidden in myth, rites, symbols, will also help us to understand both depth psychology and the historical age into which we are entering and in which we will be not only surrounded but also dominated by the "foreigner," the non-Occidentals. It will be possible to decipher the "Unconscious," as well as the Non-Western-World through the hermeneutic of the history of religions.[76]

In contrast to such a controlling function ascribed to "the hermeneutics of the history of religions" a critical feminist rhetoric sees religion as a site of feminist struggle. Insofar as it seeks to expose and to redress women's subordination, exploitation, and oppression in society and religion, it attempts to break down the structures of "othering," silencing, and exclusion inscribed in religion. By prohibiting wo/men's religious self-determination and leadership, these structures have prevented women from asking their own theological questions and from articulating religious studies in light of their own experiences of struggle. Feminist scholars in religion therefore first of all must engage a critical method that is able to theoretically explore the ways that the structures and ideological systems of kyriarchy have shaped and still shape biblical self-identity, memory, tradition, and communal practices.

As long as feminist critical reflection is motivated by the hunger and thirst for justice, it must also reclaim positively those religious visions, memories, and unrealized possibilities that can sustain resistance to oppressive structures and inspire energy and hope for their transformation. It must engage in the struggles for transforming kyriarchal religions because the "productive imagination"[77] of religion has not only sanctioned kyriocentric ideologies but also articulated visions and utopias for a more just world. In sum, the task of feminist studies in religion requires both a method of deconstructing kyriarchal religions and a method of re-articulating and re-visioning their emancipatory values in the global struggles for human dignity, justice, and the well-being of all creation

Notes

1. I use this expression not in a pejorative but in a descriptive sense. Until very recently *mainstream* scholarship has been literally *malestream*.

2. As formulated by Arvind Sharma, the editor of this volume.

3. Elisabeth Schüssler Fiorenza, *Bread Not Stone: The Challenge of Feminist Biblical Interpretation* (Boston: Beacon Press, 1985; 10th Anniversary Edition with a New Introduction, Beacon 1995).

4. Elisabeth Schüssler Fiorenza, *But She Said: Feminist Practices of Biblical Interpretation* (Boston: Beacon Press, 1992).

5. Elisabeth Schüssler Fiorenza, *Sharing Her Word. Feminist Biblical Interpretation in Context* (Boston: Beacon Press, 1998). For further discussion of my methodological and hermeneutical approach see my books *Rhetoric and Ethic. The Politics of Biblical Studies* (Minneapolis: Fortress Press, 1999); *Jesus and the Politics of Interpretation* (New York: Continuum, 2000); and *Wisdom Words. Introducing Feminist Biblical Interpretation* (Maryknoll: Orbis, 2001) which have appeared after the submission of this chapter in August 1998.

6. See the discussions in Kwok Pui-Lan and Elisabeth Schüssler Fiorenza, eds., *Women's Sacred Scriptures. Concilium 1998/3* (Maryknoll: Orbis Press, 1998).

7. See Marsha Aileen Hewitt, *Critical Theory of Religion. A Feminist Analysis* (Minneapolis: Fortress Press, 1995).

8. For the context of this expression see Maria Pilar Aquino, "Latin American Feminist Theology," *The Journal of Feminist Studies in Religion* 14 (1998): 89–108. The practice presupposes a systemic political analysis and hence it is not identical with the individualistic notion of "consciousness-raising."

9. See for instance Jean Holm with John Bowker, eds., *Women in Religion* (New York: Pinter Publishers, 1994) which discusses the status and role of wo/men in diverse religions.

10. For an exploration of the diverse voices in feminist theology see the contributions in Elisabeth Schüssler Fiorenza and Shawn Copeland, eds., *Feminist Theology in Different Contexts, Concilium 1996/1* (Maryknoll: Orbis Books, 1996).

11. I have coined this neologism in order to complexify the dualistic definition of patriarchy which is generally understood simply in terms of gender. See also the introduction to Elisabeth Schüssler Fiorenza, ed., *Searching the Scriptures* (New York: Crossroad, 1993 & 1994), 2 Vols.

12. Caroline Ramazanoglu, *Feminism and the Contradictions of Oppression* (New York: Routledge, 1998), 45

13. In order to mark the inadequacy of our language when we speak about the divine, I write G*d in such a broken form. For a discussion of the term G*d see Francis Schüssler Fiorenza and Gordon Kaufman, "God," in *Critical Terms for Religious Studies,* ed. Mark C. Taylor (Chicago: The University of Chicago Press, 1998), 136–159.

14. Caroline Ramazanoglu, *Feminism and the Contradictions of Oppression,* 33.

15. See Rosemary Hennesy, *Feminism and the Politics of Discourse* (New York: Routledge, 1993).

16. See the panel discussion at the 1982 AAR/SBL Annual meeting on my article "A Feminist Biblical Hermeneutics and Liberation Theology," in *The Challenge of Liberation Theology: A First World Response,* ed. L. Dale Richesin and Brian Mehan (New York: Orbis Books, 1981), 91–112, which was prepared for a conference at Chicago Divinity School in 1979 where I introduced the term *feminist hermeneutics*. See also the contributions in Letty M. Russell, ed. *Feminist Interpretation of the Bible* (Philadelphia: Westminster, 1985), especially her introduction.

17. John Bender and David E. Wellbery, "Rhetoricality: On the Modernist Return of Rhetoric," in *The Ends of Rhetoric. History, Theory, Practice,* ed. John Bender and David E. Wellbery (Stanford: Stanford University Press, 1990), 25–26.

18. For this emphasis see the collected essays in my book *Discipleship of Equals. A Feminist Ekklesialogy of Liberation* (New York: Crossroad, 1993).

19. See my articles "Challenging the Rhetorical Half-Turn: Feminist and Rhetorical Biblical Criticism," in *Rhetoric, Scripture, & Theology: Essays from the 1994 Pretoria Conference,* ed. Stanley E. Porter and Thomas H. Ulbricht (Sheffield, England: Sheffield University Press, 1996), 28–53 and "The Rhetoricity of Historical Knowledge: Pauline Discourse and Its Contextualizations," in *Religious Propaganda and Missionary Competition in the New Testament World: Essays Honoring Dieter Georgi,* ed. Lukas Bormann, Kelly Del Tredici, and Angela Standhartinger (Leiden: E.J. Brill, 1994), 443–470.

20. See e.g. Erin White, "Figuring and Refiguring the Female Self: Towards a Feminist Hermeneutics," in *Claiming Our Rites: Studies in Religion by Australian Women Scholars,* ed. Morny Joy and Penelope Magee (Adelaide: Australian Association for the Study of Religion, 1994), 135–155. After claiming that "feminist scholarship lacks extended discussion of hermeneutical ques-

tions," she goes on to say that Phyllis Trible's and my own works "focus on the text" and in my case "on the communities of women and men who produced the text," but that we do not focus "on the relation between text and (female) self-identity" (136). In her elaboration of my alleged position she does not refer either to my books *Bread Not Stone, But She Said,* or *Vision of a Just World* nor to any of my other hermeneutical-epistemological essays. Instead, she (mis)reads *In Memory of Her* in a positivist historical vein and claims that I do "not sufficiently recognize the place of both text and present context in the construction of any community of the past.." (138). She concedes that her critique might seem "niggardly" [*sic*] and then goes on to show how much better off we would be if we had read Ricoeur, although a reading of *Bread Not Stone* and my discussion of, e.g., Sandra Schneider's proposal could have shown that I have considered this approach but found it wanting. She caps it all by claiming that like Ricoeur I do not begin with my own life experience but with the inherited biblical text, although she could find many statements in my writings that feminist theology begins with experience and a critical feminist theology with systemically analyzed and explored experience. However, at no point does she mention that the basic difference between our feminist hermeneutical proposals is the theoretical difference between a feminist analysis in terms of gender and one in terms of the multiplicative structures of kyriarchal oppression and kyriocentric symbol systems.

21. For this section see especially also Francis Schüssler Fiorenza, "History and Hermeneutics," in *Modern Christian Thought* Vol. 2, ed. James Livingston and Francis Schüssler Fiorenza (New Jersey: Prentice Hall, 1999) and his forthcoming book *Beyond Hermeneutics* (New York: Continuum, 2003). See also the collection of essays edited by Kurt Mueller-Vollmer, *The Hermeneutics Reader* (New York: Continuum, 1988).

22. Jacques Derrida, "The Ends of Man," *Philosophy and Phenomenological Research* 30 (1969): 31–57.

23. Richard Rorty, *Philosophy and the Mirror of Nature* (Princeton: Princeton University Press, 1979), 315.

24. See Hans Georg Gadamer, *Truth and Method* and *Philosophical Hermeneutics* (Berkeley: University of California Press, 1976).

25. See Richard Bernstein, "What is the Difference that Makes a Difference? Gadamer, Habermas, and Rorty," in *Hermeneutics and Modern Philosophy*, ed. Brice R. Wachterhauser, (Albany: State University of New York Press, 1986), 343–376.

26. Paul Ricoeur's theory of interpretation has argued that action may be regarded as a text. If an action like a text is a meaningful entity, then the "paradigm of reading" can also be applied to socioreligious practices. See Paul Ricoeur, *Hermeneutics and the Human Sciences,* edited and translated by John B. Thompson (Cambridge: Cambridge University Press, 1981), 197–221.

27. See Wachterhauser, *Hermeneutics and Modern Philosophy*, 5.

28. See Ricoeur, *Hermeneutics and the Human Sciences*, 43–62.

29. Wachterhauser, *Hermeneutics and Modern Philosophy*, 8.

30. Wilhelm Dilthey, *Selected Writings*, translated and edited by H. P. Rickman (Cambridge: Cambridge University Press, 1976).

31. However, it must not be overlooked that Gadamer seeks to displace this notion through the concept of the "fusion of horizons" although in my view he still ends up with sympathetic valorization of tradition.

32. Rita M. Gross, *Feminism and Religion: An Introduction* (Boston: Beacon Press, 1996), 11–12.

33. For the role such an empathic hermeneutic plays in the rehabilitation of the Holocaust and National Socialism see Michael Brumlik, "Geisteswissenschaftlicher Revisionismus—auch eine Verharmlosung des Nationalsozialismus," in *Rechtsextremismus: Ideologie und Gewalt*, ed. Richard Faber, Hajo Funke, Gerhard Schoenberner (Berlin: Edition Hentrich, 1995).

34. Wachterhauser, *Hermeneutics and the Human Sciences*, 7.

35. See Denise Riley, *Am I That Name? Feminism and the Category of "Women"in History* (Minneapolis: University of Minnesota Press, 1988).

36. Anne-Louise Eriksson, *The Meaning of Gender in Theology: Problems and Possibilities* (Stockholm: Almqvist, 1995), 135–150, who does not understand these hermeneutical-epistemological dimensions of my work, as well as Elina Vuola, *Limits of Liberation. Praxis as Method in Latin American Liberation Theology and Feminist Theology* (Helsinki: Suomalainen Tiedekatemia, 1997), who summarizes Eriksson as follows: "It seems that the problems in Ruether's and Fiorenza's *[sic]* theology are derived from the scarcity of this sort of reflection. It is the lack of explicit theorizing of epistemological issues—with the help of non-theological feminist theory—which makes their theology vulnerable and open for different readings." Not only is the work of Radford Ruether and my own lumped together here, although they are quite different theoretically, but also our consistent engagement with feminist theory is totally overlooked. One wonders whether such failure of research is tolerated in dissertations because their advisors and publishers lack theoretical competence in feminist studies or whether it is politically motivated.

37. On religious language and hermeneutics see Dan R. Stiver, *The Philosophy of Religious Language. Sign, Symbol, and Story* (Cambridge: Blackwell Publishers, 1996), 37–111.

38. See Cheryl Glenn, *Rhetoric Retold: Regendering the Tradition from Antiquity Through the Renaissance* (Carbondale: Southern Illinois University Press, 1997); Loraine Code, *Rhetorical Spaces. Essays on Gendered Locations* (New York: Routledge, 1995).

39. Bender, and Wellbery, *The Ends of Rhetoric*, 27.

40. Wachterhauser, "History and Language in Understanding," in Wachterhauser, *Hermeneutics and the Human Sciences*, 21.

41. Wolfhart Pannenberg, "Hermeneutics and Universal History," in ibid., 135.

42. David Couzens Hoy, "Is Hermeneutic Ethnocentric?," in *The Interpretive Turn. Philosophy, Science, Culture,* ed. David R. Hiley, James F. Bowman, and Richard Shusterman (Ithaca: Cornell University Press, 1991), 165.

43. Susan Shapiro, "Rhetoric as Ideology Critique. The Gadamer-Habermas Debate Reinvented," *Journal of the American Academy of Religion* LXII/1(1997): 123–150.

44. Caputo, in Wachterhauser, *Hermeneutics and the Human Sciences*, 424.

45. David Tracy, *The Analogical Imagination: Christian Theology and the Culture of Pluralism* (New York: Crossroad, 1981), 100–155.

46. Raymond A. Morrow with David D. Baron, *Critical Theory and Methodology* (Thousand Oaks: Sage Publications, 1994), 146.

47. Michélle Barrett, *The Politics of Truth. From Marx to Foucault* (Stanford: Stanford University Press, 1991), 177.

48. Morrow with Baron, *Critical Theory and Methodology,* 130–149.

49. John B. Thompson, *Studies in the Theory of Ideology* (Cambridge: Polity Press, 1984), 254.

50. Jürgen Habermas, "Ideology," in *Modern Interpretations of Marx,* ed. Tom Bottomore (Oxford: Blackwell, 1981), 166.

51. See my article "Der 'Athenakomplex' in der theologischen Frauenforschung," in *Für Gerechtigkeit streiten. Theologie im Alltag einer bedrohten Welt,* ed. Dorothee Sölle (Gütersloh: Kaiser, 1994), 103–111.

52. See especially *But She Said,* 51–76 and 195–218 for the elaboration of this process with reference to a particular text.

53. For such a hermeneutical reading see Sandra Schneiders, *The Revelatory Text. Interpreting the New Testament as Sacred Scripture* (New York: Harper SanFrancisco, 1991).

54. Klaus Berger, *Hermeneutik des neuen Testaments* (Gütersloh: Gütersloher Verlagshaus Gerd Mohn, 1988) insists on the distinction in order to safeguard the distanciating power of exegetical-historical interpretation and the freedom of selectivity in the application of texts in contemporary situations.

55. For a critical discussion of the category of experience in feminist thought see Joan W. Scott, "Experience," in Feminists Theorize the Political, ed. Judith Butler and Joan W. Scott (New York: Routledge, 1992), 22–40.

56. "Paolo Freire, *Pedagogy of the Oppressed* (New York: The Seabury Press, 1973), 31.

57. Ibid., 33.

58. Although Anthony C. Thiselton, *New Horizons in Hermeneutics. The Theory and Practice of Transforming Biblical Reading* (London: Harper Collins Publ., 1992), 449f claims in his discussion of my work that "what is at stake is hermeneutical theory" he does not bother to discuss *Bread Not Stone* but rather focuses on a particular exegetical topic in order to show that I did not take all possible interpretations into account. Yet such a criticism overlooks the choice of genre and mistakes a work of historical reconstruction for one of hermeneutical critical theory. His apologetic concern comes to the fore in his repeated questions both as to how much a given tradition can undergo transformation before it ceases to be this tradition and in whether the transformation of which I speak comes "into being by imposing one's community values upon another in a hermeneutic of conflict, or by progress toward a universal commitment to a transcendental critique of justice and of the cross which speaks from beyond given context-bound communities in a hermeneutic of openness?" Obviously, Thiselton is not able to understand either commitment to wo/men's struggles for liberation as a universalizing stance nor feminist struggle as a commitment to a "transcendental critique of justice" or to the "cross" as the symbolic expression of such struggle.

59. The Bible and the Culture Collective, *The Postmodern Bible* (New Haven: Yale University Press, 1995), 249.

60. Toni Morrison, *Beloved,* (New York: Penguin, 1998), 88.

61. Alicia Suskin Ostriker, *Feminist Revision and the Bible* (Cambridge, Mass.: Blackwell, 1993).

62. See my book I*n Memory of Her* for the development of the notion of scripture as paradigm and prototype.

63. Page duBois, *Torture and Truth: The New Ancient World* (New York: Routledge, 1991).

64. For the notion of a feminist counter-public sphere see Rita Felski, *Beyond Feminist Aesthetics. Feminist Literature and Social Change* (Cambridge: Harvard University Press, 1989), 164–175.

65. See also Sharon Welch, *Communities of Resistance and Solidarity* (Maryknoll: Orbis Books, 1985), 7: ". . . the referent of the phrase 'liberating God' is not primarily God but liberation."

66. Especially Asian and Hispanic feminists have found this hermeneutical approach helpful. See for instance, Hyun Kyung Chung, *Struggle to be the Sun Again. Introducing Asian Women's Theology* (Maryknoll: Orbis, 1990); Kwok Pui Lan, "Discovering the Bible in the Non-Biblical World," *Semeia* 47 (1989): 25–42; Maria Pilar Aquino, *Our Cry for Life. Feminist Theology from Latin America* (New York: Orbis Books, 1993); and Ada Maria Isasi-Diaz, "The Bible and Mujerista Theology," in *Lift Every Voice: Constructing Christian Theologies from the Underside,* ed. Susan Brooks Thistlesthwaite and P. Engel (San Francisco: Harper & Row, 1990).

67. See Jonathan Smith, "Religion, Religions, Religious," in *Critical Terms in Religious Studies*, 269–284.

68. Wilfred Cantwell Smith, "The Comparative Study of Religion: Whither- and Why?," in *The History of Religions: Essays in Methodology*, ed. Mircea Eliade and Joseph Kittagawa (Chicago: University of Chicago Press, 1959), 42.

69. Patricia Hill Collins, *Fighting Words: Black Women and the Search for Justice* (Minneapolis: University of Minnesota Press, 1988), 3–11 speaks of the "outsider within" and of the feminist theologian as "resident alien."

70. See also Michelle Lelwica, "From Superstition to Enlightenment to the Race for Pure Consciousness," and the responses by Amy Richlin and Martha Ackelsberg in *JFSR* 14/2 (1998).

71. Judith Plaskow, "We are Also Your Sisters: The Development of Women's Studies in Religion," *Women's Studies Quarterly* 20/1 (1993): 9–21.

72. See Tracy Fessenden, "'Woman' and the 'Primitive' in Tillich's Life and Thought: Some Implications for the Study of Religion," *JFSR* 14/2 (1998).

73. Ursula King, ed., *Religion and Gender* (Oxford: Oxford University Press, 1995), 4.

74. Russell T. McCutcheon, *Manufacturing Religion. The Discourse on Sui Generis Religion and the Politics of Nostalgia* (New York: Oxford University Press, 1997), 26.

75. Rosalind Shaw, "Feminist Anthropology and the Gendering of Religious Studies, " in *Religion and Gender*, 73.

76. Mircea Eliade, *Journal II* (Chicago: University of Chicago Press, 1989), 69–70.

77. Paul Ricoeur, *Hermeneutics and the Human Sciences*, 38–39.

About the Contributors

Elisabeth Schüssler Fiorenza is the Krister Stendahl Professor of Scripture and Interpretation at Harvard Divinity School and past president of the Society of Biblical Literature. Among her many works are *In Memory of Her* (1984), *Revelation: Vision of a Just World* (Fortress Press, 1991), *Jesus: Miriam's Child, Sophia's Prophet* (1995), and most recently *Sharing Her Word* (1998). She is also one of the founding co-chairs of the Journal of Feminist Studies in Religion.

Rita M. Gross is the author of many books and articles dealing with gender and religion, including *Buddhism after Patriarchy: A Feminist History, Analysis, and Reconstruction of Buddhism* (SUNY, 1993) and *Feminism and Religion: An Introduction* (Beacon, 1996). She also co-edited the classic *Unspoken Worlds: Women's Religious Lives* with Nancy Auer Falk (third edition, Wadsworth, 2001). She was one of first scholars of religion to argue that gender studies must be part of religious studies if the discipline is to represent religions adequately and accurately, beginning that work in her Ph.D. dissertation written for the University of Chicago.

Constance A. Jones, Ph.D. Emory University, is Professor in the School of Consciousness and Transformation at the California Institute of Integral Studies in San Francisco, California. A sociologist of religion, she conducts research into new religious movements in the United States as part of a larger inquiry into the meeting of East and West in intellectual history and biography. Additionally, she teaches and publishes on the topic of new paradigms of research and humanistic methodologies in social science. She also publishes sociological analyses of new religions with Hindu roots. Her recent publications explore the spiritual teachings of G. I. Gurdjieff and J. Krishnamurti as examples of integral thought. As a Fulbright scholar to India in 1995–1996, she taught at Benaras Hindu University and conducted research at the Krishnamurti Study Centre.

Diane Jonte-Pace, Ph.D. 1984, Religion and Psychological Studies, University of Chicago, is Associate Professor of Religious Studies and Associate Vice Provost for Faculty Development at Santa Clara University. She serves as chair of the editorial board of *The Religious Studies Review.* Her publications include *Speaking the Unspeakable: Religion, Misogyny, and the Uncanny Mother in Freud's Cultural Texts* (University of California Press, 2001) and *Religion and Psychology: Mapping the Terrain,* co-edited with William Parsons (Routledge, 2001). She is currently editing a collection of essays, *Teaching Freud in Religious Studies,* in which contributors describe how they integrate scholarship and pedagogy.

David Kingsley was born in 1939 and taught at McMaster University in Hamilton, Ontario, Canada before he passed away in the year 2000 after making major contributions to women's studies in a cross-cultural perspective. His numerous publications include: *The Goddesses' Mirror: Vision of the Divine from East and West* (State University of New York Press, 1989); *Hindu Goddesses: Vision of the Divine Feminine in the Hindu Religious Tradition* (University of California Press, 1986); *Tantric Visions of the Feminine: The Ten Mahāvidyās* (University of California Press, 1997); *Hinduism: A Cultural Perspective* (Prentice Hall, 1982); *The Sword and the Flute: Kālī and Kṛṣṇa, Dark Visions of the Terrible and the Sublime in Hindu Mythology* (University of California Press, 1991).

Rosemary Radford Ruether is the Georgia Harkness Professor of Applied Theology at the Garrett Theological Seminary and a member of the Graduate faculty of Northwestern University in Evanston, Illinois. She is also Carpenter Professor of Feminist Theology at the Graduate Theological Union in Berkeley, California, and will join the faculty full time in the fall of 2002. She is the author or editor of twenty-five books and numerous articles in journals or book collections on feminist theology and social justice issues. Her most recent book is *Christianity and the Making of the Modern Family: Ruling Ideologies, Diverse Realities* (Beacon Press, 2000).

Arvind Sharma is the Birks Professor of Comparative Religion at McGill University in Montreal, Canada. He has edited several books on women and religion, including *Women in World Religions* (State University of New York Press, 1987), a standard text in the field. Other books edited or co-edited by him include: *Religion and Women; Today's Woman in World Religions; Feminism and World Religions* and *Women Saints in World Religions.*

Mary Ann Stenger is associate professor of Humanities at the University of Louisville, where she teaches courses in Religious Studies and Women's Studies.

She received her B.A. in Religion from Lawrence University and her Ph.D. in Religion from the University of Iowa. Her research interests include the philosophy/theology of Paul Tillich and philosophical issues of feminism and religious pluralism. She has published numerous articles and book chapters on these subjects. A current interest is fundamentalist reactions to feminism and religious pluralism. A forthcoming book is *Dialogues of Paul Tillich,* co-authored with Ronald H. Stone, published by Mercer University Press.

Katherine K. Young has a B.A. (Vermont) in philosophy and religion, and M.A. (Chicago) in the History of Religions, and a Ph.D. (McGill) in the History of Religions. Besides writing many articles in her area of specialization—the history of Tamil Vaiṣṇavism, she is in the process of finalizing her major work on this topic. In addition, she has published in the fields of gender and ethics. She has pursued her interest in comparative studies with reference to gender, collaborating, for instance, with Arvind Sharma on twelve books on women in world religions including *Feminism and World Religions,* which was selected by Choice in 1999 as an Academic Book of Excellence. She has co-authored a trilogy called Beyond the Fall of Man. The first volume has appeared under the title *Spreading Misandry: The Teaching of Contempt for Men in Popular Culture* (McGill Queen's University Press, 2001). She has written for the *Encyclopedia of Bioethics* (Macmillan) and the forthcoming *A History of Medical Ethics* (Cambridge); has edited *Hermeneutical Paths to the Sacred Worlds of India* (1994); has co-authored *Hindu Ethics* (1989); and has coedited *Religion and Law in the Global Village* (2000). Fifteen books have been published in her series McGill Studies in the History of Religions with the State University of new York Press.

Index of Names

Index of Terms

Subject Index

DATE DUE

DEMCO 38-296